Dr. Leary has assembled an outstanding, clear, and concise road map for women looking to apply to and succeed in college. It is both motivational in its presentation and incredibly practical and instructive in its content. Dr. Leary has penned a great resource for the prospective adult learner and a wonderful and thorough overview of college for new employees to the higher education sector.

—*Richard Doherty, President, Association of Independent Colleges & Universities in Massachusetts (AICUM)*

Having long witnessed Dr. Leary's tireless energy, passion, and vision for making higher education accessible to adult women, it comes as no surprise to me that she would write such an extraordinary book. The case for a woman earning a college degree is compelling: She will earn more; her children will thrive; her community will be stronger. Even more critical, when a woman achieves her higher education, the vitality of the economy and the health and well-being of American families will be secured for generations to come. I am inspired by Dr. Leary's commitment to provide an easy-to-read guide to help any woman who is trying to find her voice by incorporating higher education into her complex life.

—*Robyn Davis, Irene and George Davis Foundation; Trustee Chair Emerita, Bay Path University*

ACHIEVING THE DREAM

ACHIEVING THE DREAM

A How-to Guide
for Adult Women
Seeking a College Degree

CAROL A. LEARY, PH.D.
MICHELE BARKER, EDITOR

WHITE RIVER PRESS
AMHERST, MASSACHUSETTS

ISBN: 978-1-887043-24-3 Paperback
ISBN: 978-1-887043-25-0 eBook

First published 2016 by White River Press, PO Box 3561, Amherst, MA 01004
www.WhiteRiverPress.com

Interior and cover design by Lufkin Graphic Designs, www.LufkinGraphics.com

This work includes articles by several contributors; all articles are used by
permission:

Why College Is Important to Women – by Gina Joseph-Collins, Ph.D.; *The New
Science of Learning* – by Kathryn Wiezbicki-Stevens, Ed.D.; *Resources and Support
for Adult Women Going to College* – by Maura Devlin, Ph.D.; *Choosing a Career
and a Major* – by David Yelle; *Finding the Right College* and *The Application
Process* – by Diane Ranaldi and Veatrice Carabine; *Negotiating the Financial Aid
Maze* – by Stephanie King; *Understanding the College Curriculum* and *The Office
of the Registrar, "Keeper of Records"* – by William L. Sipple, Ph.D.; *Succeeding
in the Classroom* and *Fostering a Respectful Professor-Student Relationship* – by
Virginia Freed; *Developing a Positive Relationship with Faculty* – by Mary Lou
Di Giacomo; *Getting the Help You Need*; *Understanding Your Learning Style and
Mastering Study Skills*; and *Career Planning* – by Laureen Cirillo; *Unlock Your
College Library: The Key to Your Academic Success* – by Michael Moran; *Tips on
Technology* – by David Demers, Ph.D.; *Writing Your Way to Success* – by Suzanne
Strempek Shea; *Math in Everyday Life* – by Jane Weyant; *Cocurricular Options for
Adult Students* – by Caron Hobin; *Pursuing a Graduate Degree: Now That You
Have Your Bachelor's Degree, What's Next?* – by Melissa Morriss-Olson, Ph.D.

Cover photography by Paul Schnaittacher.
Pictured, alumnae of Bay Path University's degree programs for adult women:
Cheryl Cassidy, Aileen Lind, Maria Furlow.

Library of Congress Cataloging-in-Publication Data

Names: Leary, Carol, author.
Title: Achieving the dream : a how-to book for adult women seeking a college
   degree / Carol Leary, PhD.
Description: Amherst, Massachusetts : White River Press, 2016
Identifiers: LCCN 2016008689 (print) | LCCN 2016017179 (ebook) | ISBN
   9781887043243 (pbk. : alk. paper) | ISBN 9781887043250 ()
Subjects: LCSH: Women--Education (Higher)--United States--Handbooks,
   manuals, etc. | Women college students--United States--Handbooks, manuals,
   etc. | Adult education--United States--Handbooks, manuals, etc. | Continuing
   education--United States--Handbooks, manuals, etc. | Adult college students--
   United States.
Classification: LCC LC1756 .L386 2016 (print) | LCC LC1756 (ebook) | DDC
   378.19822--dc23
LC record available at https://lccn.loc.gov/2016008689

To my grandparents, parents, and my husband
for their passionate belief that education
opens doors of opportunity for a lifetime.

Most important for me,
they always believed in my dreams.

ACKNOWLEDGMENTS

*T*here are many individuals I wish to thank for their collaboration in bringing this book to life. I first want to acknowledge two colleagues who truly ignited my passion for adult women's education, who taught me how to create a learning environment that addressed the complexity of a woman's life and gave adult women students the opportunity to thrive: Dr William Sipple (Provost and Vice President for Academic Affairs Emeritus at Bay Path University) and Dr. Vana Nespor (Chief Learning Officer of The American Women's College Online and One Day a Week Program at Bay Path University). But the most powerful impetus for me was hearing the stories of the adult women who attended the classes on Saturdays here at Bay Path University in our One Day A Week College program and those online at The American Women's College. As they reflected on their journeys and shared their compelling stories, I sensed that other women could benefit from the lessons they learned. It was so clear: I knew I had to incorporate their experiences into a book that would help other women achieve their dream of a college education.

With a small group of faculty and staff, we outlined the project, and from there I asked experts to contribute their time and knowledge to the chapters that follow. From this initial group, the number of members of the Bay Path community who wished to share their knowledge, expertise, and encouragement for adult women students grew beyond my wildest expectations. My thanks go to Dr. Maura Devlin (Director of Liberal Studies, Writing and Assessment for The American Women's College at Bay Path University), Laureen Cirillo (Executive Director of the Sullivan Career and Life Planning Center at Bay Path University), Michael Moran (Director of Library and Information Services at Bay Path University), and Dr. Gina Joseph-Collins (former Dean of Adult and Professional Education for Adult Women at Bay Path University) for helping to lay the groundwork for the chapters and identifying the information we needed to gather for our readers.

I also want to extend my deepest appreciation to each author who contributed his or her wisdom and helped to make this book a true resource for adult women (unless stated otherwise, all are faculty or staff at Bay Path University): Veatrice Carabine, Deputy Chief Enrollment Officer at The American Women's College; Laureen Cirillo, Executive Director of the Sullivan Career and Life Planning Center; Dr. David Demers, former Vice President for Academic and Administrative Technology and Chief Operating Officer at The American Women's College Online; Dr. Maura Devlin, Director of Liberal Studies, Writing and Assessment at The American Women's College; Mary Lou Di Giacomo, Adjunct Professor; Virginia Freed, Professor Emerita of English; Caron Hobin, Chief Strategy Officer at The American Women's College; Dr. Gina Joseph-Collins, former Dean of Adult and Professional Education for Adult Women; Stephanie King, Director of Student Financial Services; Michael Moran, Director of Library and Information Services; Dr. Melissa Morriss-Olson, Provost and Vice President for Academic Affairs; Diane Ranaldi, Dean of Graduate and International Admissions; Dr. William Sipple, Provost and Vice President for Academic Affairs Emeritus at Bay Path University; Suzanne Strempek Shea, Director of Creative Writing and Writer in Residence; Jane Weyant, Chair of the Mathematics Department; Dr. Kathryn Wiezbicki-Stevens, Professor and Chair of the Psychology Department; and David Yelle, former Dean of Students. In addition, I must emphasize the tremendous technology assistance I received from Dr. David Demers throughout the writing and compilation of the material.

This book would not have been completed without the mentorship and partnership of its editor, Michele Barker. Her patience, her time-on-task skills, and her unwavering loyalty to the project allowed me to complete this labor of love. I would also like to thank author and Bay Path Writer in Residence Suzanne Strempek Shea for recommending Michele to me.

My staff—Barbara Kochon, Executive Assistant; Heather Rounsaville, Presidential Support Specialist; and Wendy Pollack, Campus Receptionist—worked diligently to ensure that the project stayed on course. My sincere appreciation to Michael Giampietro, Vice President for Finance and Administration, for his careful review of all of our legal obligations for publishing, copyright, and contracts, and to James F. Martin of Robinson Donovan, P.C., Attorneys at Law, for legal advice. Thanks, too, to Dr. William Knaus, neighbor and friend, who throughout this project offered valuable advice on publishing my final manuscript.

When I asked for students who would be willing to share their personal stories about their journey to higher education, I was overwhelmed by the response; I wish to thank the students who provided a personal story for each chapter. Thanks also to the three students who served as beta readers for the manuscript: Connie Dodds, Vanessa L. Parker, and Cecille Youmans.

In addition, I wish to thank the Board of Trustees of Bay Path University for giving me the time to write this book and for the resources to ensure the book was published. Also, I thank all the members of the Executive Team at Bay Path who encouraged and supported me. My sincerest appreciation to: Caron Hobin, Chief Strategy Officer at The American Women's College; Dr. Vana Nespor, Chief Learning Officer of The American Women's College Online and One Day a

Week Program at Bay Path University; Kathleen Bourque, Vice President of Institutional Advancement; Dr. Melissa Morriss-Olson, Provost and Vice President for Academic Affairs; Michael Giampietro, Vice President for Finance and Administrative Services; and Amanda Gould, Chief of Operational Effectiveness and Student Success.

Having Dr. Lynn Pasquerella, President of Mount Holyoke College from 2010 to 2016 and incoming President of the American Association of Colleges and Universities, write the foreword to this book is a particular honor for me because of our friendship and because of Dr. Pasquerella's commitment to the higher education of women worldwide. I would also like to acknowledge the memories of Dr. William Holmes, President Emeritus of Simmons College, and Priscilla McKee, Vice President Emerita of Simmons College, who shaped my thinking about all-women's learning environments and who believed in my potential as a college administrator. Thank you, too, to Robyn Davis, Irene and George Davis Foundation and Board Chair Emerita, Bay Path University; Richard Doherty, President of the Association of Independent Colleges and Universities of Massachusetts; Dr. Paul LeBlanc, President of Southern New Hampshire University; and Michele Ozumba, President of the Women's College Coalition, for their endorsements.

Thanks to Linda Roghaar at White River Press, Jean Stone, copyeditor, and the rest of Linda's staff for ensuring this book actually made it to press on time.

There are always those moments when you need to pull a team together for last-minute details. I wish to thank Kathleen Bourque, Vice President of Institutional Advancement; Kathleen Wroblewski, Director of Communications and Public Relations; Amanda Sbriscia, Director of Annual Giving and Alumni Relations; Leah Martin of Leah Martin Photography; and photographer Paul Schnaittacher for their tremendous assistance in arranging the photo shoot for the cover of the book. I also wish to acknowledge the alumnae of our One Day Saturday Program and The American Women's

College Online, who gave up precious time to help us: Trecia Marchand ('07, G '09), Jennifer Hotchkiss ('16, AS '15), Norma Nunnally ('01), Cheryl Cassidy ('15), Maria Furlow ('10, G '12), and Aileen Lind ('15).

Finally, many family members and friends encouraged me to complete this project. I'd like to thank my mother, Mary Gigliotti, and my two sisters, Deborah Korzak and LuAnn Mastrolembo, for their never-ending love. Finally, but most important in my life, I wish to thank my husband, Noel Leary, who never wavered in giving me his love and patience from concept to completion of this book. He has always shared my strong belief in the power of women's education.

CONTENTS

FOREWORD
BY DR. LYNN PASQUERELLA

Dr. Lynn Pasquerella is a philosopher who is committed to women's education and whose career has combined teaching and scholarship with local and global engagement. Dr. Pasquerella is a graduate of Quinebaug Valley Community College, Mount Holyoke College, and Brown University. In 2010, her alma mater, Mount Holyoke College, appointed her as its 18th president. After serving six years as president of Mount Holyoke, she will assume the presidency of the Association of American Colleges and Universities on July 1, 2016.

*T*he summer I graduated from high school, I managed to escape the factory work I had done alongside my mother the previous summer, only because I received funding under the federal Comprehensive Employment and Training Act. At the time, CETA funds were reserved for high school students who were at risk of permanent unemployment due to extreme economic and social disadvantages. That fall, I continued working 35 hours a week under a CETA grant while attending a local community college that had just opened up in the small, rural town in which I lived. I had decided to forgo a full scholarship to my state's flagship university in order to serve as a caregiver for my mother, who had become chronically ill. Two years later, I transferred to Mount Holyoke College and within another two years was headed off to Brown University for my Ph.D.

When I graduated, I vowed that I would never forget the lessons I learned in my transition from community college to the Seven Sisters and the Ivy League. As a result, throughout my career, I have been committed to promoting access to excellence in higher education, particularly for women; to championing the centrality of liberal learning; and to defending political scientist Benjamin Barber's notion of colleges and universities as "civic missions." Barber's Jeffersonian contention is that neither education nor research can prosper in an unfree society, and schooling, he thinks, is society's most promising—perhaps its only—way of producing citizens who will uphold freedom. Yet Barber goes beyond Jefferson by suggesting that we "not only have to educate every person to make [her] free, but we have to free every person to make [her] educable."[1] While there has been a good deal of rhetoric regarding the principle of universal access to higher education as an essential symbol of our nation's commitment to equality of opportunity, the reality is that many of our citizens still have "closed futures" and consequently are, in a very real sense, unfree. *Achieving the Dream* attempts to redress the growing economic segregation in higher education, but it does much more: It also highlights the personal purpose of higher education, which provides a framework for grappling with and understanding the most fundamental questions of human existence.

My own story is illustrative. Among the courses I signed up for during my first semester of college, with the help of a Pell Grant and a Perkins Loan, was an American literature class. There weren't many students in that class; most enrolled in courses that more easily translated into better jobs—or any job at all. It was held in a church basement across town from the administrative offices of the college, which were in trailers housed at a regional technical high school. Despite the lack of a physical campus, there was a true sense of community derived from the experience of embarking on a common endeavor.

One evening, my literature professor arranged for us to take a trip to Hartford for a performance of *All the Way Home*, a Pulitzer Prize-winning play by Tad Mosel. I had never attended a professional theater production before, and Hartford was a world away—known to me only as the place to which my father traveled nightly on a third-shift bus to work as a welder at Pratt and Whitney. I remember being dressed in a blue velveteen jumpsuit (it was the '70s, after all) and piling into a car with my classmates. When the lights dimmed, I was transported. In the dark—perhaps *especially* in the dark—I felt part of something important. Surrounded by classmates, I stared ahead at the stage and waited for what I could not yet see.

After the play, our class went for Chinese food and talked. The performance had raised so many big questions about faith, grief, and trust. We discussed the last act, when a wife mourns her husband's unexpected death. "I hoped he loved being," she said, recognizing the possibility that he may never have realized his own strength and potential.[2]

What that evening taught me, and why I remember it after all these years, is that we all have a right to experience "being." We are each entitled to live in our strength. We each deserve opportunities to find our best and most authentic selves.

Achieving the Dream provides a road map for women to not only find their best and most authentic selves, but also to be trailblazers in their own lives. As leaders of women's colleges, President Leary and I know that to be a trailblazer requires scanning the landscape before you and making decisions about either taking the most efficient path or the one that hasn't yet been carved out. With either route, a trailblazer faces a thicket of obstacles: a society that often treats you as invisible, a world that calls into question your right to demand justice, and a culture that tries again and again to place hurdles in your way—blocking your progress, draining your energy, and forcing you always to look down at what is making you stumble instead of looking up at the horizon in front of you. This book is about clearing away the brush so that trailblazers—like you—can keep your eyes on the limitless vista ahead.

NOTES

1. Barber, B. (1998). *A Passion for Democracy: American Essays* (p. 183). Princeton, N.J.: Princeton University Press.

2. Mosel, Tad. (1989). *All the Way Home: A Drama in Three Acts* (p. 68). New York: Samuel French, Inc.

Introduction

"The future belongs to those
who believe in the beauty of their dreams."

—*Attributed to Eleanor Roosevelt*

*F*or many women, a college education seems like an impossible dream. This dilemma is the inspiration for this book and a very personal reason why I have decided to offer my thoughts on adult women's education. Today, the number of first-generation college students of all ages has increased significantly. I am a product of that movement and have been fortunate that my parents believed that a college degree could open the door to opportunity. Neither of my parents graduated from high school. My father immigrated to America at the age of five. My Italian grandparents, with whom we lived, had no high school education, but they, too, believed in the American dream and encouraged their grandchildren to work hard in school so that college might be an option.

I was an adult student who decided to return to college for my Ph.D. after being away from higher education for 15 years. I had not been in a formal classroom during that time. I had not even had a math course since the age of 17. But I realized that if I wished to continue as an administrator in the field of higher education, I would need a Ph.D. Also, I faced a detour in my professional life when I was dissatisfied with my job and knew I would never please my boss. It was a very unhappy time for me, and my first time facing this type of dilemma in my professional career. My husband, Noel, encouraged me to quit my job and study for my doctorate. We knew we would have to live on one salary, maybe give up some of the things we were used to having. But my husband knew that the degree would help me regain my self-esteem and do something I had always wanted to do.

I provide this personal background to show that even when we think we are secure at one stage in our lives, we may be thrown a curve ball. We may have to take a step back and decide that, though making a change may be frightening and unsettling, there may be something ahead that will transform our situation into something better, more fulfilling. So it was in my case.

I was fortunate to receive a fellowship to American University in Washington, DC, and to pursue my doctorate in educational administration. I faced fear of failure, and I worried that I was too old to go back to college. My first course in statistics intimidated me, and I had to hire a tutor. I even had writer's block when doing my dissertation, and I almost gave up. Yet my course of study and writing my dissertation changed my life and allowed me to advance to the position of President of Bay Path University.

Founded in 1897 as Bay Path Institute in Springfield, Massachusetts, Bay Path became a women's college in 1945. Including my 13 years working at Simmons College (a women's college in Boston), I have dedicated my life to the education and advancement of women.

During the last 50 years, the face of higher education has changed dramatically. From a fairly homogeneous group made up of more than 60% white male students around the 1960s, the United States college population is now beginning to reflect the diversity of America. Today, nearly 60% of all college students are women, and the student population better reflects the cultural diversity of our country, though not in the percentages that we would hope. These statistics will change drastically over the next 30 years as our population includes the children of more immigrants as well as students of more diverse racial, socioeconomic, and religious profiles.[1]

One thing is certain: To have a college education is still the privilege of a few. Even with the encouragement of every administration, only 30.4% of all Americans over the age of 25 have a bachelor's degree, according to a 2012 *New York Times* article. Asian Americans take the lead, with 50.3% having achieved a bachelor's degree. Thirty-four percent of non-Hispanic whites have bachelor's degrees, while 14.1% of Hispanic Americans and 19.9% of African Americans have graduated college.[2] In 2012, the number of women earning bachelor's degrees actually surpassed the number of men who had earned them.[3]

One critical change in the profile of those seeking higher education is the increase in the number of adult students. Today, only 16% of all college students are 18–22 years old and live on a college campus.[4] This statistic is remarkably different from our expectations. The adult student population has increased significantly in all types of institutions, including the for-profit colleges and universities that have proliferated in the last 10 to 15 years. These adult students range from those who are retraining at community colleges for new career skills to obtain a certificate or associate's degree, to those who are returning after an interruption in their college journey, to those who finally have the time and motivation, or who realize that a college degree will provide a wider range of opportunities and potentially an increase in earning power over a lifetime. According to a 2000 report from the U.S. Census Bureau, those who end their education with a high school diploma will earn approximately $1.2 million in their lifetime, while those who go on to a college degree earn considerably more. An associate's degree nets graduates $1.6 million in lifetime earnings, while those with a bachelor's degree can earn as much as $2.1 million over their lifetime. At the master's level, the earning potential is even more significant.[5]

But taking that first step toward college can be intimidating. You may be afraid that you cannot learn, that an education is an unattainable goal because somewhere along the line, you were told you did not have the capacity to achieve or to learn. Or perhaps you had a number of negative educational experiences. Perhaps you were bored in elementary or secondary school. Maybe no one excited your yearning to learn, or you just wanted to get out of a system that didn't relate to you. Perhaps your life was so stressful that it was impossible to even consider sitting in a classroom or at a computer to take a course. Or maybe you had a desire to work and do something with your hands or your mind that did not involve taking a series of courses that seemed like a burden rather than a joy.

For women in particular, having children may be a reason for not starting or continuing their education. Some women may worry that their education could require their family or a spouse/partner to make too many sacrifices.

Here is where I draw the line in the sand. Education is for everyone: If you can think, you can learn. So think of today as a blank slate. You do have the capacity to learn if you're in the right frame of mind and in the right learning environment.

Somewhere along the way, perhaps you discovered that you enjoyed reading, or someone might have told you that you were creative or a good problem solver, that you were caring and kind with people, or that you might enjoy taking a few courses in an area for which you had a passion. Those courses, once accumulated, could lead to a college degree in your area of interest.

So know right from the start: We can all learn if we are in the right state of mind; if someone has inspired us to explore a topic; if we have curiosity about knowing something more fully or deeply; if someone has believed in our potential.

Finally, for women, there is no perfect time to start or return to college. There are so many different ways to achieve an education: through on-ground classes, online, hybrid (a bit of each), or competency-based learning. We may have families, but our families will eventually benefit from our college education.

As an educator for more than 45 years—33 of those at women's colleges—I have witnessed the incredible spirit and tenacity of adult women as they embark upon and continue their higher education journeys. I have been inspired by their drive and determination to achieve a college degree for personal and professional reasons. I have marveled at the obstacles they have faced and how they have overcome those challenges to continue on the path to a degree. These women are the true inspiration for this book, which I hope will be a beacon and a guide to adult women who wish to begin or continue their education.

While at Bay Path, I have been fortunate to have colleagues who fervently believe in the power of educating adult women. I particularly wish to acknowledge Dr. William Sipple (Provost and Vice President for Academic Affairs Emeritus at Bay Path University), and Dr. Vana Nespor (currently Chief Learning Officer of The American Women's College Online and One Day a Week Program at Bay Path University). Having worked with Dr. Sipple and with Dr. Nespor, I learned much about adult women's education and the best practices for addressing women's ways of learning. From offering courses at times that fit into women's busy schedules to creating accelerated degree programs, Dr. Nespor worked with our talented faculty and administrators to make a college education a reality for thousands of women who might not otherwise have been able to attend. Over the last 15 years, Bay Path's program has expanded and improved, and we are now offering our courses worldwide to women who wish to study in a supportive, inspiring, creative, and entrepreneurial online environment.

I am forever grateful to the faculty and staff of Bay Path University for their flexibility, dedication, and determination to offer degrees to all of these women. I thank our donors, who have invested millions of dollars in the education of adult women through scholarships, technological improvements, cocurricular professional development programs, leadership experiences, and internship opportunities. Donations have also ensured the small classroom size and the nurturing, supportive culture of the educational experience. Our goal is to ensure that every woman reaches her potential and beyond.

It has been a privilege to be a participant in, and an observer of, the growth of adult women's education in our country. Even more so, it has been an honor to write this book to help women around the globe earn a college degree.

I hope the topics I have addressed will provide the inspiration for women of all backgrounds to start their education. Whether you are the first in your family to obtain a degree, whether you are 60 years old, whether you have ten children or none, whether you are rich or poor, whether you are in a relationship or not, whether you believe in your potential or you don't, whether you finished high school or you didn't, you can achieve your dreams.

I started this introduction discussing the dream of a college education. While I was writing this book in Rome, Italy, my husband and I visited the National Gallery of Modern Art near Villa Borghese. As we passed through the rooms of elegant works of art, I stopped in front of an 1896 painting by Vittorio Matteo Corcos of a woman sitting on a bench. She had books next to her, and she looked out into the eyes of the Italian painter with great anticipation. I was struck by the painting and asked my husband to take a picture. I loved the composition; the look on the woman's face was timeless. It was not until later, when we bought the catalog of the gallery paintings, that we discovered the title of the painting: *Dreams*. To say I was startled would be an understatement. It seemed that she was there waiting for me to find her as the cover of my book. So I now know even more deeply that this book was meant for women of all centuries, all countries, and all circumstances . . . for *all* women who dare to dream.

Dreams by Vittorio Matteo Corcos (1859–1933)
Painting, 1896, Galleria Nazionale d'Arte Moderna, Rome.

RESOURCES:

Pelletier, S. G. (2010, Fall). Success for Adult Students. *Public Purpose*, pp. 2-6. Retrieved from www.aascu.org/uploadedFiles/AASCU/Content/Root/Media AndPublications/PublicPurposeMag azines/Issue/10fall_adultstudents.pdf

Perez-Pena, R. (2012, February 23). U.S. Bachelor Degree Rate Passes Milestone. *The New York Times*. Retrieved from www.nytimes.com/2012/02 /24/education/census-finds-bachelors-degrees-at-record-level.html ?module=Search&mabReward=relbias%3Ar%2C{%221%22%3A%22RI %3A7%22}

United States Census Bureau. (2012). *Current Population Survey*. Retrieved from www.census.gov/hhes/socdemo/education/data/cps/2012/tables.html

United States Department of Education. Institute of Education Sciences. National Center for Education Statistics. (2012). *Digest of Education Statistics*. Retrieved from nces.ed.gov/programs/digest/d12/tables/dt12_267.asp

United States Department of Labor. Bureau of Labor Statistics. (2002, Fall). More Education Means Higher Earnings—for Life. *Occupational Outlook Quarterly*. Retrieved from www.bls.gov/careeroutlook/2002/fall/oochart.pdf

NOTES:

1. United States Department of Education. Institute of Education Sciences. National Center for Education Statistics. (2012). *Digest of Education Statistics*. Retrieved from nces.ed.gov/programs/digest/d12/tables/dt12_267.asp

2. Perez-Pena, R. (2012, February 23). U.S. Bachelor Degree Rate Passes Milestone. *The New York Times*. Retrieved from www.nytimes.com/2012/02 /24/education/census-finds-bachelors-degrees-at-record-level.html ?module=Search&mabReward=relbias%3Ar%2C{%221%22%3A%22RI %3A7%22}

3. United States Census Bureau. (2012). *Current Population Survey*. Retrieved from www.census.gov/hhes/socdemo/education/data/cps/2012/tables.html

4. Pelletier, S. G. (2010, Fall). Success for Adult Students. *Public Purpose*, p. 2. Retrieved from www.aascu.org/uploadedFiles/AASCU/Content /Root/MediaAndPublications/PublicPurposeMagazines/Issue/10fall _adultstudents.pdf

5. United States Department of Labor, Bureau of Labor Statistics. (2002, Fall). More Education Means Higher Earnings—for Life. *Occupational Outlook Quarterly*. Retrieved from www.bls.gov/careeroutlook/2002/fall/oochart.pdf

Why Should You
Read this Book?

*W*e sometimes need a road map, a resource, an inspirational example, to achieve a goal. For women who do not have a college degree, the intent of this book is to provide those tools. Knowing that women lead unusually busy lives, I have designed it to guide you through a series of chapters and action steps that can be started and stopped and even repeated, if necessary. Within its pages, you will find the background you need to start the journey toward obtaining a college degree and the motivation to keep going.

The steps you will need to take come from three perspectives: First, I'll share my own years of experience in college administration, including 33 years working exclusively with women. Secondly, experts who have worked primarily with adult women students will provide advice in such areas as: selecting the appropriate educational environment for your particular goals; applying to the college of your choice; financing your education; navigating the academic culture; seeking assistance when detours present themselves; planning your career; graduating and considering postgraduate education; and more. Finally and most important, this guide will provide inspiration from students who have experienced many of the challenges and obstacles that adult women face in their lives.

Within each chapter, a series of headings will take you directly to the information you need; the chapter concludes with a list of real action steps that you can take to get closer to your goals. The recommendations will include simple, straightforward advice for overcoming hurdles that may derail your dream of a college education.

Following that, you will find a list of additional sources so that you may search the library or the web for supplemental information. For example, it would be impossible to list all the sources for scholarship assistance from the federal government, but the experts will lead you to those that staff and students have found most helpful.

In summary, here are some things that I think readers will gain from this book:

- **An Understanding of the Importance of a Degree**
  In today's increasingly technological world, a college education is more important than ever. Studies show that workers with higher education have an advantage when it comes to career advancement, promotions, and higher pay.

- **Practical Steps to Get Started**
  With the many responsibilities and roles modern women have, taking that first step toward an education can often be difficult. Family, work, aging parents, financial obligations, and limited time can all present challenges.

  Fear of failure and a lack of self-confidence can sometimes keep us from getting started. So can age. Many women fear that they are too old to go back to school. I understand this concern from my personal experience. I returned to college for my Ph.D. at age 38. I hadn't had a math class since I was 17. I often wondered if it would really be worth it. Although I might not have started in exactly the same way you might be starting, I suffered from the same fears of failure, including math phobia and writer's block. When I was close to finishing, I almost gave up. But I made it through by taking one step at a time, and so can you.

More than ever, society realizes that the typical college student is no longer 18–22 years old and living on a college campus. Today in America, the number of adult students outnumbers the number of students under age 21.[1] Older students are now taking courses not only toward degrees at the undergraduate and graduate levels, but also for career advancement or for pleasure. So take heart; you're not alone.

To keep you on the journey with signposts along the way, the few simple action steps I offer at the end of each chapter will give you the baby steps to get started and a list to check off as you complete them. In this way, you can begin that first step and have the sense that you have accomplished something. For example, I may ask you to contact a college to obtain information on a course of study in which you have an interest. As you complete each practical step, you will have accomplished a significant goal.

- **Insight Into Women's Ways of Learning**
Faculty who work with adult women will provide information that may help you understand how you learn best. You can gauge your preferred learning style based on the research, and then decide what environment for learning is best for you, how your unique ways of learning can be translated into how you will work, and how you will contribute your talents to our society.

- **Tips for Facing and Overcoming Challenges and Obstacles**
This book will also help during those times when you might hit that proverbial brick wall and feel you cannot advance any further, when you have to detour for a while. I have found that sometimes we set a direction in our lives, and then when some obstacle stands in our way, we fall

behind on the path. We then have a tough time getting started again. I have included a chapter on how to get back on the path, how to start refreshed, and how to consider an interruption as an opportunity for reflection, rest, and revitalization.

- **Advice on Balancing Work/Life/School/Family Issues**
  We realize how important a woman's family can be in her educational process, and how difficult juggling school, family, and work responsibilities can be. This book will help you with issues of balance. It can be a challenge to handle all life's obligations and still attend college. Experts will provide resources to keep you motivated and on target. You'll learn how to take advantage of networking opportunities and academic support programs that can help you balance your roles. You'll find realistic ideas for seeking support, such as bartering with your women peers for time to watch your children if you do something in return, like tutoring in math, science, etc.

  You'll also learn ways to enlist your family's help to accomplish your goals, and how your family will benefit from your obtaining a college education. If you're a mother, you'll find out how your children can learn from your example about the importance of higher education and dedication to a goal. Both men and women who return to school as adults often state that they found their inspiration from the example of a mother who attended college as an adult.

- **Information About a Variety of Options and Environments for Your Education**
  Because every student has a different learning style, this book will help you decide what type of student you are and how to select the right environment for your course of study. Today there are many alternatives available. Here are some of the choices you'll learn about:

- Women's colleges or co-ed institutions

- Private or public colleges

- On-ground or online learning

- Accelerated or traditional semester study

- Day, evening, or weekend programs

You'll learn how to use interviews and campus visits to get a feel for a place and see if it's the right fit for you. And you'll find out how to research a school's reputation and credentials and how to interpret statistical information about it.

With more than 40 years of experience in all of these educational alternatives, I can offer both objective and subjective advice on how to weigh these choices.

- **Expert Advice on Admission, Financial Aid, and More**
  Being able to take full advantage of the services available at the college you select is important. In this book, faculty and staff experts will provide perspectives on how to begin and continue your education; you'll even learn about taking your first course and about how to use a syllabus. You'll find out about using the library and doing research. And you'll find out about services like counseling and tutoring, which can help you when you get stuck.

  I've asked experts to contribute essays to this book on a number of topics, such as the admission process and how to obtain financial assistance from the government, your state, and the institution you wish to attend. You'll find advice on how to get bank or federal loans, and on what steps you need to take to ensure you can pay a loan back without penalties. You'll learn how to apply for grants and scholarships from organizations like the Rotary Club, YWCA, women's foundations, and other sources.

  You'll also learn about the different types of degrees, from certificates and associate's degrees to bachelor's and postgraduate degrees. You'll learn how to transfer credits from previous education or obtain credit for work experience, and how to get the most credit toward your degree. If you're starting from scratch, with no college experience, our experts will also advise you.

- **Insight Into Making the Most of the College Experience**
  The college experience doesn't end when you leave the classroom and the library. Today's colleges offer a range of cocurricular and extracurricular experiences to enrich students' lives. You'll learn about the wealth of information and opportunities offered by speakers, lectures, trips, and other programs that go beyond your classroom experience.

- **Career Planning Advice**
  I've included advice on planning for a career—both in the early stages of your education, when you are choosing a college or a major, and when you're looking forward to graduation. For most students, a degree that will help them find a job in a particular field is a top priority. We understand that goal, and our career planning advice stresses that you cannot wait until your last 60 credits for assistance. Students must always have their career goals front and center and make friends with the advisors in the career planning office early in their college career.

- **Advice on Life Skills**
  One benefit of a college education is the opportunity not only to become an expert in a subject, but also to learn important life skills that will enhance your well-being. For example, you will gain important knowledge in communication and leadership skills, financial literacy, community service, and philanthropy. Though many of these skills will be embedded in your course work, there will also be workshops, conferences, and extra credit available.

- **Assistance With Planning Beyond Graduation Day**
  I will help you look beyond graduation day, to answer

the question "What next?" You'll learn how your new degree may help you to advance in your present job or to get a new one. You'll also learn about options for further education, such as pursuing a postgraduate degree like a master's or a Ph.D.

- **Inspiration and Motivation**
  We sometimes need the support of a friend, family member, or mentor to help us on our journey. It is my hope that I can provide some of the inspiration, but you will also hear from women who have faced significant challenges in their life and who have successfully completed their education. Many of the chapters will provide personal stories that will inspire you and encourage you to take the first step and to continue even when you feel you cannot move forward.

- **An Opportunity to Celebrate!**
  Along the way, I ask that you do one thing for me: Celebrate. As you complete each chapter and the action steps included, I hope you will treat yourself and celebrate your success. I firmly believe that we need to pat ourselves on the back and say, "Well done!" We need to set milestones and benchmarks along the way to stay focused and on the path to an exciting and productive adventure, one that will lead to an enriched, satisfying life ahead.

  These little celebrations are really symbols of your continuing journey. You'll need to celebrate your accomplishments, even when they may seem small and insignificant in the grander plan of achieving a college degree. We all need to celebrate the markers and milestones in our lives, whether small or big. It doesn't matter as long as you celebrate.

  So I encourage you to celebrate accomplishments like:

  - Completing and sending your application to the colleges of your choice.

- Taking your first course.

- Solving a family problem while still maintaining attendance in a course to completion.

- Helping a peer with an assignment or offering to help in some other way.

- Asking a staff member or faculty member for help with an assignment.

- Attending a lecture just for the pleasure of it.

- Volunteering in your community for an hour, a day, or longer to help an organization or individual.

  Things you might do to celebrate could include:

- Inviting a faculty member or staff member to tea or coffee.

- Writing an e-mail to the college president about a course you particularly enjoyed and complimenting the faculty member.

- Inviting a classmate to have coffee or tea with you.

- Planning a party to recognize your graduation.

- And finally, thanking and celebrating those who have helped you along the way to graduation.

So let us begin our journey together. Let us consider each page as one step closer to your achieving a college degree. It may be by taking one course to start and then pursuing an associate's degree. No matter what your final destination may be, it is my hope that the chapters that follow will be an easy-to-use series of steps that get you to your goal.

Carpe diem! Seize the day. Seize the dream.

GINETTE'S STORY

For many women, returning to college can have a profound effect on their family members. Ginette went back to college after spending 20 years in the workforce and raising four successful children—one of them adopted. She didn't realize how much her college journey meant to her children until she read her daughter's proud Facebook post:

"After working three jobs for a lifetime, after purchasing her first home of her own in her 40s, after everything she's ever done for all her children, both biological and other-wise, next month my mom will be a college graduate. She is the epitome of perseverance, persistence, hard work, and dedication. She is all I aspire to be in a mother.

"She put all of her kids first, made sure we all succeeded, before doing anything for her[self]. Mom, for all the times you sat in the audience while I walked to get my diploma and degrees, you can bet that I'll be sitting in the audience while you walk to get yours! You should be so proud of yourself! And you should know that all of your kids are so proud of you!!!!! Go Mom!!"

RESOURCES:

Belenky, M. F., & Clinchy, B. M. (1997). *Women's Ways of Knowing: The Development of Self, Voice, and Mind.* New York: Basic Books.

United States Department of Education. Institute of Education Sciences. National Center for Education Statistics. (2012). *Digest of Education Statistics.* Retrieved from nces.ed.gov/programs/digest/d12/tables/dt12_267.asp

NOTES:

1. United States Department of Education. Institute of Education Sciences. National Center for Education Statistics. (2012). *Digest of Education Statistics.* Retrieved from nces.ed.gov/programs/digest/d12/tables/dt12_267.asp

2

WHY A COLLEGE EDUCATION?

*T*he world has changed dramatically in the past 40 years; women are no longer the minority in higher education. According to the educational consulting firm Ruffalo Noel Levitz's 2014–2015 *National Adult Student Priorities Report,* "Since 2000, adult learners (students age 25 and older) have become one of the fastest growing college student populations. Between 2000 and 2011, their enrollment increased by 41 percent, and is expected to grow another 14 percent through 2021. They comprise nearly 40 percent of the total student population."[1] As of 2012, more than 60% of students age 25 and older were women.[2] In a 2009 article for the National Academic Advising Association, Lisa G. Peck and Jennifer Varney noted that "...the rate of increase in female adult learners aged 30-34 has been particularly aggressive."[3]

In 2011, women of all ages comprised almost 60% of all college students.[4] So there is no excuse for not entering a world in which you will be embraced, and which will open up work opportunities at many levels of organizations. You might not be a CEO in your for-profit or not-for-profit work environment, but you will have more options for advancement than any past generation of women.

But why should you be one of those women returning to school? Here are some of the major reasons that women often cite:

- **America Needs a Better Educated Workforce to Compete in a Global Economy**

  Globalization and the rapid rise of information technology have radically changed the American job market, according to Thomas Friedman and Michael Mandelbaum's *That Used to Be Us: How America Fell Behind in the World It Invented and How We Can Come Back*. Many jobs have been eliminated entirely, and new jobs are more complex and technology oriented. These changes, according to Friedman and Mandelbaum, require "every American to be better educated than ever to secure and keep a well-paying job."[5]

  Recent data in a study at the Georgetown University Center on Education and the Workforce show that America will lose economically—both domestically and internationally—if we do not produce more college graduates. The study's authors note that:

  > ...by 2018, we will need 22 million new college degrees—**but will fall short of that number by at least 3 million post-secondary degrees, Associate's or better. In addition, we will need at least 4.7 million new workers with postsecondary certificates.** [boldface sic]

  > ...This shortfall—which amounts to a deficit of 300,000 college graduates every year between 2008 and 2018—results from burgeoning demand by employers for workers with high levels of education and training. Our calculations show that America's colleges and universities would need to increase the number of degrees they confer by 10 percent annually, a tall order.

  > ...Between 1973 and 2008, the share of jobs in the US economy which required postsecondary education increased from 28 percent to 59 percent. According to our projections, the future promises more of the same...High school graduates and dropouts will find

themselves largely left behind in the coming decade as employer demand for workers with postsecondary degrees continues to surge.[6]

A by-product of achieving a degree, not only for us, but also for our children, is our country's future health and economic vitality. An educated workforce will create products and provide services that are consumed here and overseas to keep the economic engine of our country fueled and productive.

- **An Increasing Number of Jobs Require a College Education**
  In many cases, both traditional and nontraditional students seek a college degree because it is the major qualification for a particular job. For example, if you want to be a nurse, teacher, lawyer, doctor, or accountant, there are specific courses required to achieve proficiency and certification in the field. Today, the bachelor's degree is still a privilege, but it is becoming a requirement for more and more positions. Some jobs that required only a high school education when our parents were in the job market now demand a bachelor's degree.

  With technology expanding in every profession, more and more jobs require computer skills for which an advanced education is needed. In fact, as our country moves toward running on more of a service-based economy, we will need the technological skills to maneuver through any profession, but more important, we will need the critical thinking and analytical skills that come with the study of a discipline or major.

- **A Degree Can Lead to a Promotion or Pay Raise**
  Career advancement is another reason for seeking a college education. In our country today, the earning power of those with an advanced degree is significantly higher than for those with a high school education. As noted in the introduction, lifetime earnings can be as much as

$900,000 more for a worker with a bachelor's degree than for someone with only a high school diploma.[7]

If you're trying to get a promotion or a salary increase in your present job, a college degree can be an advantage. After several years at a job, women often realize that a degree is essential, and they often return to college to seek a degree that will offer more upward mobility.

In some cases, employers will pay you to attend college, offering tuition reimbursements of anywhere from 10% to 100% of course expenses. Employers usually have guidelines for such assistance; for example, you may need to achieve a minimum grade to be eligible. Employers sometimes will not reimburse an employee until a course is successfully completed, so be prepared to pay up front.

- **A Degree Can Improve Your Standard of Living**
  Another reason for a college education is to improve one's standard of living. In its study on jobs and education requirements, the Georgetown University Center on Education and the Workforce states that:

  > In 1970, 26 percent of the middle class had postsecondary education and training. By 2007, 61 percent of middle class workers had postsecondary education and training.

  > Workers with postsecondary education and training are moving into the upper class. That is, the educational composition of the upper class also favors workers with some college or better. In 1970, 44 percent of the upper class had postsecondary education and training. By 2007, 81 percent of upper class workers had postsecondary education and training.[8]

  Our standard of living and ease of providing for our family is enhanced with a college degree. Today, we can offer the next generation a college degree at an earlier age, when we may not have had that opportunity.

- **A Change in Life Circumstances May Lead You to College**

For many adult women, a change in personal or professional circumstances—from an unexpected move to a new city, to divorce or separation, to a bad employment situation—may be the reason for seeking a degree. In a larger city, a job that you previously did with little or no higher education may now demand a degree.

A move is often cited as a reason for seeking a degree. For example, a military wife must start and stop her life every time her husband is recommissioned, which in many cases can be as often as every two to three years. In this case, an online degree might make the most sense; applying for such degrees will be discussed in the chapter on admissions.

- **Parenthood Might Have Delayed Your Higher Education**

Deciding to have children can delay or prevent a woman from seeking a degree. If you find a circumstance in which raising children has delayed your education, there is always hope. At Bay Path, we have had women at age 50 who have raised their families, worked in some entrepreneurial venture, or had a satisfying career while raising children, who often decide that they wish to have a bachelor's degree or a graduate degree.

A by-product of a mother's studying for and completing a degree is that she will be an excellent model for her children to follow. No matter the circumstances, there are few downsides to a child's watching his or her mother study and graduate. Although there are adjustments to be made in a family, women state that, in the end, they wish to be a good role model for their children.

The family can even become a part of the education process. Children will learn to respect their mother's study time. Women might even seek the assistance of their teenage or grown children with courses that are challenging.

I love this image of the child as the tutor. The most satisfying moments for me as a college president are those shouts at commencement: "Way to go, Mom!"

- **A Degree Can Provide Self-Fulfillment**
Finally, there is the woman who wants the degree for the degree itself. She might not need it for a profession or to advance in her career, but it is her dream. For some women, it promotes self-esteem to have a college degree. For others, it is the pursuit of knowledge with others that drives them forward. Many times these women are not under time constraints to complete their education and can savor every class as they travel toward a college degree.

My assumption in writing this book is that adult women are beginning their education or are returning to college to learn a professional skill, perhaps eventually to attend graduate school. Whatever the goal, the general education courses you take in the first few years of an associate's or bachelor's degree will enrich your life forever. Through the study of a discipline, you start by taking courses that give you a broad view of your world. Colleges are structured to provide this liberal education in addition to teaching a specific major or professional goal.

In many cases, women discover a love of art, history, or science because of a general education course they take as a requirement for graduation. For example, I started my education with the goal of studying a foreign language and working with those seeking American citizenship. Because of a series of excellent professors in political science and international relations, I changed my major at the end of my sophomore year and finally graduated with a political science degree. My interest in the subject matter, my fascination with the professors who skillfully and passionately shared their knowledge, changed my course of study.

Can you be educated without a college degree? Of course. We all know brilliant writers, business professionals, and entrepreneurs who have succeeded without a college degree. There is a talent or drive that distinguishes such individuals from the rest. But for most of us, a college degree is necessary to advance in our work lives or to provide a sense of fulfillment in learning for learning's sake. An educated woman is someone with great curiosity about our world or about one particular subject and who pursues that interest by being taught or by doing research on her own. I know women who have never attended college but are very well-read on a number of subjects. So it is not the college degree that makes an educated woman. It is a mind-set for learning, a curiosity about life around us. The degree is merely one tool. If we keep this definition close at heart throughout our lifetime, we will seek education in the daily news, in reading a book for pleasure, in formal classroom and online settings, in a Google search, wherever, whenever we can.

So why an education? Edith Hamilton, educator and writer (1867-1963), may have said it best: "It has always seemed strange to me that in our endless discussions about education so little stress is laid on the pleasure of becoming an educated person, the enormous interest it adds to life. To be able to be caught up into the world of thought—that is to be educated."[9]

In the end, the "why" of achieving a college degree is personal. This book can help you, whatever your reason. This book will give you the steps to the end result—the dream.

KEY POINTS TO REMEMBER:

- Women make up more than half of the college population today.

- America needs more college graduates to be competitive in the global marketplace.

- An increasing number of jobs require a degree.

- A degree can be the key to a promotion, a raise, a better job, or a higher standard of living.

- No matter what your life circumstances, a degree is attainable.

- A degree is valuable for its own sake; it can lead to self-fulfillment and higher self-esteem.

ACTION STEPS:

1. Pick two college-educated people whom you admire and ask them about their college experience. What did they study? Has it been beneficial? What did they gain from the experience and would they do it again? What advice can they give you about going back to college?

2. Are there jobs that have always interested you? Go to the Bureau of Labor Statistics website: www.bls.gov/ooh. Look up several jobs that interest you; find out about minimum requirements, salary range, and the jobs' future outlook.

3. On a sheet of paper, draw two columns. At the top of one, write "pros"; at the top of the other, write "cons." Then make your list of pros and cons for a college education in each column.

MICHELLE'S STORY

Michelle had been accepted at a college after graduating high school, but decided to go to work as a legal secretary in order to help her family pay the bills. "This seemed fine for a while," she said, "but I always felt I was capable of more—much more." After a divorce in her early 30s, she "began to reassess [her] goals."

"[T]o remain competitive in the job market," she began taking classes at a local community college. "I was hooked," she said, "and continued with classes, never thinking I would finally obtain an associate's degree . . . Along the way, I also gave birth to a beautiful daughter—a bonus! I now was determined to not only achieve higher academic success but to also set a positive example for her." She studied for a second associate's degree and graduated as co-valedictorian of her class. "The graduation ceremony . . . will always remain one of the high points of my life."

RESOURCES:

Carneval, A. P. (2010, June). Executive Summary. In *Help Wanted: Projections of Jobs and Education Requirements through 2013*. Washington, DC: Georgetown University Center on Education and the Workforce. Retrieved from georgetown.app.box.com/s/28gamdlhtll4fsmyh48k

Friedman, T. L. (2011). *That Used To Be Us: How America Fell Behind in the World It Invented and How We Can Come Back*. New York: Farrar, Straus and Giroux.

Hamilton, E. (1959). *Bryn Mawr Bulletin*. As cited in K. Olson. (2009). *Wounded by School: Recapturing the Joy in Learning and Standing Up to Old School Culture* (p. 30). New York: Teachers College Press.

Peck, L. J. (2009). *Advising IS Teaching: Providing Adult Learners with Strategies for Self-Advocation*. Retrieved from www.nacada.ksu.edu/Resources /Clearinghouse/View-Articles/Providing-adult-learners-with-strategies-for-self-advocation.aspx

Ruffalo Noel Levitz. (2015). *2014-2015 National Adult Student Priorities Report*. Retrieved from www.noellevitz.com/Benchmark

United States Department of Education. Institute of Education Sciences. National Center for Education Statistics. (2012). *Digest of Education Statistics, Table 303.40*. Retrieved from nces.ed.gov/programs/digest/d13/tables/dt13_303 .40.asp

United States Department of Labor. Bureau of Labor Statistics. (2002, Fall). More Education Means Higher Earnings—for Life. *Occupational Outlook Quarterly*. Retrieved from www.bls.gov/careeroutlook/2002/fall/oochart.pdf

United States Department of Labor. Bureau of Labor Statistics. (2014, January 8). *Occupational Outlook Handbook*. Retrieved from www.bls.gov/ooh

NOTES:

1. Ruffalo Noel Levitz. (2015). *2014-2015 National Adult Student Priorities Report* (p. 2). Cedar Rapids, IA: Ruffalo Noel Levitz. Retrieved from www .noellevitz.com/Benchmark

2. United States Department of Education. Institute of Education Sciences. National Center for Education Statistics. (2012). *Digest of Education Statistics, Table 303.40*. Retrieved from nces.ed.gov/programs/digest/d13/tables /dt13_303.40.asp

3. Peck, L. J. & Varney, J. (2009). *Advising IS Teaching: Providing Adult Learners with Strategies for Self-Advocation*. Retrieved from www.nacada.ksu.edu /Resources/Clearinghouse/View-Articles/Providing-adult-learners-with-strategies-for-self-advocation.aspx

4. United States Department of Education, 2012.

5. Friedman, T. & Mandelbaum, M. (2011). *That Used To Be Us: How America Fell Behind in the World It Invented and How We Can Come Back* (p. 20). New York: Farrar, Straus and Giroux.

6. Carneval, A. P. (2010, June). Executive Summary. In *Help Wanted: Projections of Jobs and Education Requirements through 2013*. Washington, DC: Georgetown University Center on Education and the Workforce. Retrieved from georgetown.app.box.com/s/28gamdlhtll4fsmyh48k

7. United States Department of Labor. Bureau of Labor Statistics. (2002, Fall). More Education Means Higher Earnings—for Life. *Occupational Outlook Quarterly*. Retrieved from www.bls.gov/careeroutlook/2002/fall/oochart.pdf

8. Carneval et al.

9. Hamilton, E. (1959). *Bryn Mawr Bulletin*. As cited in K. Olson. (2009). *Wounded by School: Recapturing the Joy in Learning and Standing Up to Old School Culture* (p. 30). New York: Teachers College Press.

3

Understanding
How Adult Women Learn

*I*n the previous chapter, you have learned why it is important to seek a college degree. But there is also a way for you to define your learning styles so that you can select the best environment in which to seek your degree.

Having worked at public and private, small and large, secular and religious, predominately male and all-female colleges, I have experienced a wide variety of learning environments. I am not a graduate of an all-women's college, but my first experience with single-sex education at Simmons College in Boston was an eye-opener for me. The women were engaged in every aspect of their education. There was a deep respect and an appreciation for learning and for those who taught, whether in or out of the classroom. But more important, the classes and the cocurricular environment motivated women to achieve their potential.

We all learn in unique and different ways. Some students can study while listening to music; others must have complete silence for concentration. Some women learn best by reading, by teaching the material they are learning to someone else, by experiencing the information, or by memorizing. Whatever your learning style, there are some simple principles about learning that can help you pursue your preferred style, while enticing you to think and understand how others learn. A wonderful resource is Howard Gardner's *Multiple Intelligences: New Horizons in Theory and Practice* (Basic Books). This seminal classic of 1993 was updated in 2008, and is used by readers from parents to college professors for understanding how people learn.

Women's Ways of Knowing: The Development of Self, Voice, and Mind was a breakthrough book in the 1980s by Mary Field Belenky, Blythe Mcvicker Clinchy, Nancy Rule Goldberger, and Jill Mattuck Tarule, professors at institutions that included the University of Vermont, the Fielding Institute (now named Fielding Graduate University) in California, and Wellesley College, a women's college in Massachusetts. In that book, the authors stress that women learn differently from men. Perhaps it is the way we have been raised. Perhaps it is just part of being a woman. No matter what your perspective on gender differences in learning, there seems to be evidence that women look at the world in different ways and therefore learn best when the educational environment reflects their ways of knowing the world. Our experts will share their insights, and you can decide if their advice can assist you in selecting the right learning environment for you.[1]

For some women, learning can be an intimidating process. Carol Gilligan at Harvard, who wrote *In a Different Voice: Psychological Theory and Women's Development*, explained why some young girls lose their voice by puberty and have a hard time finding the strong, confident voice they had as children.[2]

In *Men and Women of the Corporation*, Dr. Rosabeth Moss Kanter showed why men have held the leadership positions in major companies for hundreds of years, but also how women's styles of management could be an important part of the way we structure and lead our organizations in the future. Her prognosis has certainly been important to the rise of women in corporate America.[3] Margaret Hennig and Anne Jardim took the concept of women's management styles one step further in their groundbreaking book *The Managerial Woman*.[4]

Whether you attend an all-women's or a co-ed college, the point of this chapter is to understand how women learn. Experts who have taught women for decades will provide the context for you to determine how you learn best. That will be an important part of your decision-making process when selecting a college.

The first expert I include is Dr. Gina Joseph-Collins, who has had a career working with students of all ages, but particularly adult women. As former Dean of Adult and Professional Education for Adult Women at Bay Path University, she has observed the teaching and learning process as a faculty member as well as a mentor and advisor to women. She draws from her expertise to offer the thoughts that follow.

WHY COLLEGE IS IMPORTANT TO WOMEN
BY GINA JOSEPH-COLLINS, PH.D.

"WE ACCEPT LIFE AS A WORK IN PROGRESS WHERE ROLES AND THE MEANING OF ROLES CHANGE OVER TIME, WHERE WE ARE CONTINUALLY DEVELOPING, WHERE LEARNING, UNLEARNING AND RELEARNING ARE CONSTANTLY GOING ON."

—*Elizabeth Hayes and Daniele D. Flannery*
with Ann K. Brooks, Elizabeth J. Tisdell and Jane M. Hugo,
Women as Learners: The Significance of Gender
in Adult Learning[5]

Economics, culture, politics, and social contexts all play a role in the ways that women approach and benefit from college. The number of women who have enrolled in college has more than doubled over the past three decades. College is important to women because it gives them a chance to exercise their intellects and liberate their spirits. Women tend to view higher education as a way to prove their worth and advance their interests. When women enroll in college programs, they want to demonstrate to others (families, children, friends, employers, communities, etc.) that they can achieve success by learning and doing new things. This includes advancing their knowledge and improving their skills so they can support themselves and others. Like all learners, women are enriched by the knowledge they gain, motivated by the relationships they form, and inspired by the possibilities inherent in expanded worldviews and deeper personal insights.

The status of women across the globe is constantly evolving as more and more women graduate from college. Women are experiencing college as a way to discover their individual and collective voice, strength, and potential. Some women who enroll in college are interested in challenging the norms that society establishes for women, while others want to conform to traditional women's roles, albeit at higher levels. Women are overrepresented in career fields such as teaching and nursing and underrepresented in fields such as engineering and computer science. In many fields, including business and science, women are still creating pathways to the top. Through education, women can transform their lives because they gain a greater sense of themselves and a better understanding of the world.

As caregivers and nurturers, women pursue a college education because it gives them a chance to serve families, organizations, and communities with excellence. Women are also generally interested in social justice and the advancement of our society. Women use their education in the workplace and also as volunteers and entrepreneurs. College has been an important force for change; it has affirmed the worth of women, and it has empowered women to make a difference.

- **How Do Women Learn?**
  ". . . [W]omen learn much more than subject matter or skills. They learn implicit and explicit lessons about themselves as women . . ." —Hayes et al., *Women as Learners*[6]

Education is a powerful force because it engages the mind, body, and spirit in pursuit of our individual and collective well-being. Academic discipline requires study, reflection, planning, and results. Research reveals that the learning process gives women a chance to explore and transform their identity and circumstances. Ultimately, learning is tied to self-esteem for women, and it gives them a way to validate their experiences.

Studies confirm that women learn as much about themselves as they do about their world when pursuing education. Through the teaching and learning process, women are able to question old beliefs and create new knowledge concerning who they want to be and what they want to do in the world. Many women describe this as "finding their voice." In *Women as Learners: The Significance of Gender in Adult Learning*, Elizabeth Hayes and her co-authors Daniele D. Flannery, Ann K. Brooks, Elizabeth J. Tisdell, and Jane M. Hugo explain that voice has many meanings for women. It is "active—implying the ability to express thoughts and feelings so that they can be heard and understood by others."[7] Voice is also connection, image, expression, identity, power, and influence.

Holistic teaching and learning techniques are especially helpful to women because the cognitive, emotional, and physical dimensions of life are interconnected. Such techniques include critical reflection, storytelling, perspectives on practice, experiential learning, team building, dialogue, and diverse approaches for gathering and analyzing information. Hayes and her co-authors remind us that storytelling touches our hearts, puts a human face on the abstract world of ideas, moves our spirits, and encourages action.[8] Through critical reflection and practice we learn how to know, be, and do.

According to *Women as Learners*, feminist pedagogy is an approach to learning that encourages learners to become "more fully the authors of their own lives." In this sense educators must plan for learning activities that combine rational and cognitive models with affective relationship and connections. The idea of feminist pedagogy is that it "facilitates both women's development and structural social change for women."[9]

Women also learn best and more as they gain confidence. Confidence in these terms means that through the educational process women can become more conscious of their power. With increased faith in their abilities, they can then act in the most effective ways to achieve success. Therefore, the teaching and learning process for women must include activities that affirm the potential and promise of women so they will commit to lifelong learning and growth. An environment infused with storytelling, connections, critical reflection, and active participation ensures that this can happen.

Now you have a sense why so many educators like Dr. Joseph-Collins believe in the education and power of women returning to college. Dr. Kathryn Wiezbicki-Stevens is another expert educator who understands the depth and importance of learning. Dr. Wiezbicki-Stevens has been Professor and Chair of the Psychology Department at Bay Path University for a number of years. She did her doctoral dissertation on *Metacognition: Developing Self-Knowledge through Guided Reflection*, and has a deep insight into how we learn as individuals. She believes that by understanding how learning takes place, you will find great insight into yourself and how you will succeed as a student. She has compiled her thoughts (below) to help you understand your preferred learning style and to help you appreciate the variety and breadth of learning and teaching styles.

THE NEW SCIENCE OF LEARNING
by Kathryn Wiezbicki-Stevens, Ed.D.

Recent decades have seen a consolidated effort from neuroscientists, cognitive psychologists, and educators to interpret and synthesize research on learning and memory to help students. Years ago, your classes—either high school or college—were probably lectures in which you were expected to sit quietly and take notes. Basically, you were expected to be a passive recipient of the knowledge your teacher was sharing with you. You would show what you knew on an exam that probably produced a good deal of anxiety as you studied. Did you reread your notes? Did you memorize the facts? Did you cram at the last minute? These study strategies might have helped you pass, but did you feel as though you truly understood the content? More important, how much of that course content did you remember weeks, months, years later?

Key findings from a national report, *How People Learn: Brain, Mind, Experience, and School*, from the U.S. Department of Education's Office of Research and Improvement, all point to the concept of "deep learning" as the goal of educational experiences.[10] Deep learning entails personal involvement in a learning task, interest and relevance of content to the learner, seeking underlying meanings in the material, practical exercises that require analysis and synthesis rather than factual responses, and the use of participatory and engaging learning strategies.[11] College educators who embrace this approach create an entirely different dynamic in the classroom. Learning becomes an active process. It is more engaging, exciting, and meaningful for you. It is not just learning for learning's sake; it is learning with a purpose. How can you, the student, develop strategies to achieve deep learning?

A starting point is to address what happens when we are presented with new information. In order to build deep learning, it helps if we consider what we already know about a topic, if we have any preconceived notions or information that shares some kind of similarity. How does new information relate to what we already know? For example, a psychology class introduces the theory on social learning. When you hear about role models as part of this theory, you may remember seeing a recent article in a magazine or a show on TV discussing how the antics of some celebrities and professional athletes make them poor role models for our children. You've made a connection! We want our brains to search for an existing neural network into which new information can fit. The new information then expands the existing network by linking more neural connections, so that more becomes known. Now we have a place where the new information resides, so any further information on a topic can be linked, especially as we attempt to build a framework for understanding it. Those simple questions have helped you engage with that class topic. The vocabulary used in that theory, the implications, etc., all of it, can now be built on that first connection you made. Making a connection with new knowledge is crucial because the brain cannot organize what it does not have.[12]

Once new information has been integrated into your neural network (i.e., learning has begun), what sustains the learning over time (i.e., turns it into long-term memory)? Newly formed connections in a neural network are fragile. If they are not, in essence, exercised, the connection is lost. The common phrase "use it or lose it" is a helpful metaphor for this process.[13] Exercise, or repeated activation of new neural networks, can occur with frequent exposure. The more exposure to the various linked factors involving a new topic, the more a durable and sustained neural network is achieved. This is called "elaborative rehearsal," and involves numerous learning strategies that enhance your understanding and retention of information.[14] Examples include reading about a topic, discussing it, watching a video on it, writing about it, applying it to a case study, and role playing, to name a few. In addition, researchers have discovered a phenomenon called the "testing effect," which is another strategy for deep learning.[15] Frequent attempts to answer questions about topics from class or your reading enhance your memory. It is the act of retrieving information again and again that strengthens your neural network and builds your memory. Textbooks often embed review questions throughout a chapter. Your professors may frequently ask questions as a review when you discuss a topic in class. Quizzing yourself with flash cards can also help. These are the kinds of learning strategies that you'll find in a classroom dedicated to active learning, and you can certainly use these strategies on your own to rehearse your understanding, and ultimately achieve deep learning.

Two specific learning theories also address active strategies that will benefit you in your college studies. The first is the constructivist approach, the view that learning is a process of constructing one's own knowledge, as opposed to passively receiving it from an expert. Making sense of new information involves the individual process of adaptation and assemblage as well as a socially interactive exchange. If you are engaged with others in determining what is meaningful on a particular topic, and reflect on diverse views, then the topic becomes more relevant, interesting, and better understood.[16] You are also developing skills such as enhanced communication, understanding group dynamics, critical thinking, and reaching consensus (or agreeing not to!)—all valuable in today's work world.[17] Feminist theory in learning posits that women tend to be "connected learners" who possess skills for engaging others to participate in sharing knowledge.[18] A sense of community and connectedness is formed with classmates and the professor. Taking these approaches in your education creates an entirely different dynamic from what you may remember from school days of old; these approaches are engaging, active, interesting, and create a much richer and more fulfilling experience.

One last finding from *How People Learn* that you should know about refers to the role that metacognition plays in our learning process.[19] Metacognition is our awareness of the psychological processes involved in memory, thinking, and learning.[20] Regarded as the executive strategies of our cognitive abilities, metacognition involves the use of strategies to assist learners in an efficient pursuit of understanding. Metacognitive skills are recognized as an integral part of academic competence, ultimately influencing lifelong learning.[21]

Examples of metacognitive strategies include:

- **Predicting the Difficulty of a Learning Task**
  For example, how challenging will it be to write an essay or analyze a case study? Have you done anything like this before? What helped or did not help last time?

- **Planning the Way to Approach a Task**
  What are the steps needed to get started?

- **Monitoring Comprehension**
  If something seems unclear, how do you find an answer?

- **Sustaining Effort Over Time**
  What will help motivate you?

- **Evaluating Progress**
  Are you missing anything? Have you double-checked your work?

- **Knowing Your Strengths and Weaknesses as a Learner**
  In what aspects of this assignment are you confident? In what areas could you benefit from more time spent on the task, or help from someone such as a tutor?

From the combined experience of my experts and myself, what we now know about memory and the learning process means that college can be the relevant and rewarding experience you've always wanted it to be. Having an awareness of elements such as active learning, neural networking, frequency of exposure, the value of collaboration, and metacognitive strategies can make you a better learner, a more efficient learner. You can do this!

KEY POINTS TO REMEMBER:

- A college education can help women find their individual voice, strength, and potential.

- Women learn about both the world and themselves when pursuing education.

- Holistic learning (learning through many dimensions) is especially helpful to women.

- Women learn best as they gain confidence.

- Deep learning is an active process: learning with a purpose.

- To build deep learning, make connections between new material and what you already know.

- Repetition, exercise, and retrieval of information help learners retain information.

- Learning with others improves understanding and retention of information.

ACTION STEPS:

1. Select a college-educated woman whom you admire. Ask her what tips she has for achieving a degree or for getting through a difficult course.

2. Ask this same woman how her classes were structured in college. Does she have tips for learning and deciding what the best learning environment is for an adult woman who does not have a degree?

$\mathcal{T}$RECIA'S STORY

When Trecia was a child, her teachers told her that she was "a great kid but not exactly college material." As a result of this, she said, "I believed college would not be for me."

She added that "[F]ear, doubt and disbelief [had] an immobilizing effect" on her. After a divorce, she realized that "the lack of a college education" could impede her progress. One day she picked her child up from day care, and she saw a brochure for a one-day-a-week academic program at a local college. This happy accident "gave me hope beyond my wildest dreams," she said. "I picked up the brochure, and my life has never been the same." She had to face her fears in order to apply, but she said that it was worth it. She now has a Bachelor of Science degree in business administration and an MBA in entrepreneurial thinking and innovative practices. She had to juggle family, work, and school. "I've had to overcome many obstacles to stay in school," she said, but "I had finally stuck with something, a [previous] shortcoming for me, and I had achieved a college degree, something no one in my family had." She credited her college experience with giving her "resilience, innovation, authenticity, courage, and change."

RESOURCES:

Bandura, A. (1997). *Self-Efficacy: The Exercise of Control*. New York: W.H. Freeman.

Baxter Magolda, M. (1991). *Knowing and Reasoning in College: Gender-Related Patterns in Students' Intellectual Development*. San Francisco: Jossey-Bass.

Belenky, M. F. & Clinchy, B. M. (1991). *Women's Ways of Knowing: The Development of Self, Voice, and Mind*. New York: Basic Books.

Biggs, J. B. (1989). Approaches to the Enhancement of Tertiary Teaching. *Higher Education Research and Development, 8*(1), 7–25.

Bransford, J., Brown, A. L. & Cocking, R. R. (2000). *How People Learn: Brain, Mind, Experience and School*. Washington, DC: National Academy Press.

Chickering, A. W. & Gamson, Z. F. (1987). Seven Principles for Good Practice in Undergraduate Education. *American Association for Higher Education Bulletin, 39*(7), 3–7.

Cross, K. P. (1999). What Do We Know about Students' Learning and How Do We Know It? *Innovative Higher Education, 23*(4), 255–270.

Gilligan, C. (1982). *In a Different Voice: Psychological Theory and Women's Development*. Cambridge, Massachusetts: Harvard University Press.

Hayes, E. et al. (2002). *Women as Learners: The Significance of Gender in Adult Learning*. San Francisco: Jossey-Bass.

Hennig, M. & Jardim, A. (1997). *The Managerial Woman*. Garden City, New York: Anchor Press/Doubleday.

Kanter, R. M. (1993). *Men and Women of the Corporation*. New York: Basic Books.

Leamnson, R. (2000). Learning as Biological Brain Change. *Change, 32*(6), 34–41.

Pellegrino, J. W., Chudowsky, N. & Glaser, E. (Eds.). (2001). *Knowing What Students Know: The Science and Design of Educational Assessment*. Washington, DC: National Academy Press.

Pintrich, P. R. (2002). The Role of Metacognitive Knowledge in Learning, Teaching, and Assessment. *Theory into Practice, 41*(4), 220–227.

Roediger, H. L., III & Karpicke, J. D. (2006). Test-Enhanced Learning: Taking Memory Tests Improves Long-Term Retention. *Psychological Science, 17*(3), 249–255.

Säljö, R. (1981). Learning Approach and Outcome: Some Empirical Observations. *Instructional Science, 10*, 41–65.

Scheckly, B. G. & Bell, S. (2006). Experience, Consciousness, and Learning: Implications for Instruction. In S. Johnson & K. Taylor (Eds.). *The Neuroscience of Adult Learning* (pp. 43–52). San Francisco: Jossey-Bass.

Wolfe, P. (2001). *Brain Matters: Translating Research into Classroom Practice*. Alexandria, Virginia: Association for Supervision & Curriculum Development.

Zimmerman, B. J. (1990). Self-Regulated Learning and Academic Achievement: An Overview. *Educational Psychologist, 25*(1), 3–17.

NOTES:

1. Belenky, M. F. & Clinchy, B. M. (1997). *Women's Ways of Knowing: The Development of Self, Voice, and Mind.* New York: Basic Books.

2. Gilligan, C. (1982). *In a Different Voice: Psychological Theory and Women's Development.* Cambridge, Massachusetts: Harvard University Press.

3. Kanter, R. M. (1993). *Men and Women of the Corporation,* New York: Basic Books.

4. Hennig, M. & Jardim, A. (1977). *The Managerial Woman,* Garden City, New York: Anchor Press/Doubleday.

5. Hayes, E. et al. (2002). *Women as Learners: The Significance of Gender in Adult Learning* (p. v). San Francisco: Jossey-Bass.

6. Ibid, 51.

7. Ibid, 80.

8. Ibid, 80.

9. Ibid, 15.

10. Bransford, J., Brown, A. L. & Cocking, R. R. (2000). *How People Learn: Brain, Mind, Experience and School.* Washington, DC: National Academy Press.

11. Biggs, J. B. (1989). Approaches to the Enhancement of Tertiary Teaching. *Higher Education Research and Development 8*(1), 7–25. Chickering, A. W. & Gamson, Z. F. (1987). Seven Principles for Good Practice in Undergraduate Education. *American Association for Higher Education Bulletin 39*(7), 3–7. Pellegrino, J. W., Chudowsky, N. & Glaser, R. (Eds.). (2001). *Knowing What Students Know: The Science and Design of Educational Assessment.* Washington, DC: National Academy Press. Säljö, R. (1981). Learning Approach and Outcome: Some Empirical Observations. *Instructional Science 10,* 41–65.

12. Scheckly, B. G. & Bell, S. (2006). Experience, Consciousness, and Learning: Implications for Instruction. In S. Johnson & K. Taylor (Eds.), *The Neuroscience of Adult Learning* (pp. 43–52). San Francisco: Jossey-Bass.

13. Leamnson, R. (2000). Learning as Biological Brain Change. *Change, 32*(6), 34–41.

14. Wolfe, P. (2001). *Brain Matters: Translating Research into Classroom Practice.* Alexandria, VA: Association for Supervision & Curriculum Development.

15. Roediger, H. L. III & Karpicke, J. D. (2006). Test-Enhanced Learning: Taking Memory Tests Improves Long-Term Retention. *Psychological Science, 17*(3), 249–255.

16. Cross, K. P. (1999). What Do We Know about Students' Learning and How Do We Know It? *Innovative Higher Education, 23*(4), 255–270.

17. Baxter Magolda, M. (1992). *Knowing and Reasoning in College: Gender-Related Patterns in Students' Intellectual Development.* San Francisco: Jossey-Bass.

18. Belenky & Clinchy, 1997.

19. Bransford et al., 2000.

20. Bostrum, L. & Lassen, L. M. (2006). Unraveling Learning, Learning Styles, Learning Strategies and Meta-cognition. *Education and Training*, *48*(2/3), 178–189.

21. Bandura, A. (1997). *Self-Efficacy: The Exercise of Control*. New York: W.H. Freeman. Pintrich, P. R. (2002). The Role of Metacognitive Knowledge in Learning, Teaching, and Assessment. *Theory into Practice*, *41*(4), 220–227. Zimmerman, B. J. (1990). Self-Regulated Learning and Academic Achievement: An Overview. *Educational Psychologist*, *25*(1), 3–17.

4

THE JOURNEY:
TAKING THE FIRST STEPS

*O*ften, we realize that something is missing from our lives. We might be yearning for a new or better relationship with our family members, or our job might not be satisfying any longer, or we might want to accomplish something that we have put off for many years. For many adult women in our country, the unmet need is the desire to continue their education. The motivation for achieving a college degree may take many forms, and, as I wrote in Chapter 2, the goal may be more of a necessity today than a pure desire for education. Whatever the reason, there are some major direct financial benefits. A college degree can help you earn more in your lifetime and enable you to purchase a home, provide educational opportunities for your children, and help you lead a more satisfying life.

It is often said that it is the journey, not the destination, that is the joy. I think that, in many respects, this book is about the journey as well the destination. The destination of a college degree is the major focus of this guide. But the self-discovery of how you live and use your time along the way will help you achieve other dreams and goals throughout your lifetime. So use the concepts, guideposts, and benchmarks in this book as a way to achieve a college education and also to reach your goals in life . . . step by step.

- **Overcome Your Fears**

  For many women, taking the first step is the hardest part of the journey. Whether it is fear of failure, too many obligations in your personal life, lack of finances, or inertia, you need a way to address these issues boldly. In the last chapter, you saw that you are not alone in your quest for a degree. Many others have faced the same fears and anxieties as you have, and they have succeeded. Viewing your college degree as a step-by-step journey can make the process less intimidating. Break the process down into small, attainable steps. Succeeding at small tasks can help you overcome your fears and tackle increasingly larger goals. Successfully taking that first step can motivate you to achieve your goal.

- **Use Flexibility to Manage Your Life's Demands**

  Once you have the motivation and have bypassed the fear factor, how can you view your life during the journey? In *CEO of Me: Creating a Life that Works in the Flexible Job Age*, authors Ellen Ernst Kossek and Brenda A. Lautsch outline a concept I find very appealing; I have used it when speaking to groups of women business leaders and nonprofit administrators who are seeking advancement or a way to balance their many responsibilities. The concept is simple: It is all about flexibility and "how you are currently using flexibility in your life and whether how you are using it makes your life better or worse." Take some time to think about that. We often say that we have no spare time, that every minute is spent working or caring for others. But in *CEO of Me*, the authors believe "you can take control of your life to make flexibility work for you instead of against you." They then present a number of suggestions for how to do so, such as finding your most effective "Flexstyle"—how you best integrate work and personal lives. Some people, they argue, work best by blending work and personal life; others work better when they keep those sectors of their life separate. A third type, according to Kossek and Lautsch, moves back and forth between the two sectors. You may want to pick up a copy of their book for some helpful advice on negotiating a balance among work, family, and school responsibilities, and for some practical ways to use their Flexstyle strategy.[1]

- **Take Charge of Your Life**
  I take the concept of being the CEO of one's life one step further. I think that as the CEO of our own life, we must do what CEOs do when leading an organization: They must be visionaries who organize their staff to accomplish goals and to improve productivity. Being a CEO means setting goals and finding the right people to help achieve those goals, whether it is improving the organization's finances, the product, the marketing, or the stock price. In the end, being your own CEO is all about improving your organization, or in personal terms, your life. Just as a corporate CEO is in charge of a company's destiny, so you are in charge of your own destiny.

- **Set Goals**
  You need to set goals—in this case, the achievement of a college degree—and then you need to talk to those who will help you accomplish those goals. It may mean figuring out how to get the support of family members who will need to understand the sacrifices the whole family must face. It may mean convincing your supervisor that reimbursing you for your tuition will help you grow and contribute to the success of your organization. Or it may mean figuring out with a financial aid officer how to pay for your education and determine the best grants or loans to underwrite your investment. You may even need to do some marketing. You will need to apply to a college or two and sell yourself as the student they wish to admit and have as an alumna.

  The concept of setting goals as if you were the CEO of your own life is simple and clear, and I hope you will keep it in mind as you take your first steps to achieving a college education.

- **Make Decisions and Avoid Procrastination**

  Another helpful source is *Leading from the Front: No-Excuse Leadership Tactics for Women* by Angie Morgan and Courtney Lynch, two former Marines. Using their military training and their work as leadership consultants, they help individuals follow their dreams to become leaders of their own destinies. They emphasize the importance of making decisions and acting upon them promptly. The authors suggest, and I firmly believe, that "Decision-making can be stressful. Recognize that you will rarely have 100 percent of the information you need to make a perfect choice. Making a decision will get you one step closer to your objective."[2] This is excellent advice. Inaction is worse than taking one small action.

  Procrastination can be a stumbling block for anyone attempting to make a change in her life. Sometimes we become paralyzed and can't seem to move forward. For many, according to Morgan and Lynch, "procrastination is a choice all on its own . . . By taking no action at all, you may pass up important, valuable opportunities." Breaking a large task into smaller, manageable chunks is one strategy to defeat procrastination.[3]

  Dr. William J. Knaus is the author of several books on this subject, and is a recognized expert on curing procrastination. If procrastination is a particular problem for you, you may want to check out some of his books, which are listed in the "Resources" section at the end of this chapter.

- **Take Responsibility and Avoid Blaming Others**

  Morgan and Lynch also stress taking responsibility for your choices and your future. They write: "In order to lead the life you want, you need to make decisions. Avoiding decisions means that you've handed off decision-making power to others. That is, others are controlling *your* future."[4]

This concept can easily be applied to achieving a college degree. We can avoid taking the first step toward our goals by blaming others or using fear to derail the first move. Instead of blaming others for our difficulties, we must take responsibility and move forward. For example, if you call a college and don't get a good response, that is not the end. Try another college and see what the response may be.

It is also easy to blame your state in life for not being able to move forward to achieve the dream of a college education: a divorce; a lack of money; a lack of encouragement; all life's challenges that delayed your college education. But true leaders get past the challenges and focus on the action steps to take them where they wish to go.

The essence of taking that first step toward college is all about knowing what you want, setting up a series of action steps to get there, and then acting.

In the May 20, 2012 *Boston Globe*, a wonderful article written by Yvonne Abraham epitomizes the courage and the commitment it takes to return to college. Abraham writes about Northern Essex Community College graduate Pat Lundin, who took 45 years to achieve her degree, graduating with an associate's in general studies and with high honors.

She had taken her first course in 1967. Why did it take her so long? As in many women's lives, Lundin's dreams took a back seat to the needs of others around her. When she graduated from high school, her family could not afford to send her to college, so she began to work and took one math course at night. That was all her father could afford. Then she married and had two children. Unexpectedly, at age 27, her husband had a massive coronary and had to change jobs, so he went to college to retrain. Journalist Yvonne Abraham wrote that, through it all, Lundin never gave up on her dream to return to finish her degree. She took a course, but then found herself pregnant with her second child, so again she put her studies on the back burner. By 1997, she found a window of opportunity to return to school when her children were out on their own or about to be. She was laid off from her job; her husband worked a second job to earn the tuition money for her. Another obstacle arose: Lundin had vertigo and could not drive, so her daughter would drive her and wait as long as three hours to pick her up. When she had a difficult time understanding algebra (which happens to be one of those courses women often dread taking), her son tutored her. As Lundin finished her degree and proudly accepted it with her wheelchair-bound parents watching from the audience, Abraham asked Lundin about her incredible determination and what she might have done with her life and career if she had been able to finish sooner. Lundin replied that she'd never thought about that. "I'm one that thinks . . . there's a reason you go a certain path," she said.[5]

I share this story because it is so typical of the women who will read this book. For some, the journey will be long, with many obstacles to overcome. But in the end, success will be worth the effort. We should have no regrets, just a sense of appreciation for what we have and what is ahead.

When looking at my computer's keyboard, I realized that the plus sign and the equal sign are linked. That is a good analogy for how we can look at our goal of achieving a college education. In the book *Leading from Front*, the authors have a whole chapter on the pluses that equal success. They say, "Goals and objectives can be fairly simple, such as catching up on your overdue expense reports, or more challenging, like earning a college degree." They add, "Objectives help us stay focused on where we're headed; they help to prevent us from getting off the track and wasting time in a pursuit that doesn't move us closer to accomplishing our dream, such as quitting college to accept a full-time job when the desired goal is to earn a college degree. Goals give us a target to hit and keep our energies and efforts directed toward achieving success."[6]

Leaders and CEOs must stay focused on their goals and objectives to build successful organizations. Viewing yourself as the CEO of your own destiny can help you focus on your own goals and objectives for your life's journey.

KEY POINTS TO REMEMBER:

- Set clear goals and objectives.

- Remember that making a decision is better than not acting at all.

- Take responsibility for your life; put blame behind you.

- Take charge—be the CEO of your life.

ACTION STEPS:

1. Ask any CEO of a company or organization about the best parts of her job and the worst. Do you see parallels with asking yourself this question about your life? Maybe the best part of being a CEO is the ability to set a vision for where the company should go and then leading the organization to complete that vision. See the parallels with setting your own vision for what you want in life. Maybe the difficult part of being a CEO is supervising employees, firing, motivating. If you have children, can you see the parallels between employees and children?

2. Have you made a decision about something you really wanted and pushed for it? How did you feel afterward? Were you successful? Why or why not? Did you try again? Why or why not?

3. Take a typical 24-hour day and write down all the things you did. Can you find one or two hours in that day to do something you want to do for yourself?

4. Perhaps you have not yet been in a position to take charge of something—either a family decision or a decision at work. Start small. See what opportunities for decision-making and leadership are open for you. It could be volunteering to lead a project at your child's school, to plan the family vacation, or to help your supervisor tackle a problem. When you've completed the task, think about how it felt to be in charge.

$\mathcal{W}$HITNEY'S STORY

Whitney's college career was thrown off course when her grandmother was diagnosed with cancer. Whitney moved back home to support her family and help take care of her grandmother. Although she was glad to be available for her family, she said, "I felt horrible about not being in school. It made me feel unproductive, a failure, a disappointment." Whitney was bringing in the mail one day when a letter fell out of the mailbox. It was a mailing about a weekend college program, and it helped her realize she could assist her grandmother but still pursue her dream of higher education. "If I've learned anything from my own story," she said, "and what I hope other women are able to learn from my story as well, it's that when life happens, you may be knocked down by an unexpected bump in the road or by life's twists and turns, but don't allow yourself to be knocked out. Get back in the ring, keep fighting, and keep doing your best to achieve all that you know you are truly capable of! Turn your discouragement into encouragement, because you never know what blessing or opportunity could be right around the corner . . . or, as in my case, right on your doorstep."

RESOURCES:

Abraham, Y. (2012, May 20). A Long Time Coming. *The Boston Globe*. Retrieved from www.bostonglobe.com/metro/2012/05/19/woman-graduates-years-after -taking-her-first-class/sfcjT8w5ltygT0iVj0MoOO/story.html

Knaus, W. J. (1998). *Do It Now! Break the Procrastination Habit*. New York: J. Wiley.

Knaus, W. J. (2002). *The Procrastination Workbook: Your Personalized Program for Breaking Free from the Patterns that Hold You Back*. Oakland, California: New Harbinger.

Knaus, W. J. (2010). *End Procrastination Now! Get It Done with a Proven Psychological Approach*. New York: McGraw-Hill.

Kossek, E. E. & Lautsch, B. A. (2007). *CEO of Me: Creating a Life that Works in the Flexible Job Age*. Upper Saddle River, New Jersey: Wharton School.

Morgan, A. & Lynch, C. (2006). *Leading from the Front: No-Excuse Leadership Tactics for Women*. New York: McGraw-Hill.

NOTES:

1. Kossek, E. E. & Lautsch, B. A. (2007). *CEO of Me: Creating a Life that Works in the Flexible Job Age* (pp. 19–34). Upper Saddle River, New Jersey: Wharton School.

2. Morgan, A. & Lynch, C. (2006). *Leading from the Front: No-Excuse Leadership Tactics for Women* (p. 51). New York: McGraw-Hill.

3. Ibid., p. 51.

4. Ibid., p. 51.

5. Abraham, Y. (2012, May 20). A Long Time Coming. *The Boston Globe*. Retrieved from www.bostonglobe.com/metro/2012/05/19/woman-graduates -years-after-taking-her-first-class/sfcjT8w5ltygT0iVj0MoOO/story.html

6. Morgan & Lynch, p. 126.

5

Challenges and Obstacles

"Open yourself to possibilities —
life abounds with teachers and lessons."

—*Lee G. Bolman and Terrence E. Deal*, Leading with Soul

*F*or many women, taking that first step on the journey to college is not a simple task; it may seem impossible. You may be asking yourself how you can overcome obstacles to your dream. What hints or advice can remove the brick walls that stand between you and a college degree? In previous chapters, you've received advice on having a mind-set for taking the first step toward college and for planning your life in such a way that you can have confidence that a degree is within your reach.

But for some women who are interested in enrolling in college, having a mind-set for college may not be enough. Their high school track record may seem to be a barrier. For example, some may have dropped out of high school, while others may not have focused on their studies in high school, which resulted in high school transcripts that might prevent them from being accepted. If either of these scenarios is your situation, you don't have to give up your dream of attaining a college degree. A high school diploma or a GED (General Education Development) diploma is almost always required for admission to college. If you didn't earn a high school diploma, you will want to explore ways to get your GED, which is the most widely accepted high school equivalency credential. Check out www.ged.com for more information. Also, local community colleges may have resources such as GED classes and practice tests to help you prepare. If your high school record is not strong, you may want to seek open-enrollment institutions, which accept almost all applicants. Community colleges are generally open enrollment, as well as some four-year institutions. The admissions pages of colleges' websites and college guidebooks available at local libraries will be helpful in determining admissions requirements.

Even if you've held the dream of a college degree for a long time, life happens, as we all know. Sometimes time passes with no particular challenge or obstacle. We follow where the path may lead. But no matter what the situation, there are often roadblocks and detours that send us down a different path from the one on which we started. In some cases, these challenges strengthen us and allow us to see our lives differently, and the result may improve our situation. But in other cases, obstacles and challenges may seem insurmountable, and we lose our way. We become stuck in a scenario that appears to be our course in life, and we fear venturing off.

Obstacles come in all shapes and sizes. Fear is one of the most significant. Sometimes it is a function of our age. How can we open our minds to new ideas and concepts the way young people do? You may be asking yourself: How will I manage to pass algebra when I failed in high school? What if I can't finish a course and I lose all my money? How can I attend classes when I have two children and a sick parent? Am I really capable of studying?

Guilt is a common reaction when women return to college, particularly regarding the care of family members, especially children. Women who return to work after having children have the same misgivings about how their work may affect others. There is no simple answer to the complicated lives women face, but research has shown that having a mother who works outside the home does not mean a child will be less well-adjusted than one with a stay-at-home mother.

Support systems are essential. Women who return to college often find soul mates in class who are experiencing or have already experienced the same challenges. Many times sharing a challenge and asking how another woman handled it will provide some simple, straightforward, successful strategies.

In this chapter, we will discuss facing obstacles and fears so that, at any step along the way, you will be able to return to this chapter to be encouraged, learn from the advice of other students and experts, and get back on track.

Another expert with whom I have been privileged to work is Dr. Maura Devlin, Director of Liberal Studies, Writing and Assessment for The American Women's College at Bay Path University. Dr. Devlin has been working with students for more than two decades and has found her niche in offering adult women ways to be successful no matter what their personal circumstances. She has also been influential in helping women network while in college in order to find the job of their dreams. In the advice that follows, she addresses many of the issues I have mentioned. Her perspective provides another vantage point from which you can launch yourself onto a successful academic journey.

RESOURCES AND SUPPORT FOR
ADULT WOMEN GOING TO COLLEGE
BY MAURA DEVLIN, PH.D.

As you consider enrolling in college, you're most likely thinking about the many roles that you fulfill and the people and things for which you care. You're possibly worried that you can't add college student to your list of multiple selves.

You may be worried about your academic skills and how you will succeed. This chapter addresses the specific fears you're facing, fears that are common among adult women as they contemplate returning to college. It will help you find local resources, both in your community and within the college you're considering, to manage your various roles. It will also encourage you not to forget to take care of yourself while you care for others, and help you see that YES, YOU CAN!

Here, you will find resources to answer questions such as:

- **I'm a mother, wife, daughter, employee, chauffeur, homeowner, financial planner, friend, grocery shopper, chief cook and bottle washer. How will I be able to care for all the people and things I care for now if I return to school?**

- **What about me? Will I have enough energy and time left to take care of myself?**

- **How can I possibly do college-level work? I've been out of school for so long. I didn't do so well when I was younger.**

Let's tackle the first question, as it's probably the most important one on your mind. Bear in mind that as you enroll in college, you probably will need to free up your schedule. You will need to attend classes, and you'll need time to study outside of class. College-level academic work is more self-directed than high school work, which means you will spend more time on your academic work out of class than in class each week. To gauge how much time you'll need, check with the admissions officers at institutions that you are considering. These professionals have been working with adult students who are going to college, and they have experience with their institution's academic programs and requirements. They have fielded similar questions from other prospective students.

Remember, no one expects you to be a superwoman. You will likely need to enlist some support from family and friends. You may need to tap into a wider network of resources, too. Part of your college journey will include an assessment of what your priorities are, what is important for you to undertake, what can be passed onto someone else, and what is "good enough." Many women struggle with the belief that they have to be perfect in all of their roles, all at the same time. That just isn't possible. So keep that in mind as we discuss ways you can find help in your key roles.

One resource for referrals to local community services is the 2-1-1 telephone service. Most residents throughout the United States have access, as 2-1-1 currently serves over 90% of Americans in all 50 states. The 2-1-1 service is a partnership between the United Way and the Association of Information and Referral Services; it works like 9-1-1, but provides telephone referrals to agencies in the caller's local area that correspond to the caller's needs. This would be a good starting place for any need that you may have.

Below we'll discuss some of the specific roles women take on, and ways that you can find support in your community to assist you.

- **Your Role as Student**
  My reading, writing, and math skills aren't where they should be. How will I succeed in school? I have a disability (mental, physical and/or emotional) that might cause me to do poorly in my classes. How can I get help? How can I possibly catch up to younger students on technology so that I will be successful?

  Advice:
  Some institutions, and the vast majority of community colleges, offer remedial courses in reading, writing, and math (and other subjects as well) to get students ready to take college-level courses. These courses are usually numbered below the 100 level, and often the credits earned do not count toward a student's degree, but they may be

exactly what a woman whose skills are sub-par may need. As you work with admissions counselors and academic advisors at any college that you're interested in attending, share your academic concerns and see what they advise. Many colleges also offer placement tests, which help take the guesswork out of course selection.

Colleges are required by law to provide support and accommodation services to students with disabilities. College websites, advisors, and counselors can direct you to the office or person responsible for helping students needing accommodations and support. These resources will vary based on each student's needs, but they are intended to help each student succeed. You will probably need to share any documentation you have about your particular situation, but don't be shy! Disability coordinators have worked with many students just like you. They don't judge, and they ensure that the college helps you succeed.

Many colleges, like other institutions in the United States, rely heavily on technology. Colleges often have online student portals, which allow students to see their schedules, choose classes, and view their financial aid and billing. Colleges also increasingly use technology for their classes, by putting some aspects of a course, such as the syllabus, or the entire course, online. Because computer systems are now used so much, college IT professionals often train students on the basic "how-tos" at required orientation sessions and in optional workshops. Because colleges also recognize the need for students to understand how to work with the software that they will use for assignments—such as Microsoft Word and PowerPoint— classes in these programs are typically also offered. Your advisors will be able to help you determine how and when to take advantage of the training you might need.

- **Your Role as Mother**
  Who will care for my children if I return to school? Will my children be okay if I devote less time to them? How can I keep up

*with their growing needs as they age, especially when I have my
nose in my own schoolbooks?*

Advice:
Whether you have an infant, young children, kids in
elementary school, or teens, you spend a good amount
of your time guiding, mentoring, teaching, disciplining,
caring for, and playing with them. This is probably an
area of responsibility for which you'll have to negotiate
for time with someone else who can help fulfill these
roles—a spouse or partner, girlfriends, parents, neighbors,
or babysitters. Maybe you can barter for childcare if you
have some ability or talent you can provide in return—on
school breaks.

Before they begin a college program, women are often
unsure whether their children will be okay without them.
They are usually happily surprised to see the benefits that
being in school can provide. Many college women notice
that their children demonstrate increased interest in
school and earn higher grades. You can create this kind of
environment by including your children in your studies.
For example, you can have your children quiz you with
flash cards that you create. You can post your good grades
on hard exams on the fridge alongside theirs. Younger
children like to mimic their studying mothers by working
on schoolbooks and coloring books. It's a good idea to
have your children visit your campus so they can visualize
where Mommy goes, and you may find that it helps them
be supportive.

Depending on your family and your personal
situations, you will know when your best chunks of study
time will be—after young children are in bed, while older
children are doing their homework, before the household
gets up in the morning, or weekend mornings when you
don't have to go to work. Some adult women students have
been successful by identifying pockets of time during the
week that are often not used productively. For example,

taking books to work and studying on your lunch hour may be a way to get assignments done. Another pocket of "found" time adult women talk about is all the time they spend waiting for their children. Bring books and study materials to the carpool line, to the doctor's office, to sporting events—you may be surprised by how much you can read and get done.

With older children, you may need more support in your parenting. Teenagers who are close to leaving the nest tend to challenge their parents' authority, and this can cause some family clashes. Local family therapy groups, which you can find through your medical care providers, online and print directories of local services (like the Yellow Pages—available online at www.yellowpages.com), or the 2-1-1 service, can provide some counseling and parenting strategies, if needed. Your child's high school may also have some adjustment counselors who can help with those tricky teenage years.

You may also wonder how you can help your teen get to college. Your school's guidance counselors can be a terrific resource with college planning. Schools in which your teen is interested may offer open houses you can attend to gather more information. College Goal Sunday, a joint program between the national YMCA and the Lumina Foundation, offers college recruitment workshops and fairs and counseling about the financial aid process. You can find state-by-state information on each state's website: www.collegegoalsundayusa.org. Another Lumina Foundation project provides general information about the college process at www.knowhow2go.org.

- **Your Role as Spouse/Partner**
  How can I take care of my relationship while I'm a student? Will my partner feel neglected? What if my partner and I need more serious help while I'm in school?

Advice:

If you're married or are in a long-term committed relationship, you may already have your strongest supporter and favorite cheerleader as you pursue your education. Including your spouse or partner in your schoolwork is critical to maintaining that person's enthusiasm, as is sharing what the educational journey means to you. It's probably a good idea to give your significant other a sense of the emotional roller coaster you're about to board, a sense that you'll soon be experiencing academic excitement about burgeoning knowledge as well as crushing moments when a bad grade may seem to define you . . . but not for long!

Be sure to cast aside your books sometimes and keep romance a part of your life. But know that there are resources for rockier times, too. If you and your partner need healthcare resources, try outreach programs at your local hospitals. Or try your area's 2-1-1 service for referrals to health-related agencies. Your local human services agencies, which you can locate through your town or city's resources, Internet searches for local services, or in-print directories, can also assist with life basics that you and your partner may need, such as clothing, food, housing, and transportation.

New roles can be stressful, even when negotiated in advance and agreed upon happily. If you and your spouse or partner experience extreme stress in your relationship, you could consider counseling as a way to look at your roles, behaviors, and needs in a new light. College campuses have mental health counseling services, so this may be a good place to start. There are family and couples' counselors throughout the nation who can help, and your health plan administrators can point out the ones whom your insurance provider will approve. Your medical care providers and local 2-1-1 service can point you to family and couples' counseling programs, too.

- **Your Role as Daughter**
  I provide care for my elderly parents. Who will help my parents if I'm devoting more time to school? And what if they need more help as they age?

  Advice:
  Your parents were there for you, and you want to be there for them. You can still be, even while going to college; you just might need to get some help. Check the elderly resources in your local human services directory, which you can find by reviewing your town or city's website or senior center. Your parents' medical care providers also may be able to refer you to services. There may be programs that provide companionship, meals and food resources, rides to appointments, grooming care, and social activities. Even if you need assistance with more substantial concerns, such as legal and financial resources, eldercare agencies are still a good place to start. The staff there might be able to direct you to more specialized services, such as attorneys who work in eldercare law.

  It will probably be helpful for your studies if you have frank conversations with your family members about your school responsibilities and your need for help in caring for aging parents. Often, staff members who work in eldercare services can provide guidance on how to split time-consuming care work among siblings and family members. You may decide to rotate driving and food-shopping responsibilities, or to collectively pay for a service provider to fulfill some of these functions.

- **Your Role as Financial Planner**
  How will I be able to keep up with bills and related paperwork? What resources are available for keeping me financially savvy?

  Advice:
  Financial matters can be daunting, even if you aren't going to college. Fortunately, colleges and universities are

increasingly offering financial management and literacy workshops, and sometimes these events are open to the public. Your institution may be able to refer you to financial planners in the area, too. Financial aid offices can be invaluable resources, not only for financial aid processing, but they might also have ideas on scholarships and tax credits for students. Your 2-1-1 service can refer you to credit and debt management resources and legal resources, such as the National Legal Aid and Defender Association and Legal Services Corporation (www.nlada.org).

- **Your Role as Employee**
  But I work, too! Will my job performance suffer? How can I get my boss on board with my college plans?

Advice:
You may be apprehensive about returning to school while working at the same time, but chances are your boss and company would support such a decision because of the new knowledge and perspectives that you will bring to work. So don't hesitate to discuss your college aspirations with your boss; this would be a good start to developing a support network. Also, check your employer's benefits. You may be eligible for tuition reimbursement programs.

A good way to sound out work/life balance challenges and career thoughts is to find a mentor, either at your workplace or within your industry. If this person also attended school as an adult, that would be ideal. But if not, a trusted mentor can still give you advice and help you see challenges in a new way. So how do you get a mentor? Just by asking! Most people are flattered to be asked and have a genuine interest in advancing the careers of others. They also understand that most working adults have multiple roles, and they can help you determine priorities. Consider joining the professional association in your field or in the field you are considering as you enter college. Many professional associations have student rates, even for adult students, and this can be a good way to find mentors in your field and to keep up the motivation for your schoolwork. Some cities and states have women's organizations, such as the Junior League or women's chambers of commerce, which offer mentoring for other women. Searching "mentoring for adult women" in a web browser will help you identify such organizations in your area.

- **Your Role as Homemaker/Homeowner/Tenant**
  How will I be able to take care of my home?

Advice:
Another of the roles you manage is that of homeowner or tenant, and, of course, you'll need to maintain your home. But you may be surprised to learn how many chores and tasks can be minimized or let go of during periods of busy schoolwork. For example, vacuuming and changing the bedsheets less frequently may give you some newfound time. Get together with those with whom you make a home, determine the minimum cleaning standards you can tolerate, and then assign responsibilities to everyone. Even children can help out with chores. Check online for suggested chores for children or "chore chart" templates that can give ideas and tools you may find useful. Printable chore charts are available on www.kidpointz.com, and www.pinterest.com offers many ideas about ways children can track chores and tasks. Enlist help, too, for seasonal tasks, such as raking and shoveling snow. Or consider hiring teens; your local high school's guidance department or a community center might help you find someone who will do yard work. For more substantial home maintenance guidance, check out the federal government's guides for energy-efficient heating and cooling, lawn and garden care, and reconstruction at www.usa.gov/repairing-home.

- **Your Role as a Meal Planner and Cook**
  I'm the primary provider of our family meals. How will I keep up with shopping and preparation of food? Also, I don't want my nutrition to be sacrificed!

Advice:
Preparing food is important for health, for sustaining family and ethnic traditions, and even for ceremonial reasons. Fortunately, more (and better!) food resources and tools are now available than ever before. For example, you could sign up for a grocery delivery service, if your area has one. Or check out online grocery lists, such as at www .grocerylists.org/ultimatest or www.plantoeat.com; you could even share the responsibility by asking family members to add any item they polish off onto a running grocery list. Teaching other family members, including children, to cook simple meals can help spread the responsibility.

For nutrition resources, a good place to start is the federal government's website: www.nutrition.gov. Your college's food service department probably has nutrition tips and resources for you. Also, many tools are available via online recipe sites, such as www.allrecipes.com, www .foodnetwork.com, and www.epicurious.com; there are even recipe apps, such as Big Oven. These can be good sources for learning time-saving cooking tips and for making a meal with what you have on hand; simply search for recipes based on the food items you have. Slow cookers can be kitchen time-savers, too, and you'll find plenty of recipes for those online.

- **Your Role in Taking Care of Yourself!**
  I'm worried that I will be so busy I won't be able to take care of myself, but I know this is so important!

Advice:
Taking care of yourself is extremely important, even though it often comes last on many women's lists. Make

sure that you make time for yourself. This could include relaxing with your spouse and children or with other family members or girlfriends—be sure to keep them part of your life, even while letting them know that your get-togethers may not be as frequent while school is in session. Maintaining your social relationships can be a significant source of stress relief.

Exercise, too, will help you manage stress. Fortunately, most colleges recognize this and have fitness centers and recreation programs. Check out the resources that may be available to you for free or at a reduced cost as a student; they might even include personalized fitness consultations with a trainer. Exercise is also an activity that you can do with your family and friends, so it's a good way to keep connected.

The college you are considering most likely has health services and mental health counseling services, should you feel you need them. Check out their offerings; you may be surprised at all that is available to you. In addition, your employer might offer an Employee Assistance Program (EAP), a confidential telephone counseling service. Trained mental health providers know how to coach clients over the phone and how to refer to local providers if necessary.

The last—but maybe the most important—way to take care of yourself is to realize that you are not alone. Even though going back to college later in life may seem odd to you, it's not. Millions have done it before you, and millions more are doing it now. There are websites created just for older women going back to college. Lumina Foundation's Adult College Completion Network has a wide variety of resources and advice for adult students; their website is www.adultcollegecompletion.org/blog/2. Be sure to also check out websites and/or resources for nontraditional students; you'll be surprised at the tips, chat forums, and communities that are out there. For example, www.mycollegeguide.org has a question-and-answer page for adults returning to college. Your college, too, may have an office dedicated to older students who faced the questions you face; it may even have a web-based community for its adult students.

- **Your Role in Handling Detours and Bumps Along Your Path**
  I am committed to returning to college, but I also know there will be bumps and surprises along the way. How can I handle the unexpected?

  Advice:
  Despite the best management of your multiple life roles, you may face situations that make it impossible to take courses for a period of time. You may find that you need to stop out for a spell. This is common with adult students, and it does not mean that your journey toward your college degree has ended for good. If you need to, you can reduce your course load, take a semester off, or take a leave of absence from your college. Consult your advisor and the staff in your registrar's office. They will be able to tell you the college's policies on leaves. They will also be able to tell you how reducing the number of courses you take or "stopping out" (temporarily putting your studies on hold) will affect your academic standing and progress and your financial aid award. (If they can't answer your financial questions, consult your financial aid office). They will also clarify any policies and requirements regarding your return to campus. Remember, stops and restarts are common among adult college students, but you want to minimize them whenever you can so that you can continue to make progress toward your ultimate goal—your college degree!

- **Your Role as a New Student**
  It's been so many years; this is all new to me. How can I get started with the least amount of confusion or stress?

Advice:

If you are wondering—a little anxiously—how you'll get up to speed on navigating your college experience, fortunately your college's staff knows that incoming students need guidance. They offer orientation programs to help you gain comfort. Even if you aren't apprehensive, you should make every effort possible to attend these sessions. At orientation, you will learn how to pick your classes, how to work with your advisor and your professors, how to find out about your assignments, and how to locate your books, whether they are in print or accessible online. You may be given a student ID, probably in both a physical ID card format and an online format that will give you access to the college's computer system. Most colleges provide students with e-mail and learning management systems, which complement instruction in the courses themselves. The orientation staff will make sure that incoming students are familiar with these programs. You'll hear about campus resources, policies, and procedures. Such information will make your academic life much easier and productive down the line.

Last, and possibly most important, you'll meet other incoming adult students. You'll see that there are others like you, adult women who are returning to school. You may even make some new friends. So make every effort to attend your orientation, but if you cannot, make sure to talk to your admissions counselor about what steps you need to take to get yourself ready.

In this chapter, I discussed the barriers and fears that adult women have expressed as they have considered getting a college degree. I have provided some guidance for each of the multiple roles that most adult women fulfill in their demanding lives. There are ways to identify resources and help for most of these roles. Perhaps just knowing that resources exist and that there are supports in place to help women succeed in all their roles might make attaining a college degree seem that much closer.

KEY POINTS TO REMEMBER:

- Don't try to be superwoman! Ask for support from family, friends, college staff, and others.

- Your local 2-1-1 service can help you locate a wealth of support services.

- Getting your children involved in your education can help win their support and improve their studies.

- Keep books and study materials with you so that you can use "found time" between chores and errands and while waiting at doctors' offices, etc. for studying.

- If you have a partner, don't forget to nurture your relationship while working on your education.

- Use your local senior services to help with care of elderly parents.

- Discuss your college plans with your work supervisor; you may be eligible for tuition reimbursements.

- It's okay to let the housework go in order to make time to study.

- Don't forget to take care of yourself—pay attention to nutrition and exercise.

ACTION STEPS:

1. What is your biggest concern out of the items mentioned in this chapter? Select one of the resources listed and get information on where you might find assistance before you meet with an admissions representative or start your first class.

2. Make a list of all the concerns you have regarding your children, your spouse, or your partner. Ask friends, neighbors, or colleagues at work how they have addressed these issues.

3. If you think that your spouse or partner, your children, or your employer will have issues with your returning to college, make a list of all the reasons you feel it will be beneficial to them. This will help you if you meet with any resistance.

4. Make a list of all the concerns you have regarding your academic success. Then look at college websites to see what programs and offerings are available to help support students with these concerns. If some of your concerns aren't addressed, talk to advisors at the college about them. Identify academic supports outside the college, such as GED workshops, as necessary.

5. Do you have any friends who have faced a huge obstacle in life and yet are successful and happy? Why not ask some of those friends how they faced that obstacle?

Melody's Story

A mother at age 17, Melody dropped out of high school to raise her children. She got her GED in her early 20s and resolved to finish her education one day. A diagnosis of breast cancer, however, pushed her to take action. She wrote, "That is when I decided that it was time to start fulfilling some of my goals and dreams." Melody struggled to balance her schoolwork with her responsibilities as a mother, and found that she had to develop some creative strategies to get her study time in. "Balancing the guilt of putting myself first versus being an involved mother was the hardest obstacle to overcome," she wrote. "The way I handled it was to bring my homework to [her children's] baseball and football practices and complete it in the car. That way, I didn't feel guilty when I was enjoying the actual games. It was also extremely quiet in the car, and reading to myself out loud looked like I was singing. Doing this the first couple of times brought some strange glances from other parents at the fields, but now, three years later, if they see me without my books, they ask me where they are."

She found that her studies helped put her in touch with her sons' school life. "Being in the education field, I am relearning some of the things they are currently learning in school. This has helped me be able to relate to three teenage boys, which in another setting, I may have not been able to [do.]" She stressed the importance of developing a routine and staying with it. "Another challenge is having only one day a week to get household things done. Going back to school

> takes scheduling and planning. I have my routine and have to stick to it—otherwise my week is off track. I work Monday through Friday, go to school for 11 hours on Saturday, and do the household chores and grocery shopping on Sunday."

RESOURCES:

Allrecipes.com. (n.d.). *Allrecipes.com*. Retrieved from allrecipes.com/

American Council on Education. (2014). *KnowHow2Go*. Retrieved from www .knowhow2go.org

BigOven. (n.d.). *BigOven*. Retrieved from www.bigoven.com

Bolman, L. G., & Deal, T. E. (2011). *Leading with Soul: An Uncommon Journey of Spirit*. San Francisco: Jossey-Bass.

College Goal Sunday. (2014). *College Goal Sunday*. Retrieved from www .collegegoalsundayusa.org

Condé Nast. (2014). *Epicurious*. Retrieved from www.epicurious.com/

Fungaroli, C. S. (2000). *Traditional Degrees for Nontraditional Students: How to Earn a Top Diploma from America's Great Colleges at Any Age*. New York: Farrar, Straus and Giroux.

GED Testing Service LLC. (2014). *GED Testing Service*. Retrieved from www.ged.com

Goodman, M. (n.d.). *Kid Pointz*. Retrieved from www.kidpointz.com

Ivery, E. F., & Kirk, S. (2003). *How to Earn a College Degree When You Think You Are Too Old, Too Busy, Too Broke, Too Scared: An Educational Planning Guide for Adult Learners*. Scottsdale, Arizona: Education Advisory Services.

Kantrowitz, M. (2014). Financial Aid for Older and Nontraditional Students. *FinAid! The Smart Student Guide to Financial Aid*. Retrieved from www.finaid .org/otheraid/nontraditional.phtml

Keaggy, B. (2014). The Grocery List Collection. *The Ultimatest Grocery Lists*. Retrieved from www.grocerylists.org/ultimatest

My College Guide. (2014). *My College Guide*. Retrieved from www.mycollegeguide.org

National Legal Aid and Defender Association. (2014). NLADA: *National Legal Aid and Defender Association*. Retrieved from www.nlada.org

Plan to Eat, LLC. (2014). *Plan to Eat*. Retrieved from www.plantoeat.com

Television Food Network GP. (2014). *Food Network*. Retrieved from www.foodnetwork.com

United States Department of Agriculture. (2014, November 6). Nutrition Information for You. *Nutrition.gov: Smart Nutrition Starts Here.* Retrieved from: www.nutrition.gov

United States Government. (n.d.). Repairing and Improving a Home. *USA.gov.* Retrieved from www.usa.gov/repairing-home

Western Interstate Commission for Higher Education. (n.d.). *Adult College Completion Network.* Retrieved from www.adultcollegecompletion.org

6

Choosing a Career Path and a Major

"Somewhere along the line of development we discover who we really are, and then we make our real decision for which we are responsible. Make that decision primarily for yourself because you can never really live anyone else's life . . . The influence you exert is through your own life and what you become yourself."

—*Eleanor Roosevelt (June 1941 letter to Trude Lash)*

*O*ne of the most important steps in the college journey is selecting a major—the course of study on which you'll concentrate as you work toward your degree. As we discussed in previous chapters, a college degree may be a way to achieve higher earning potential, a promotion in your current career, or personal enrichment. No matter what the reason, the process in selecting what to study is both an art and a science. By that I mean you need to use both the creative and analytical sides of your brain; you need to understand how you wish to use the degree before you select your major.

There are many fine books that can help you decide what your passions in life are. One of the most famous is *What Color is Your Parachute?* by Richard N. Bolles. This book includes many exercises that may prove helpful in choosing a major. In a chapter entitled "You Need to Understand More Fully Who You Are," a series of questionnaires about your past and your likes and dislikes leads you to identify your areas of expertise, special skills, and work environment preferences. Bolles also provides a grid to help you set priorities and assign a numerical rating if you need to choose among preferences that initially may seem equally strong. Working your way through the exercises may be time-consuming and challenging, but when you're finished, you'll have an in-depth analysis of your skills, interests, strengths, weaknesses, and preferred work situations. There are also many tests and computer programs at college career offices and in public libraries that can help.

A good way to know if you really understand what a major entails is to network and shadow someone in the profession you are seeking for a day or a week. For example, I have witnessed many students who enter the field of education, but they don't realize that teaching is not for them until they do their first practicum. If they had experienced the field before selecting it, they would have saved both time and money.

It's important to remember that if you seek one degree, set out to take the specialized courses required for that degree, and then change your mind, you may face a longer period of time in college and more expense. This is not to say that you can't change your mind while you are in college. Most students don't decide on their majors until they have had experience in a number of introductory courses. That was my situation when I was an undergraduate. I changed majors twice, but I had enough time to complete my core requirements (general education requirements in humanities, social sciences, and sciences) and the number of credits required for the major.

Adults who are more specific about what they want and who have life or work experience as a foundation usually have a much firmer understanding of the major they wish to pursue. I suggest asking the college admissions officer or dean if there are ways you can have some practical experience as part of your college work and get credit for that experience. Many colleges have supervised independent study or internship opportunities for their adult students, which often result in an offer of a job upon completion of the degree. More and more, I believe this will be an important part of what colleges offer students who seek career advancement or who are starting out on a new career path.

Once you have a major selected or have a pretty good idea of what you may wish to do, it's important to explore what jobs may be available in that field. Government reports on careers and their potential earning power can be found in the U.S. Department of Labor's *Occupational Outlook Handbook*, which is available at most libraries or online at www.bls.gov/ooh.

David Yelle has had several careers during his 35-year work life. He was a criminal justice major who worked in law enforcement; he moved to the insurance industry as an assistant vice president at MassMutual Financial Group; then he started working at Bay Path University in 2006. He recently retired from his position as Bay Path's Dean of Students. His skills are many, but one thing is certain: He has trained and retrained to find the best career for the right time in his life. At Bay Path, he was considered the go-to person for information on the Predictive Index Test, which provides insights into a person's working style and personality. For team building and for hiring, this test can be highly effective. Needless to say, David's own background and his countless career coaching sessions with women and men make him the perfect person to add his thoughts to this important chapter on choosing a career and major.

CHOOSING A CAREER AND A MAJOR
BY DAVID YELLE

Choosing a career can be one of the most challenging decisions to make. With thousands of different careers to choose from, this decision can seem overwhelming. The first thing to keep in mind is that you are not alone. While no one can make this decision for you, there are tools and resources that can help. These tools include, but are not limited to, Internet research, advice from career professionals, books and periodicals, and, most important, education. Education is the one resource that never loses its relevance, no matter what stage of life you find yourself in.

Students who are entering or coming back to college after a gap of several years from their last classroom experience will no doubt be unsure and anxious. This feeling is especially common among women students, who have a host of additional responsibilities to juggle. Doing things like figuring out class schedules, juggling parenting responsibilities, and holding down a job can often seem insurmountable. Try to understand that this feeling is normal, and that there are a variety of resources available to assist you.

- **Assessing Your Personality**

  When choosing a career, understanding what excites you is essential. Often, we are asked to talk about things about which we are passionate, those things that get us excited to get up every morning. For some, such things are easy to identify, but for others, finding their passion is an elusive task. Finding your passion doesn't have to be difficult. Keep in mind that we are all motivated differently. Some may find that their passion is mission driven; perhaps a particular charity or cause energizes them, which can often become a career. For those who struggle with finding their passion, the best place to start is with increasing self-awareness. Developing a deeper understanding of your personality and building strong self-awareness are wonderful places to start. To begin this process, you may want to use one of the various personality instruments listed below. While there may be some minor differences among instruments, essentially the goal is the same. The primary purpose is to develop your self-awareness, allowing you to make more informed decisions about careers. For example, the Predictive Index (PI) focuses on motivating needs, those things that you are naturally drawn to because you enjoy them. Most are affordable and will provide a rich resource of personal information that you can continue to tap into. Some of the most commonly used personality assessment tests are:

- **Myers Briggs Type Indicator (MBTI)**

- **Predictive Index (PI)**

- **DiSC Profile**

- **Keirsey Temperament Sorter (KTS-II)**

You can find out about these tests at the websites listed in the "Resources" section of this chapter. Before you sign up for any of the above assessments, you should check with the career service department of the college you are thinking about attending to see if they offer any assessment services for current or prospective students. In addition, the opportunity to sit with one of the college's trained career professionals to interpret those results is invaluable.

As you begin to develop a better sense of self-awareness, it will become increasingly important to understand what type of work aligns with your personality. For example, if you are an extrovert with little patience or interest in repetitive and detailed work, a job that requires you to do the same things over and over, with little variety and minimal opportunity to interact with others, would be a poor choice. Instead, you should be looking for something that provides a lot of interaction with people, has a great deal of variety, and rewards skills such as relationship building. This is a much better alignment of your career with your personality. How many times have you listened to friends or family members express how unhappy they are at work? Often, when you drill down, you find that the type of work they are doing is completely opposite to their core personality. Subsequently, the behaviors that are encouraged and rewarded in their jobs are not the natural behaviors they possess. This is a classic example of being out of alignment, which can be avoided with a little bit of work up front. So remember to do your homework!

As mentioned above, taking the time to truly understand what motivates you behaviorally is critically important. As an extrovert with little patience, I have learned that I get my energy from other people and that variety in my work is essential for my job satisfaction. By paying attention to these needs, I know that the opportunity to interact with people face-to-face is a must for me. I also know that a job that is highly repetitive will frustrate me.

As you begin your journey exploring your self-awareness and your own motivating needs, there are some things that can help. Spending some time exploring internship or volunteer opportunities can be extremely helpful. One of the great benefits of expanding your self-awareness is that you tend to become more observant. Learn to ask yourself questions. If you find that you are enjoying a particular experience—perhaps some volunteer work you are engaged in—ask yourself, "Why do I seem to enjoy this so much?" And, "What is it about this experience that seems to ignite my passion?"

This concept of self-conversation may seem foreign, but give it a try. It can really be a helpful way to stimulate the thought process. Remember, all we are trying to do is tap into the "Why?" Instead of just sensing that something works, we want to start understanding why it works.

Once you have decided on a career that motivates and excites you, it is time to discuss a major. The most important thing to remember when choosing a major is that it's perfectly normal to change your mind. Many, if not most, students change their mind about their major at some point along their journey. To minimize making too many changes, stick to the same methodology you used when choosing a career. Start by looking at what types of jobs you decided on and in what field they exist. That same process will help you when choosing a major. For example, if you find that you have a diligent personality and are one who enjoys working alone or in small groups and becoming a subject-matter expert in your field, you should be looking for jobs that reward these qualities. Some examples would be careers in the areas of research and analysis, laboratory work, or computer and information technology.

The key is to understand that, while it's not necessary for your personality to be an exact match for a career, making sure that at least one or two aspects are in alignment is important. By taking the time on the front end to do the research, develop better self-awareness, and establish realistic goals, you will avoid many pitfalls down the road.

- **Planning to Succeed**
  As you start to build a plan to succeed, some basic questions need to be answered. It will be extremely difficult to move forward until you have addressed the following:

  - **What are my geographical limitations? Where am I willing to go?**

  - **What is my timetable? What do I want to have done, and when?**

  - **What educational requirements do I have?**

  - **What is my goal? What do I expect to achieve?**

  - **What's important? What won't I compromise on?**

  Build a list with these questions, and be honest with your answers. Be mindful that the time you devote to meeting your objectives will need to align with your goals. For example, if you have a goal that requires a graduate degree, but you can only commit to a part-time schedule, you will need to account for that. It's important that you set yourself up to succeed by having reachable goals.

- **Building Your Safety Net**

   Now that you have followed all the steps and have a plan about which you are excited, there is one last thing that you will need to do to ensure your success: Build your safety net. Even the best plans often go astray, and while it may look as though you have thought of everything, chances are you haven't. Building a safety net will be your saving grace.

   When I refer to a safety net, I am speaking of those resources that will be there for you when you need them. One of the best resources for support will be family and friends, particularly those with whom you live. If you are out on your own and have a roommate, she or he will be an important person to have as part of your safety net. Other sources may be career professionals at your college, faculty members with whom you have built strong relationships, and anyone else you know who wants to see you succeed. Remember that it's easy to be supportive when everything is going well and others are not inconvenienced. Those individuals who will be there for you when things go off track will be critical to your success.

   Meet with folks who are part of your safety net and who share your plan. Getting their buy-in up front will be a huge help, and sharing your plan is a great way to do that.

Keep in mind as you follow these steps that the single most important thing is to be honest with yourself. Take the time to make sure your goals are realistic and that you are not taking on more than you can manage. It's great to stretch yourself, but it is dangerous to set yourself up for failure. Building self-confidence by achieving small successes will go a long way toward ensuring that you stick it out and reach your goals.

Finally, remember to enjoy the process. While it can be nerve-racking, it is also an exciting time in your life. The decision to enter or continue college will be one of the best decisions you will ever make. Remember to find your passion, know yourself and what excites you, develop a plan and stick to it, and involve others in achieving your goals. You can do it!

KEY POINTS TO REMEMBER:

- Personality assessment tests and other resources can help you uncover your passions and guide you toward a career path that fits you.

- To help you to choose your major, learn the training requirements for specific careers.

- Build a safety net of reliable people who can help you stay on track.

ACTION STEPS:

1. What are you passionate about? Make a list of subjects and activities that excite your interest.

2. What courses did you like the most when you last were in school? In what courses did you do your best work? Think about what those courses had in common and why you enjoyed them.

3. Are there professions that you admire and have always wanted to pursue as a career? What type of degree is necessary to become a professional in that field? Google the career and find out what its educational requirements are.

4. Ask the career office of the college or university you are considering if there are any career and/or personality tests that you can take to help you figure out what you may wish to major in.

5. Ask three college-educated friends or colleagues what their first choice was for a major when they entered college. Did that change along the way? What degree did they leave with?

6. Share your career dreams with close family members or friends. See what their reactions are.

*T*ANYA'S STORY

When she graduated high school, Tanya was eight months pregnant and working a part-time job. College was "not an option" at that time.

"I was not an exceptional student in school and did not apply all of my skills," she said, "so the idea of motherhood seemed so much more inviting than school." But she added, once her son started school, "it was time for me to think about where I was going career-wise." She had a part-time job, but explained, "While this was a fun job, I knew that it wasn't what I had seen . . . myself doing for the rest of my life. This was not my gift to the world!"

She eventually got a job at a healthcare staffing firm, which was a satisfying position, but she soon realized that most of the staff, if not everyone, in her position had a higher-level education background. "[T]he fear of someone asking me about my education level seemed to paralyze me."

Still, Tanya continued in the job for another ten years and eventually became unhappy in her position. "I felt trapped . . . I felt like the job was ruining my life and that I was not in control!"

Then she attended a seminar at a local college, where she took a personality inventory that was designed to determine how people change their natural behavior to suit their work environment. "When the instructor took a look at my scores," Tanya said, "she said to me, 'Boy, you're not happy at all where you work; look at how much you are changing who you naturally are.'" As Tanya talked about the test results with the instructor, she began to cry. The instructor said, "Tears are just a sign that change needs to happen."

With support from her husband, Tanya filled out a college application and was soon going back to school after 17 years away from the classroom. "I am on the path of finding what my gift to the world is, as well as appreciating the gift that I gave myself: control over my life!"

RESOURCES:

Bolles, R. N. (2013). *What Color Is Your Parachute? A Practical Manual for Job-Hunters and Career-Changers*. Berkeley, California: Ten Speed Press.

Buckingham, M., & Clifton, D. O. (2001). *Now, Discover Your Strengths*. New York: Free Press.

Buckingham, M., & Coffman, C. (1999). *First, Break All the Rules: What the World's Greatest Managers Do Differently*. New York: Simon & Schuster.

Inscape Publishing, Inc. (2014). Take the DiSC Test Online Now. *Your Life's Path Consulting and Team Building*. Retrieved from www.thediscpersonalitytest.com

Keirsey, D. M. (n.d.). *Welcome to the Keirsey Temperament Sorter (KTS-II)*. Retrieved from keirsey.com/sorter/instruments2.aspx

Myers & Briggs Foundation. (2014). *The Myers & Briggs Foundation*. Retrieved from www.myersbriggs.org

PI Worldwide. (2014). *PI Worldwide*. Retrieved from piworldwide.com

United States Department of Labor. Bureau of Labor Statistics. (2014, January 8). *Occupational Outlook Handbook*. Retrieved from www.bls.gov/ooh

7

FINDING THE RIGHT COLLEGE

*T*o be sure you have what I believe is the most valuable information available regarding your college choices, I have co-written this chapter with two experts who have years of experience in adult education and advising adult students: Diane Ranaldi, Dean of Graduate and International Admissions at Bay Path University, and Veatrice Carabine, Deputy Chief Enrollment Officer at The American Women's College at Bay Path University. The content that follows is a compilation of our thoughts and suggestions.

First, when considering a college, one of your best sources of information will be the college's admissions office. The admissions office serves prospective students, but it also has a duty to meet the enrollment needs of the institution. This chapter is designed to give you the information you need to make the most of your time in talking with admissions office staff. It will help you identify which questions to ask and how to identify potential pitfalls, deadlines, and requirements. At the end of the chapter is a helpful checklist, which you can use to gather information and make decisions about which college to attend.

Once you finally decide that the time is right, choosing the type of college to attend can be daunting. It's important that you give some thought to what you wish to study, how much you can afford, and what model of education suits you.

You may or may not know your end goal for a particular degree, but most colleges can start you toward that goal, depending on what point you've reached in your education. An important question to consider will be: Are you just beginning your degree and need the basics for a skill like bookkeeping or information technology, or do you need a liberal arts core of courses to begin to study at a higher level, like biology at the bachelor's level?

Another vital question is: What type of college will meet your needs for your educational goals? Today in America, there are many choices for higher education. That is why we are the envy of the world.

Depending on your goals, colleges and universities offer a wide range of opportunities. You can obtain certificates that will enhance your current job or give you skills for specialized fields such as computers, healthcare, or business. For example, you may wish to take only a few courses as you begin. Some colleges offer five- or six-course certificates that do not give you a degree but provide the basic skills necessary to apply for certain jobs.

For those who wish to have a more intensive educational experience that provides a focus on a subject matter or discipline or major, degrees can range from associate's to bachelor's to master's to doctoral degrees. If you continue beyond a bachelor's degree, graduate school degrees are more specialized and can range from Master of Science in a particular field to a specialized course like a Master of Occupational Therapy (MOT) or a Master of Business Administration (MBA). The specialization can last from one year to as much as two years of intensive study, to a three-year law degree (Juris Doctor), or a medical degree with internship and residency. Whatever your destination, be sure to ask questions about how many credits you need, because every course toward a degree has a cost to it.

In this book, we will provide the steps toward achieving an associate's or a bachelor's degree. What is the difference? The associate's degree usually can be completed in two years when the student attends college full-time. At most colleges this consists of 20 courses or 60 credit hours. For example, you can earn an associate's degree in paralegal studies. The bachelor's degree can be completed in four years when the student attends full-time, and it typically takes 40 courses or 120 credits. The total number of credits required for a degree can vary, depending on the institution and how many credits are awarded per course.

Full-time college attendance is the path that an 18- to 20-year-old student would normally follow. However, for adult women students, the length of time to degree completion, days of the week for study, and choice of in-class or online learning can vary and are matters of personal choice.

Many colleges assign three credits to each course. The number of credits is determined by the amount of time the student must spend in class. For a three-credit course, a student usually needs to spend 42–45 hours in class over the semester, or about three hours a week. Some colleges and degree programs use different systems. For example, courses in which the students spend 30 hours in class might be given only two credits. It is important to ask how your college assigns credits. For a variety of reasons, some colleges may assign two credits or four credits per course. For example, science courses that require a lab in addition to classroom time are almost always four or more credits, due to the extra work involved.

Today with online education, the number of hours spent in a class has a whole new meaning. As students absorb material on their own schedules, some students may find that they are spending many more hours of reading, writing, or chatting online in open chat lines than they would sitting in a classroom.

Some degrees require accreditation or certification from an external body, that is, an organization that is separate from the college or university. For example, for majors in education or in health-related fields like occupational therapy or physical therapy, there are specific, required steps for completion of the degree. For many occupations, there are state or professional licensing requirements to demonstrate competence in a series of subjects before students can move on to the final two or three years of degree completion. Take education, for example. To be an elementary school teacher, states are now requiring that students prove competence in reading, science, history, etc., before graduation and certification. Because of this, colleges will now accept you to study for your first two years, then allow you to take the teachers' exam before your junior or senior years to see if you pass. If you do not, most colleges will not advance you to the junior or senior year as an education major. They do not wish to have you take all your courses, complete your student teaching, and then fail the licensing exam at the end of your senior year, leaving you unable to teach.

Therefore, it is critical that you ask the following questions when looking at colleges:

- **When will you officially be enrolled as an education major or an occupational therapy major or other major?**

- **What steps do you need to take to achieve the degree you desire?**

- **What if you start as an education major and don't pass the required tests?**

- **What are your options for getting a degree that you can complete and use?**

Your admissions advisor or registrar can be very helpful in answering these questions.

- **Types of Colleges**

  First, it is important to ask yourself about the kind of learning environment that appeals to you. Are you someone who needs a small class size and personal attention, or would you thrive in a large lecture hall? Can you independently navigate the institutional structure fairly well, or would you prefer having someone who can guide you through the process of admissions and registration? Is the mission and focus of the institution important? There are several different types of colleges and universities, and it is important to choose the one that best meets your needs.

  - **Community (two-year) or four-year college.** Community colleges are usually career focused and less expensive than four-year programs. They usually have an open enrollment model for admissions. Today, many students who cannot afford a state university or a private college use the community college as a stepping-stone to transfer to a four-year college.

    Four-year state or private colleges are beneficial for the continuity of learning environment and as a way to significantly invest your time and energy into the college culture and its many extracurricular and co-curricular opportunities, and to build relationships with faculty, staff, and fellow students.

  - **State or private college.** Would you like a state college or a private college? Those students who choose a state college are often drawn to the lower tuition of a state institution versus the higher tuition of a private college. But there are different advantages to each type of environment. Often a state college is large and the classes contain 50 or more students, whereas a private college usually keeps classes small. The smaller classroom gives students more opportunity to have contact with the professor or to receive some personalized attention.

- **Co-ed or women's college.** Then, there is the choice of a co-ed institution versus a women's college. There are currently about 50 women's colleges in the United States. Some women prefer the single-gender classroom; they feel it is more conducive to enhancing their participation in the classroom and in having faculty more accessible. A women's college can also help you understand the potential you have as a woman student and future employee. But whatever your preference for the environment, there are still more decisions to make regarding the type of learning format.

- **Not-for-profit or for-profit college.** There are also important distinctions to make in choosing a college that is not-for-profit versus a college that is for-profit. Most traditional state and private colleges and universities are not-for-profit, with an essential purpose of educating students, whereas a for-profit college is set up as a business with an obligation to shareholders and investors to generate a profit. As the world of higher education is rapidly evolving, no matter what college you choose—nonprofit or for-profit—do your research about cost, reputation, accreditation, and graduation rates.

- **Accreditation**
  Whether you are selecting a for-profit or a not-for-profit college, accreditation is a key consideration. In the United States, accreditation is a regional process that ensures the institution you select has met a series of minimum standards for its mission, curriculum, faculty, student life, facilities, and finances. If a college has met the standards for accreditation, it will be clearly identified on its website or in its catalog. Choosing an unaccredited college or university could result in your having a future employer refuse to recognize your hard-earned degree.

- **Scheduling**

  Another important concern for many adult learners
  is scheduling classes around their work and family
  obligations. Flexible scheduling is designed to assist
  working adults to take classes at a convenient time, and
  complete their degree program quickly. Many colleges
  and universities offer schedules that can vary among
  weekday, evening, or weekend classes, and online courses.
  Some offer hybrid schedules that combine two or more of
  these elements. Usually students make their choices based
  upon their availability. However, sometimes a particular
  program might be offered only on weekdays, therefore
  making it inaccessible to some. Often students will search
  for colleges that both have their degree program and
  offer classes at times that work in tandem with their other
  commitments and responsibilities. Many working adults
  choose an evening or weekend class schedule, which
  sometimes provides courses in an accelerated format. An
  accelerated format typically includes more hours per week
  in fewer sessions. For example, instead of three hours per
  week for 14 weeks, a course might be five or six hours a
  week for eight weeks.

  Keep in mind that sometimes certain majors are
  offered only during the day. Usually these are courses
  in education or nursing that may require a practicum.
  Sometimes you can achieve all the prerequisites in an
  evening or weekend college and then use the final year
  for your student teaching or practicum. Questions about
  scheduling are important to ask when choosing a major.

- **Online vs. On-site Courses**

  Many colleges offer on-campus classes, online classes,
  or hybrid classes. On-campus classes are those delivered
  entirely on-site at the college. Online classes are delivered
  entirely online or through a learning website. Then there
  are hybrid classes that combine both the on-campus
  classroom experience with some online classes and

assignments. Today, most colleges offer these options, and it is a personal decision whether to take classes on campus or online. Some people enjoy the face-to-face discussion that takes place in the classroom and do not want to lose that opportunity to interact with their classmates and professors. Other students enjoy the self-management of the online classes and use chat rooms and e-mails to connect with other students and faculty.

For some students it is important to start college in a face-to-face situation to gain confidence in studying, to connect with a faculty member, to find another student who may be a study partner, to have social engagement, and to see if the college is the right option for them. The beauty of higher education today is that the choice is with the student. Having access to so many colleges online has widened the opportunities for women who must stay at home to care for a child or parent. So now the decision is yours. You can experiment among so many options that there is no longer the excuse that a college is not within commuting distance.

An important question to ask about online classes is whether the classes are offered in an *asynchronous* or a *synchronous* format. Asynchronous means that you can log in to the classroom any time you want to complete the assignments, based on the deadlines and requirements outlined in the course's syllabus. Synchronous means that the classes will meet online at a particular day and time, and you will need to make sure that you are available at that time.

If you are interested in applying to a college that offers online programs, then your best way to investigate these options is through an Internet search. Your search will turn up many colleges, and making a decision might be difficult. You can always make your choice based upon price and reputation of the college.

- **Where to Find Information About Colleges**

  Once you determine your prospective major, the detailed information that you'll find on the Internet is probably your best source. Colleges do have printed materials and catalogs, but more and more are using the web as the main point of access. There are also numerous guidebooks for colleges and universities, including: *Peterson's* (www.petersons.com), *Princeton Review* (www.princetonreview.com), and *U.S. News & World Report* (colleges.usnews.rankingsandreviews.com/best-colleges), all of which have both print and online guidebooks.

  The best way to begin your college search is to investigate the local market. You can use the Internet or the phone book to gather the names and phone numbers of the colleges in your area. Do some research online or at the library to find out which colleges offer the degree you want, and then either make appointments to visit the admissions office or ask that information be mailed to your home. The admissions office will give you all the information you need about the college, its degree programs, and format for course delivery.

- **What to Do if You Don't Know What You Want to Major In**

  It is important to know that you can begin the college process even if you are not entirely sure what major or program of study interests you the most. An important consideration will be how many college credits you have already completed. If you have little or no college experience, you may have more flexibility in your degree program to try out different majors and see what fits, as well as more time to work with the career services office before you need to commit to a particular major. If you have quite a few transfer credits, you might be required to make decisions earlier. Either way, your admissions counselor will be able to help you determine where you stand and what your options are for degree programs.

- **Questions to Ask When Evaluating a College**

  - **Is it accredited?** As previously mentioned, accreditation is a very important consideration in choosing a college. There are many different types of accreditation; however, most colleges fall under a regional or national accrediting agency. Traditional state and private colleges are usually regionally accredited. The United States is divided into six regional accrediting organizations, and credits earned at a regionally accredited college or university are generally transferable to any other regionally accredited college or university across the country. It is important to note that in most cases, credits earned from a nationally accredited institution will not necessarily transfer to a regionally accredited institution. (You will learn more about transfer credits in Chapter 11: "The Registrar's Office.") The Council for Higher Education Accreditation (www.chea.org) is a valuable resource for understanding accreditation. This site provides tutorials and videos to help you understand the different types of accreditation and the important role it plays in choosing a college. Another helpful website dealing with accreditation is hosted by the U.S. Department of Education at: ope.ed.gov/accreditation.

  - **Does it have good ratings in guidebooks and/or online guides?** A number of guidebooks and websites provide ratings for colleges and universities. The *Princeton Review* and *U.S. News & World Report* college guides mentioned earlier in this chapter are two popular sources for ratings. The U.S. Department of Education's Institute of Education Sciences and National Center for Education Statistics maintains an online database called the Integrated Postsecondary Education Data System (IPEDS) that allows you to compare institutions based on a number of variables. You can find the IPEDS Data Center online at nces

.ed.gov/ipeds/. Keep in mind, though, that statistics and ratings can sometimes be deceiving. Sometimes colleges that don't have great retention or graduation rates are colleges that specialize in working with first-generation, nontraditional students who need to drop in and out to pay for their education. Sometimes smaller colleges will have low ratings, but might provide personalized resources and support needed by adult learners.

- **Does it give course credit for previous training and/or work experience?** It's important to find out whether the college to which you're applying will give you credit for any previous college courses you have taken, any professional training you've received, or for your work/life experience. Each college has its own policy for accepting transfer credits, which includes the level of course work, the minimum grade, and the total number of transfer credits that can be accepted. For example, if you completed 10 courses at another college and you achieved at least a grade of C, in most cases credit for those courses would be transferred. By transferring these credits, you would not have to retake those 10 courses at your new college. This is an excellent way to reduce the number of courses you will need to complete your degree. Each college has its own policies regarding transfer credits, so it's a good idea to ask about that policy when you are investigating colleges.

  Keep in mind that credit from some of your previous courses might not be transferable. Here are a few reasons they may not transfer:

  - *The courses are in a technical skill such as typing, shorthand, or hairdressing that is not relevant to the degree that you are seeking.* These courses will not count, in most cases, toward the requirements listed in the catalog of your new college.

- *The course may have been taken a long time ago in a field such as information technology that has changed considerably in the intervening years.* The knowledge today might be so much more advanced and different that your new college may require you to take the course again.

- *Some colleges have strict curricular guidelines that require the admissions officer and the registrar to review what your course covered compared to what the course entails at the new college.* These judgments should be questioned to ensure you are not retaking something that you have already studied. Retaking courses will cost you time and money, and that is why it is your right to ask why a course in English Literature 100, for example, was not accepted.

Some colleges offer credit for college-level learning that you may have gained outside of the classroom through your work, volunteer experience, or other training. Typically, awarding credit for life or work experience requires that students complete a portfolio to document how they achieved the college-level knowledge in a particular subject. Most colleges follow the standards for assessment issued by the Council for Adult and Experiential Learning (CAEL). These standards require that credit can only be given for work or experience that equates to actual college-level learning, not work experience alone. For more information on credit for life or work experience, visit the CAEL website at www.cael.org.

Another common way that students earn transferable credit is through the College Level Exam Program (CLEP) exam (clep.collegeboard.org/exam). CLEP credits are typically accepted at any regionally accredited college or university; they allow students to save both time and money by taking a test on a particular subject. If the student passes, she is awarded a predetermined number of college credits for that subject. CLEP credits can be a great option for students who have a lot of knowledge on a particular subject, as well as for students who are able to study independently using resources like CLEP Study Guides. There are also several websites available to help prepare students to pass the CLEP; for instance, students can have unlimited access to study guides for all CLEP subject tests for a small monthly fee at www.instantcert.com. In addition, www.CLEP. collegeboard.org offers more information on how to take advantage of CLEP credits as well as how to order transcripts for prior CLEP courses you may have completed.

- **How does the college staff respond to you as a consumer?** In seeking a college or university to meet your needs, the institution's customer-service ability is often ignored, and yet that is one of the most critical characteristics. In many ways, it will give you insights into how the college or university works with you as the consumer. Today, there are over 3,500 options for higher education. Every college is willing to work with students, but some are more customer service oriented than others. Some large colleges may have too many students to deal with, and so do not have enough time to spend one-on-one answering questions; or adult students might not be a central focus of the college, but merely an add-on to a mission strictly focused on educating traditional students. This is not a reflection on the value of the education you would receive, but merely an indication that adult students are not always a major priority.

  You will sense this when you call the colleges in which you are interested. Listen carefully:

- *How are you greeted?*

- *How quickly do you receive the information you need by mail or e-mail?*

- *Will you have a specific counselor with whom you will be working, or will you be required to work with anyone who might be available?*

Other questions you should ask are:

- *Is there a dedicated staff for adult women students, and, if so, how many are on the staff?*

- *What services does the college offer in addition to the degree? Career advice? Financial aid? Specific scholarships for adult women?*

- **What is the cost?** The cost of tuition is often an important factor in determining which college you will attend. During your conversation with admissions, it is important to ask what the tuition rate is, and if there is financial aid available for adult students. You should also ask if the tuition increases each year and what the typical rate of increase has been. Many private and state colleges increase their tuition every year to cover the growing costs of providing services. Be sure to ask if books are included in the tuition or if they are an additional cost, and what other costs and fees are required. Some colleges charge a fee for online services, parking, laboratory charges, student services, etc. Chapter 9: "The Financial Aid Process" will cover all of the important details you need to know regarding how to pay for your education. Your costs can vary greatly, depending on your personal situation and the amount of scholarships and grants you are able to receive. It is important that you not immediately discount attending a college until you see your financial aid award.

- **Do you have any special needs?** If you have a learning disability or require any accommodations for a physical disability, you should ask your admissions representative about the services provided. You will want to find out who the special needs contact person is on campus and arrange a private meeting with that individual to ensure that the college or university will be able to meet your needs before you enroll.

- **Setting up an Interview or Campus Tour**
  If the college or university is local, it is a good idea to arrange a time to visit the campus and tour the classrooms, libraries, and other facilities. You will want to observe the people on campus, both other students and the faculty and staff. Do they seem welcoming and friendly? Do you feel as though you would fit into this environment? You should also pay attention to the physical appearance of the institution. Are the buildings and grounds clean and well maintained? Take a look at the classrooms where you will be spending most of your time. Are the desks suitable for adult students, with adequate space for textbooks, notebooks, and possibly even a tablet or a laptop? What type of technology is available? Are computer labs available for students to use between classes? What type of technology is available for the instructor? Does it appear to be up to date and well maintained? Is parking available? How far away is the parking from the main classroom buildings? Finally, you will want to know about the safety of the local area. You might wish to request a copy of the crime report from the campus public safety office.

- **Prioritizing Your College Options**
  Sometimes colleges meet their class-size quotas quickly, especially in high-demand fields like nursing or forensic science. Therefore, it is always a good idea to have your colleges selected in order of priority, with the understanding that your admission may not have anything

to do with your credentials, but with the quota for your major being filled.

As you can see, colleges and universities come in all shapes and sizes and missions. It's worth your time and effort to research prospective colleges thoroughly. Finding the one that best matches your goals and learning style can be a challenge, but in the end will provide you with a rewarding college experience.

KEY POINTS TO REMEMBER:

- There is a variety of colleges and degree programs; do your homework to find one that best meets your needs and your work style.

- Take advantage of flexible scheduling and/or online classes to find a program that works well with your family and job demands.

- Use print and online guides and information on accreditation to help in your evaluation of colleges.

- Many colleges will give course credit for previous educational or work experience.

ACTION STEPS:

1. Check out some of the websites listed in this chapter or go to the library to review some of the guidebooks mentioned. Using the questions and advice in this chapter, make a list of colleges that interest you.

2. Call or e-mail any college in which you're interested and ask: Do you have a continuing education program for adult students who wish to obtain a college degree?

When do you offer the courses in which I wish to major: days, evenings, or weekends? May I have the name of the person who can give me further information, so I can make an appointment?

3. Call an admissions resource person and ask all the questions you have about admission, financial aid, etc. Remember: Colleges and universities are the providers; you are the consumer, and you are paying for the opportunity to receive a college degree. You will learn much about what a college or university thinks about adult students just by how they answer your questions.

4. Visit the college, if possible, or look more carefully at its website. What sense do you have about this college and how it educates adult women? Are reviews from adult students who have attended available online?

5. Call and set up an appointment to talk to an admissions representative at your convenience. Was it easy to do? How long did you have to wait to meet with an admissions representative?

QUESTIONS TO ASK THE ADMISSIONS REPRESENTATIVE:

These questions will provide a guide when you meet with the admissions representative or communicate online with the college.

1. Do you offer a degree in _____?

2. What type of accreditation does this institution carry?

3. Is there a program specific to adult students? Are there student services specific to adult students?

4. When are classes offered? Days, evenings, weekends, 24/7?

5. Are online classes available? Can I complete my entire degree online?

6. Are online classes offered in synchronous or asynchronous format?

7. What is the tuition? What types of financial aid are available? Are tuition rates variable by degree program; i.e., will occupational therapy cost more than an English major? Does the tuition vary by format—online versus on-ground, weekend versus weekday?

8. How many credits are required for this degree?

9. How many transfer credits will you accept? Is there an expiration date on allowable transfer credits? What is the minimum grade that can be transferred?

10. Do you accept CLEP credits? Is there a limit on the number of CLEP credits I can transfer in?

11. Do you offer credit for life/work experience? What type of proof do you require for this?

12. What criteria are considered for admission?

13. What do I need to do to apply? What is the deadline to apply? If I miss the deadline, when is the next time I can start the program?

14. Are any placement tests or standardized tests required?

15. What types of tutoring support services are available for adult students?

16. What type of support is available for students with a documented learning disability?

17. Are the classrooms accessible?

18. When are acceptance decisions made?

19. Is a deposit required for enrollment? Is this an extra fee, or is it applied to my tuition bill?

20. Is there an orientation program for new students?

21. Do you have childcare facilities or options?

22. Is there someone in the financial aid office who has special knowledge of adult financial aid options?

23. What will be the ages of the students with whom I will be studying? Will I be studying with students who are 18–22 years old, or will there be many older students in my classes?

24. (If you are attending an all-women's college) Will there be men in my classes at any time?

$\mathcal{L}$ISA'S STORY

Lisa, a 38-year-old woman with three children and a full-time job, asked herself, "Am I nuts? ... Can I really do this?" when she set out to get her degree. It was "the scariest thing I did in my adult life, yet it was the best decision I ever made," she wrote. "The thought of a college degree always seemed more of a dream than [a] reality for me. I had not one credit to my name and was scared to death of falling on my face." A meeting with an admissions counselor convinced her. "This woman couldn't have been nicer and made our conversation very enjoyable and gave me my first step to my future." Attending an orientation, Lisa said, "[I] compared my nerves to how a kindergartener must feel on their first day of school." Listening to Bay Path President Dr. Carol Leary's orientation speech was an inspiring moment for Lisa. "I [got] the chills, and tears came to my eyes, and I thought, 'Wow, this dream of a college education means so much to me, and I want to do everything in [my] power to finish this race.'" By the end of her first year, Lisa was on the dean's list, in spite of "sleep-deprived nights, hours writing papers, time spent at the computer, minutes pulling my hair out and crying, and my lost time spent with my family." For Lisa, all the sacrifices were worth it. She said, "I have gained confidence in myself that I NEVER thought I had. Classes are great, professors are wonderful, and everyone I have come into contact with has been supportive and helpful."

RESOURCES:

College Board. (2014). CLEP Exams. *CLEP.* Retrieved from clep.collegeboard
.org/exam

Council for Adult and Experiential Learning. (2014). *CAEL: Linking Learning and Work.* Retrieved from www.cael.org/

Council for Higher Education Accreditation. (2014, October 10). *Directories: Regional Accrediting Organizations,* 2014-2015. Retrieved from www.chea.org
/Directories/regional.asp

Edvisors Network, Inc. (2014). *Edvisors.* Retrieved from www.edvisors.com

InstantCert Academy. (n.d.). *InstantCert Academy.* Retrieved from www.instantcert.com

Peterson's, a Nelnet Company. (2014). *Peterson's.* Retrieved from www.petersons.com

TPR Education IP Holdings, LLC. (2014). *Princeton Review.* Retrieved from www
.princetonreview.com

U.S. News & World Report L.P. (2014). Best Colleges: U.S. News & World Report Rankings. *U.S. News & World Report: Education.* Retrieved from colleges
.usnews.rankingsandreviews.com/best-colleges

United States Department of Education. (n.d.). *The Database of Accredited Postsecondary Institutions and Programs.* Retrieved from ope.ed.gov/accreditation

United States Department of Education. Institute of Education Sciences. National Center for Education Statistics. (n.d.). *The College Navigator.* Retrieved from nces.ed.gov/collegenavigator

United States Department of Education. Institute of Education Sciences. National Center for Education Statistics. (n.d.). *Integrated Postsecondary Education Data System.* Retrieved from nces.ed.gov/ipeds

8

THE APPLICATION PROCESS

*T*o be sure you have what I believe is the most valuable information available regarding your college choices, as with Chapter 7, I have co-written this chapter with Diane Ranaldi, Dean of Graduate and International Admissions at Bay Path University, and Veatrice Carabine, Deputy Chief Enrollment Officer at The American Women's College at Bay Path University. The content that follows is a compilation of our thoughts and suggestions.

Once you have determined the college that will be the best fit for you, it is time to begin the application process. It is important that you ask the admissions office exactly what is required to apply, in what format, and when the materials need to arrive.

Most colleges offer online applications that can be downloaded from their website, or they will mail you the application along with catalogs and brochures. The application is usually one to four pages in length and asks general information about your prior education, work history, interests, degree interests, and why you are considering college. This last part—why you are considering college—is usually a goal statement, and you need to be clear about your goals. After reading your goal statement, the admissions counselor can better advise you and point you in the right direction regarding your degree choice.

- **Assembling Your Credentials**

  Before you begin preparing your application, you'll want to assemble your credentials: records of past education and work experience relevant to your application. You'll need to submit official transcripts from any secondary schools and colleges where you have taken any college courses in the past. Often when you meet with an admissions representative, he or she can review an unofficial copy of your transcripts, but an official copy is typically required before you can be accepted. (See Chapter 11: "The Registrar's Office" for more information on the differences between an official and unofficial transcript.) Also, if you've taken any College Level Exam Program (CLEP) exams, you'll want to have those test results.

  You can usually obtain your high school transcript by calling the school's main office. For college transcripts, contact the registrar's office at that school. Most schools and colleges will require you to sign a written release and pay a small fee, typically $3 to $5, in order for them to send your official transcripts.

  Regardless of how long ago you attended high school or college, you can get a copy of your transcript. If your school or college has closed and you cannot locate a phone number, then you will need to call your state's department of education, which is always located in the capital city. This department will tell you how to obtain a copy of your transcripts.

- **Placement Tests**

  Sometimes exams are required, such as placement tests in math or English. These help the college to place you in the best classes for your level of knowledge. In some cases, colleges might also require other tests, such as the SAT (Scholastic Aptitude Test) or ACT (American College Testing) exam. These tests are administered by the College Board, which can be located on the Internet at www.collegeboard.org. Or, if you are a recent high school graduate, your high school guidance counselor can assist you in learning about them and how to register to take one. However, for adults entering college for the first time or returning to college, the SAT and ACT tests are not usually required.

- **Fees**

  Application fees are common and usually range from $25 to $50, depending upon the institution. You may find that the fee will be waived if you apply online or attend a college information session. If a waiver is not offered, ask the admissions counselor if the application fee can be waived. It is important that you understand the admissions timeline and when materials are due. Some colleges only accept students once or twice a year and have strict deadlines for when materials must be received. Other colleges offer rolling admissions and will accept students throughout the year. Either way, most colleges offer final enrollment deadlines. In order to start classes in a given semester or session, you must understand what these dates are and complete all the necessary steps on time.

- **What Happens Next?**

  Once the college has received all of the information required to complete your application, the school will make a decision on your acceptance. Although many colleges do accept students on a rolling basis, some colleges, and in particular some very competitive programs, may make acceptance decisions all at once. Once you have been accepted, you will receive formal notification of this decision along with information on next steps. Most colleges will require you to pay a deposit, which typically ranges from $75 to $300. This deposit lets the college know you are committed to attending, and it confirms your enrollment; once you have paid it, you are considered an enrolled student and will then receive more information about registering for classes and attending a new student orientation. Be sure to ask if the deposit is considered an extra fee or if it will be applied to your cost of tuition. You should also ask if the deposit is refundable if you change your mind or are unable to attend.

Usually there are set dates by which monies paid are refundable. Always read the catalog to find out what those dates are for the deposit and/or tuition payments that you make in advance of your first class. Life happens, and there may be times when you must delay your studies. Knowing the college's deadlines in advance will help you avoid unnecessary expense or disappointment.

- **What if You Are Denied Acceptance?**
  If for some reason you are not accepted to the college, you should contact the admissions office and speak either to your admissions counselor or the director. Ask why you were denied and what options you might have. For example, ask if you can attend a certain number of courses as a nonmatriculated student (a student who is not formally enrolled in a degree program). (Note: financial aid is often not available to nonmatriculated students.) Find out when can you reapply, and if there is something you can do to strengthen your application. Be sure to ask what the timeline is for appealing the decision. Remember that acceptance decisions vary from college to college, so you may want to apply to another college or to a few additional colleges.

  As previously mentioned, often a denial has nothing to do with your qualifications. It may be caused by a limited class size; for example, many nursing programs keep their entering classes small to ensure they meet the students' learning needs and the accrediting standards of the nursing profession. Sometimes, your grades from your previous college are not adequate for a certain program of study, like chemistry or engineering. That is why the initial conversation with an admissions counselor is important, so that you totally understand the minimum requirements for acceptance and the consequences of submitting your application for a particular program of study.

Most important, don't be intimidated by the application process. By carefully gathering the needed information and paying attention to deadlines for submitting forms and fees, you should take some of the stress out of the process.

KEY POINTS TO REMEMBER:

- Make sure your credentials are in order: school transcripts, work and volunteer experience, and letters of recommendation.

- Application fees are sometimes waived for online applications.

- Be alert to deadlines and submission requirements.

- If you are denied acceptance, you may be able to appeal or reapply.

ACTION STEPS:

1. Go to your prospective college's website and download the application form, or call the college and ask that the form be mailed to you.

2. Assemble your credentials. Request transcripts, test results, letters of recommendation, and any other materials needed for your application.

3. Mark your calendar with application deadlines for the colleges in which you're interested, and plan to have your application finished well before those deadlines.

Qiana's Story

Dissatisfaction with a job led Qiana to return to school. She was a medical assistant at a surgeons' office and had watched several of her friends earn degrees at a local college. "I said to myself that I needed to make a change," Qiana said, "and if I didn't do it now, I would probably never do it." So she sent in an application and within a month was "officially a college student." A weekend school schedule allowed her to juggle her classes around a 40-hour workweek and her responsibilities as a mother. She eagerly looked forward to graduation. "To walk across that stage with my peers and get my degree so I can open up my world and that of my family to new experiences. What a blessing!"

9

The Financial Aid Process

*T*oo often, adult women do not believe they are eligible for financial aid. Today, more than ever, colleges and universities consider adult students as critical to their missions and will provide scholarships dedicated to adult students, or will assist them with information on how to obtain state, federal, or private dollars to pay for tuition. In addition, good financial aid officers will help you search for loans that will provide low interest rates and good payback options, and will also help you explore tuition reimbursement benefits from employers. Colleges may also offer payment plans to help you spread out your tuition bill over a reasonable period of time.

In some cases, colleges and universities have a lower tuition for adult students, so, in essence, a scholarship is integrated in the cost. For example, an 18- to 20-year-old who experiences student activities, athletics, and other on-campus services will pay a higher rate than an adult student who takes courses online. Never hesitate to ask if there are varying tuition rates for adults.

Perhaps one of the most difficult questions for women to come to grips with is: How can I achieve my education without sacrificing the needs of my family, my children, my job, etc.? That essential question was addressed in Chapter 5: "Challenges and Obstacles," but it is important to mention it again from the perspective of a financial aid officer.

From a personal standpoint, I would like to provide some insight into the question of sacrifice and how women can make their finances work to afford a college education.

As I mentioned in my introduction, I returned to college for my doctorate after many years away from the classroom. My husband and I both earned fairly good salaries, enjoyed taking vacations, buying some of the name-brand products on the market, and dining out quite a bit. We both had cars, although we did not drive luxury models. When I quit my job, I feared that we would never enjoy any of life's finer pleasures again. But I must admit, in all honesty, that was not the case. Now, granted, I did not have to pay tuition, and I received a $10,000 work stipend as part of my fellowship. But we lost almost two full years of salary. For the 2-1/2 years that I studied full-time, we seemed to be able to do the same things we always had. We didn't save anything for our retirement, but the end result in earning power certainly offset those years. As I became a college vice president and then president, my salary almost doubled in my first year, and certainly has been very satisfying as I near retirement.

If we are truly the CEOs of our own destiny, that destiny must always be one of our top priorities in life. If we are not truly fulfilled, it will show up in our relationships with children, spouses or significant others, family, friends, or co-workers as resentment, depression, sadness, yearning, or any number of negative emotions. If you truly believe that being a CEO of your destiny includes your education, I can assure you that the sacrifices will be small in comparison to the rewards. Your outlook on life will improve; your self-esteem will be enhanced; your earning power (with clear and strong action steps toward a career) will increase; your children will benefit and perhaps will be encouraged to seek their own higher education.

I say all of this with some trepidation, because I cannot promise any of the above. But in a large percentage of cases, a college degree does bring those benefits.

Also, be aware that financial problems are one of the major reasons for marital and relationship discord and breakups. Both partners must understand the implications of obtaining a degree and the hardships it may cause. Both partners must realize that there will be periods of anxiety, confusion, and resentment that need to be anticipated and discussed.

Knowing your own financial situation will help you determine what type of college you can afford. If cost is a real issue, and there are no scholarships or potential for tuition reimbursement, the public college option is always there. Public institutions are founded on the premise that education is a societal good, and the populace should support it. So take advantage of a public college if you cannot afford a private education. Your tax dollars are essentially helping to support and subsidize lower tuition levels at public colleges. Private colleges must depend on donors to help them offer scholarships, or they set aside part of their operating budget to offer financial aid to students in the form of grants.

Don't assume, however, that your only option is public education. In some cases, private education may be a good option if the (usually) small class sizes or a focus on a particular major is what you are seeking, or if sufficient scholarships are offered. To understand your options, it's essential to seek the advice of a financial aid counselor at both a private and a public college.

Taking out loans is also an option. Many women fear adding another burden on top of financial responsibilities like paying rent, daily living expenses, or childcare. Work with the financial aid office of the college you choose, and staff will provide written guidelines on the questions you should ask and the issues you should consider when taking out a loan. Be sure to understand the payback provisions. Prepare a list of questions to ask a financial aid officer, and get the details about potential loans in writing. (You can find a list of sample questions later in this chapter.)

Today, more and more companies, and even some nonprofit organizations, will pay for some or all of your education. Organizations realize that to recruit and retain key employees, ongoing education is important for achieving the organization's goals and for ensuring that the organization grows and thrives. If you are employed, a first step would be to meet with your human resources office to see what assistance may be available. Usually there are certain requirements and expectations. For example, you may need to be employed for at least one year before the benefit is offered. Such a restriction could determine your timeline for beginning a college program. Your company might pay 100% of your tuition; however, some companies limit what they are willing to offer. Some put an annual cap on the amount you can have for tuition assistance. Other companies require you to pay up front for your courses and then to show you have received a minimum grade before being reimbursed. Some colleges allow students to sign up and take a course with the expectation that the employer will pay; but know that if it doesn't, the student is responsible. My advice is to carefully seek out information on tuition reimbursement and be sure you know what requirements you must fulfill to take advantage of the benefit and what results your company expects you to achieve.

Be sure to research how you can receive financial aid in whatever form is offered, discuss it openly with those who will be affected by your decision, and know that the reward at the end could significantly improve your earning power over a lifetime.

Mastering the world of college financial aid is an art and a science. Good financial aid officers are constantly updating their records for new scholarship opportunities and offering sessions on how to complete the sometimes-complicated forms for financial assistance from the federal government. The expertise of a good financial aid officer is worth gold in the admission and financial aid process. And whatever choice you make, be sure to decide how you can best finance your education prior to enrolling.

Stephanie King, the Director of Student Financial Services at Bay Path University, has been involved as a financial aid expert for 16 years. She has worked with thousands of women with all types of circumstances and financial profiles. She offers the advice that follows; it is simple and clear. With this advice, you will no longer see financial aid as a mystery or a maze of inexplicable questions.

NEGOTIATING THE FINANCIAL AID MAZE
BY STEPHANIE KING

To prevent any mistakes and to avoid pitfalls in applying for financial aid, carefully research college financial aid websites for specific programs for which you may be eligible, along with their application requirements and deadlines. Talk to a financial aid advisor about your specific questions. Never be embarrassed, shy, or hesitant to talk with a financial aid administrator. The more information you share about your specific situation, the better the financial aid office administrator can assist you in affording a college degree. Talk with a financial aid administrator about the cost of education, the financial aid application process, and the types of financial aid you may be eligible to receive.

Here are answers to some of the most frequently asked questions about financial aid:

- **What Is the Cost of Education?**
  While researching a particular school that interests you, begin by reviewing the college's website to learn the costs associated with attending that particular college. The comprehensive cost of attendance is comprised of two parts. The first part consists of direct educational expenses, including tuition and fees, along with room and board for those students who may reside on campus. The second part includes indirect costs such as books, personal expenses, and travel. Although you see only

direct expenses such as tuition, fees, and room and board for resident students on the college billing statements, the comprehensive cost determines your eligibility for financial aid. Actual expenses will vary depending upon whether you attend a public or private school.

- **How Do You Apply for Financial Aid?**

  As you search for a college to attend, look at the financial aid application requirements on the college's website. Colleges have different requirements to apply for financial aid. Be mindful of deadlines to apply for specific scholarships or grants awarded through the college. All students must complete the Free Application for Federal Student Aid (FAFSA) to apply for federal funds and for some state grant programs. In addition to the FAFSA, a college may require its own financial aid application and copies of your most recently completed federal tax return documents to apply for institutional grant or scholarship aid. You will need to submit a financial aid application every year that you attend the college.

  Prior to completing the FAFSA, apply for your Personal Identification Number (PIN) online at www.pin.ed.gov. The PIN allows you to complete and sign the FAFSA form online, sign a master promissory note if borrowing a Federal Direct Student Loan, and obtain your student loan history.

  The FAFSA is usually available between January 1 and June 30 of each year. Complete the FAFSA online at www.fafsa.gov. The electronic filing of the FAFSA is the fastest and easiest process and reduces the chances for errors. You will need a copy of your prior year's federal tax return to complete the FAFSA. You may also be able to use the IRS Data Retrieval Tool to view and transfer your tax information from the IRS directly to your FAFSA form; the FAFSA electronic process will walk you through the IRS Data Retrieval Tool process. If applying before your tax return is completed, estimate your income. You will be able to update the FAFSA when the tax return is completed. If you need assistance completing the FAFSA, contact the financial aid office at the college you plan to attend. You may also contact the U.S. Department of Education at www.studentaid.ed.gov or call 1-800-433-3243.

- **What Types of Financial Aid Might You Receive?**
  There are a variety of aid programs available, some based on the student's financial needs, others based on the student's talents in academics, athletics, or other fields, or on a number of other characteristics, such as relationship to college alumnae.

  - **Need-based aid.** For institutional, federal or state assistance, a student must demonstrate financial need to qualify. A student's financial aid need is determined by the cost of attendance at the college less the Expected Family Contribution, (EFC). (The EFC is not the amount of money your family is expected to pay for college. Rather, according to the FAFSA website, it is "a measure of your family's financial strength.") The EFC is calculated according to a formula established by the federal government. The information you report on the FAFSA is used to calculate your EFC. The college you apply to will use the EFC to calculate the amount of financial aid you are eligible to receive.

  - **Merit aid.** Financial aid awarded based on academic achievement, merit, or any other non-need-based reason is considered merit aid. A college may offer, for example, a Legacy Scholarship to an immediate family member of an alumna from the college.

  All financial aid programs fall into one of four categories: grants, scholarships, loans, or employment.

  - **Grants** are outright gifts of money and do not have to be repaid or earned by working for an employer.

Grants are awarded on the basis of financial need and not based on merit. Students must demonstrate financial need to qualify for a grant.

- **Scholarships** are gifts of money that are provided to students on the basis of need, merit, or academic criteria and do not have to be repaid. Scholarships may be determined, for example, by the scholastic achievement of the student.

- **Loans** are borrowed money that must be repaid with interest.

- **Employment** through the Federal Work-Study Program (FWS) allows students to work and earn money needed for college costs. In some circumstances, students who do not qualify for FWS might be eligible for other jobs on campus. (At some institutions, these opportunities might be restricted to undergraduate students between 18–22 years old, whose parents are paying for most of their education.)

In addition to the financial aid programs mentioned above, the federal government offers programs that are often called Title IV Programs because they fall under Title IV of the Higher Education Act of 1965, as amended. The Title IV Programs include: Federal Pell Grants, Federal Perkins Loans, Federal Supplemental Educational Opportunity Grants, Federal Work Study, Federal Direct Subsidized and Unsubsidized Loans. Students apply for all these financial aid programs by completing the FAFSA. The results of the FAFSA will determine your eligibility for federal aid programs. For further information about federal aid programs, visit www.studentaid.ed.gov.

State grants may also be available from your home state. State requirements differ in application processes and eligibility. All require the FAFSA, but some require additional application documentation. You can contact your state higher education agency to inquire about these grants.

Colleges may offer assistance through need-based grant or scholarship aid. Review the financial aid section of the websites for the colleges in which you are interested for information on any specific grants and scholarships they might offer. Such aid will typically be based on specific criteria, such as your major, whether you're an adult student returning to college, whether you're a first-generation college student, and so on.

- **How Is Your Financial Aid Determined?**
  Most colleges will use the same consistent method to determine the student's financial aid eligibility. The college financial aid office will determine a student's financial aid need by subtracting the EFC (Expected Family Contribution) from the total cost of attendance at the institution. The EFC is determined based on the information reported on the FAFSA, and is subjected to a formula set by the U.S. Department of Education. Colleges may also determine institutional need-based grant aid after reviewing the FAFSA and the college's financial aid application. Students who have financial need are eligible to receive funds from one or more of a variety of sources. Most colleges and universities provide aid to the extent that resources are available from the federal and state governments and the college itself. There may be a gap between the student's financial aid need and the amount of financial aid offered. Resources from the federal and state governments, in addition to colleges, may not fully cover the cost of tuition and fees.

  The merit awards are based on a student's academic, athletic, artistic or other abilities; a student's involvement in her community may also be considered when merit-award applications are reviewed. Colleges determine if a student is qualified.

- **How Are You Notified About Your Financial Aid?**

  The financial aid office will review the results of the FAFSA, along with any other application or tax documents submitted, and will determine your financial aid award package. The package may consist of grant, scholarship, and loan funds for a semester or academic year. The college will then send a financial aid award letter detailing the amount of assistance that you are eligible to receive from federal, state, and institutional sources. Review the financial aid award letter carefully. The college may require you to sign and accept the financial aid offered. *Be careful to adhere to any deadlines for responding to the college in accepting a financial aid package; this is critical.* If you do not respond, the financial aid office will assume you have not accepted the award and may then award your dollars to another deserving student. Therefore, never miss a deadline when it involves financial aid, or you may risk losing some very valuable dollars toward your education. For example, Massachusetts has a state grant program with a FAFSA application deadline of May 1st to apply for the upcoming academic year. Several students who were late completing the FAFSA lost eligibility for the MassGrant program in the amount of a $1,700 award for the year. Grant aid is "free" money, and each year students apply too late to receive the funding.

  If you have any questions about the award letter or the next steps with the financial aid process, contact the financial aid office or schedule an appointment to talk to a financial aid administrator.

- **Other Sources of Aid**

  Veteran's Education Benefits may be available to student veterans or spouses of veterans. Check with your local Veterans Affairs Office for further information.

  Miscellaneous sources of private scholarships and/or loans include banks, schools, fraternal organizations (such as Lions, Kiwanis, Zonta, Rotary, etc.), churches, local community foundations, and corporations that provide scholarships, tuition reimbursement, or loans for employees, and more. The college's financial aid website might provide information on specific scholarships for which you may apply. These are often quite competitive, but students are encouraged to look for all scholarships for which they might qualify. In addition, scholarships might be available specifically for adult women returning to college. Talk with a financial aid counselor to see if she or he can recommend websites for scholarships geared toward adult women.

Students are required to notify the financial aid office if they receive any private scholarship awards. You can search for scholarships at www.studentaid.ed.gov/scholarships or www.fastweb.com or www.finaid.org.

- **What Should You Know About Borrowing a Federal Student Loan?**
  In the Federal Direct Loan Program (FDL), you borrow from the federal government rather than from a bank. The loan is credited to your tuition account at the college. Loan amounts are based on the year you are in school and have maximum limits you are eligible to borrow each year. For example, a first-year independent student's maximum eligibility per year is $6,500; a sophomore student's maximum eligibility per year is $7,500. A credit check process is not required to apply for a Federal Direct Loan. By completing the financial aid application process for the college you plan to attend, you may receive a Federal Direct Loan as part of your financial aid award package. A financial aid offer may contain one or both types of Direct Loans:

  - **Federal Direct Subsidized Loan.** The FDSL is awarded based on a student's demonstrated financial need. The federal government pays the interest that accrues while a student attends college at least half time (six or more credits per semester). No payment is necessary until six months after leaving college or going below half time. The federal government sets maximum loan amounts for each academic year.

- **Federal Direct Unsubsidized Loan.** Additional funds may be available via the Federal Direct Unsubsidized Loan Program. The borrower can either pay the interest while in school, or defer the interest payments and have the interest capitalized onto the principal balance once the borrower is no longer enrolled in college or after the student drops below half time (six credits). Maximum loan amounts are set by the federal government.

You may be eligible for a loan forgiveness program or the Public Service Loan Forgiveness Program. Forgiveness loans are loans that may be given to you for a particular major or for a special location in our country in need of assistance from doctors, teachers, etc. You can research loan forgiveness online. Information about Teacher Loan Forgiveness is online at: www .studentaid.ed.gov/repay-loans/forgiveness-cancellation /charts/teacher. Information about Public Services Loan Forgiveness is online at: www.studentaid.ed.gov/repay -loans/forgiveness-cancellation/charts/public-service.

You will need to check with the federal government for information on these types of loans, or your financial aid officer may be able to help.

Please note that a promissory note means you will repay the government for the loans you take at a certain interest rate and with specific guidelines for when you need to start repaying the loans. Student loans must be repaid even if you do not complete your education, can't find a job related to your program of study, or are unhappy with the education you paid for with your loan. However, under certain circumstances, your loans may be forgiven, cancelled, or discharged. Understand each of these options very carefully in order to plan for repayment in light of your other financial obligations, like a mortgage or credit card payments.

- **How Do You Repay Your Student Loans?**
  You have several options for loan repayment schedules and terms, which can be adapted to your particular situation. You might wish to repay your entire loan in a standard 10- to 25-year term; or you might choose a plan with a monthly payment that is relatively low for the first few years, then increases as you advance in your career. Choosing an option that fits well with your individual situation will make paying your monthly student loan bill less burdensome. There are repayment plans that extend repayment periods, offer smaller payments for a period of time, or base payments on how much money a borrower makes. It is important to know that you will pay more money with these alternative payment plans than with a standard repayment plan, due to the increased amount of interest that will accrue on the loans. Students may find details and examples of repayment calculators online at www.studentaid.ed.gov/repaying. Remember: Know what you owe. Being late on your federal student loan payments can severely damage your credit score and increase the amount you owe. If you fall behind on your payments it can be difficult to catch up. You can obtain your financial aid history and details, including whom to contact with repayment questions, through your loan servicer, online with the National Student Loan Data System (NSLDS). The NSDLS is the U.S. Department of Education's central database for federal student aid records. It receives data from schools, loan guarantor agencies, and U.S. Department of Education programs. To gain access to the NSLDS, visit the website www.nslds.ed.gov. You will need your Personal Identification Number (PIN) from your FAFSA to log onto the site.

- **What if You Want to Appeal Your Financial Aid Award, or What if Your Circumstances Change?**

  If you are denied financial aid, or if you feel your financial aid award is not sufficient, you may appeal the award to request additional aid, but you should first contact the financial aid office to discuss the particulars of the circumstances surrounding the appeal. The basis for the appeal might be any reason that affects a family's ability to pay for the cost of college, including loss of income, retirement, high medical bills, or any other circumstance that may be unique to a family. Colleges may require a specific application for the appeal process. If an appeal is sent, be sure to detail your reasons for appealing, and always save a copy of your appeal. Such details should include specific reference to the actual dollar amounts of lost income or indebtedness, why the income will be lost, how the indebtedness occurred, and any other appropriate details. Supporting documentation must accompany the request for consideration. A financial aid administrator may use professional judgment to adjust the student's Expected Family Contribution (EFC).

- **What Other Financing Options Are Available?**

  If the amount of financial aid offered does not cover your entire tuition costs, you may want to consider other financing options, such as a payment plan through the college or a tuition reimbursement program from your employer.

  Colleges typically offer students a payment plan by which you can spread out all or part of your education expenses over a period of time. Research college websites for the types of payment options offered to students. Talk with a financial aid administrator about payment options to pay your cost of education.

  Employer tuition reimbursement may be an option to help pay your college expenses. Talk with your employer and find out if they offer a tuition reimbursement program to assist employees with paying for college. Contact the financial aid office or business office at the college you plan to attend, and inquire about ways in which you can use your tuition reimbursement program from your employer.

- **Are Income Tax Credits Available for Students?**
  Education credits are available to qualifying students to help reduce the amount of your income tax. The education tax credits are the American Opportunity Credit and the Lifetime Learning Credit. For further information, see IRS regulations at www.irs.gov/Individuals/Students.

- **Are Foreign Students Eligible for Financial Aid?**
  Students who are not citizens of the United States might be eligible for financial aid under certain conditions.

  - **Green Card students.** A student who has a Green Card is eligible for federal, state, and institutional aid.

  - **International students.** International students might be eligible for institutional aid at the college they attend. International students should inquire about the type and amount of institutional aid a college may provide. International students do not qualify for federal or state aid, as they are not citizens or eligible noncitizens of the United States.

- **What if You Are Divorced or Have Children?**

  - **Divorced women.** A woman who is divorced will complete the financial aid application process and indicate if she receives any alimony or child support. A student in this situation is not treated any differently for calculating her financial aid need.

  - **Women with children.** If a woman has children under the age of 24 whom she supports, the FAFSA calculations factor in the number of family members to determine the EFC (Expected Family Contribution).

The EFC is based on the number of family members in the student's household, along with the number in college. If the adult student has a dependent child attending college, her EFC may be less, and therefore she may qualify for more aid, since there are two in the family attending college.

As Ms. King has demonstrated, understanding financial aid can be one of the most important parts of achieving a college degree. If you are lucky enough to finance your education through your own resources, congratulations. But if not, this information will give you some steps to take to financing your education. No matter what, always be forthright and honest with your financial aid counselor if your circumstances change—if you need to drop out for a while or reduce the number of courses you are taking due to a divorce, an illness, or a job loss—because there are penalties that may occur, or you might have to begin paying back loans earlier than you realize. In some cases, you may lose your scholarships and may need to reapply, with the risk that there might not be funds left to assist you. Talking about your finances may seem private and embarrassing, but it is worth it to prevent unnecessary financial hardships as a result of a seemingly innocent action. Remember, finances can be the number one reason students drop out of college today. Please don't add to that statistic because of one missed meeting with your counselor or one simple phone call.

Financial aid counselors will assist you through all aspects of financing your education, from explaining the application process to providing guidance on funding opportunities. They can provide you with the pathway to planning the financing of your education. No matter how many questions you may have on financing your education, a financial aid counselor will be available to help you navigate through the process.

KEY POINTS TO REMEMBER:

- Don't forget to include indirect costs like books, personal expenses, and travel when calculating your college expenses.

- Don't assume you can't afford college. There is a wide variety of financial assistance available, including grants, scholarships, loans, and employment (work-study programs).

- Be sure to check for all available financial aid sources from federal and state governments, from your college, and from private scholarship funds.

- Ask your employer if your company offers tuition reimbursements for employees who return to college.

- Pay close attention to deadlines for filing FAFSA and other financial aid paperwork; a missed deadline could jeopardize your financial aid.

- Be alert to deadlines and payment schedules for student loans; missing payments can increase the amount you owe.

- Contact your college's financial aid office as soon as possible if your financial circumstances change (you lose your job, have a family illness, etc.)

ACTION STEPS:

1. Call a public college or university financial aid office and ask if they have scholarships for adult women who wish to attend college. Call a private college with the same question.

2. When offered a financial aid package from a private college, compare tuition prices, fees, books, etc. with the cost to attend a public college to see what the net result would be. Often, a private college will cost almost the same as a public college if need-based aid and/or merit aid are received.

3. Call your local Lion's Club, Rotary Club, Community Foundation, or other local fraternal or service organizations and ask whether they have scholarships for adult women.

4. Check out the websites listed in this chapter and make a list of potential financial aid sources.

5. Ask your employer if the organization has a tuition reimbursement program. Find out about the details for applying, the maximum amount offered yearly, and any minimum grade per class needed to receive this benefit.

6. Make a list of the cash and savings you have on hand. Make a list of all your debts and credit card bills. These steps will be necessary when filling out the paperwork for federal financial assistance and any type of loan, so taking the time now will save you time later. Finding the information is a good first step.

QUESTIONS TO ASK
A FINANCIAL AID COUNSELOR

1. What types of financial aid do you offer?

2. How do I apply for financial aid? What application forms are required?

3. Is there a deadline to apply for financial aid?

4. When will I receive my financial aid award letter?

5. If my financial circumstances change, can I appeal for additional financial aid?

6. Where can I find other sources of financial aid?

7. If I borrow a student loan, what is the interest rate, and when do I begin repayment on my loan?

8. How much debt do students usually have when they graduate?

9. Do you offer a payment plan to stretch my tuition payments over monthly installments during the academic year?

10. If I receive a private scholarship from a local organization do you reduce my financial aid?

Danielle's Story

Danielle's college career was a series of starts and stops. She'd attended a community college in the late 1990s, but she explained, "The timing just wasn't right for me for so many reasons." It took a number of unsuccessful efforts before she found a college program that worked with her schedule. "My prayer was that I really wanted a school where I could find balance: family, work, school, and ministry work," she said. A Saturday college program gave her that balance. A happy surprise occurred when she discovered that her job provided tuition reimbursement. She advised other women in her situation, "It is worth it! Your life is waiting for you!"

RESOURCES:

Fastweb. (2014). *Fastweb!* Retrieved from www.fastweb.com

Kantrowitz, M. (2014). *FinAid! The Smart Student Guide to Financial Aid.* Retrieved from www.finaid.org

Kantrowitz, M. (2015). Financial Aid for Female Students. *FinAid! The Smart Student Guide to Financial Aid.* Retrieved from www.finaid.org/otheraid /female.phtml

Kantrowitz, M. (2015). Minority Students. *FinAid! The Smart Student Guide to Financial Aid.* Retrieved from: www.finaid.org/otheraid/minority.phtml

United States Department of Education. (2014, September 21). Get Help Paying for College: Submit a Free Application for Federal Student Aid (FAFSA). *Federal Student Aid: An Office of the U.S. Department of Education.* Retrieved from www.fafsa.ed.gov

United States Department of Education. (n.d.). *Federal Student Aid: An Office of the U.S. Department of Education.* Retrieved from studentaid.ed.gov

United States Department of Education. (n.d.). If You Work Full-Time in a Public Service Job, You May Qualify for Public Service Loan Forgiveness. *Federal Student Aid: An Office of the U.S. Department of Education.* Retrieved from www .studentaid.ed.gov/repay-loans/forgiveness-cancellation/charts/public-service

United States Department of Education. (n.d.). *National Student Loan Data System.* Retrieved from nslds.ed.gov

United States Department of Education. (n.d.). *StudentLoans.gov.* Retrieved from studentloans.gov/myDirectLoan/index.action

United States Department of Education. (n.d.). Wondering Whether You Can Get Your Federal Student Loans Forgiven or Canceled for Your Service as a Teacher? *Federal Student Aid: An Office of the U.S. Department of Education.* Retrieved from www.studentaid.ed.gov/repay-loans/forgiveness-cancellation /charts/teacher

United States Internal Revenue Service. (2014, October 30). *Tax Information for Students.* Retrieved from www.irs.gov/Individuals/Students

10

THE COLLEGE CURRICULUM

*O*nce you have been accepted into the college of your choice, you will probably be eager to plunge into courses leading to the career skills you would like to acquire. But in your first year or two of study, you will be required to take a number of courses that seem to have nothing to do with your major—these are called core courses. You may wonder why you must take English composition, for example, if you're planning to major in biology. But all colleges have this type of core curriculum: a set of courses all students are required to take before they can pursue a specialized major.

Sometimes students do not understand why they are required to take core courses. There are many important reasons: A college education is meant to be both broad and deep, not only providing students with detailed knowledge of a specific subject, but also with a general background in the humanities, social sciences, and natural sciences. Core curricula are developed based on the belief that students should have a shared general knowledge base before they move on to specialized studies; thus the curricula provide a background for and a complement to your major course of studies. Taking courses in the core curriculum also gives you the opportunity to explore fields outside your major and perhaps discover interests and talents you didn't know you had.

Dr. William Sipple is Provost and Vice President for Academic Affairs Emeritus at Bay Path University. Dr. Sipple's explanation of the rationale for the college curriculum will help you see that both required courses and electives are part of a logical progression toward your degree.

UNDERSTANDING THE COLLEGE CURRICULUM
BY WILLIAM L. SIPPLE, PH.D.

Many adults returning to college or starting college for the first time question the purpose and structure of the college curriculum. Yet they fear asking about it at the risk of feeling as though they are asking stupid questions. Moreover, many adults are investing in their education at significant personal costs, both in time and finances, and they want their studies to be directly related to their personal goals. What academic administrators hear most often is that adult students do not want to have to take courses that are unrelated to their majors or career interests or that repeat areas where they maintain they already have experience or expertise. This is a reasonable expectation, and most colleges take these concerns into consideration when designing curricula for adult students. Nevertheless, while the focus may well be on career preparation, the abiding purpose of a college degree extends far beyond this tangible goal. The well-constructed college curriculum is comprised of many individual courses that flow one into another and ultimately result in a coherent educational experience.

There is a fundamental difference between training and education, even though in higher education today the two often overlap in significant ways. Training focuses primarily on preparation for employment, with all the educational experiences directly related to the goal of the job. For example, training to become a medical technician or a welder provides the learner with knowledge and experience for these fields. On a much higher level, medical school both educates and trains physicians and surgeons with a blend of classroom knowledge and clinical training. Today, adult learners have come to expect that as a result of their college experience they will be trained for a career and will be employed or advanced upon graduation or sooner.

Education, on the other hand, is a much more elusive goal: how does one become an educated person? What, in fact, is an educated person? This question has been answered and debated for centuries, and our higher education curriculum has been significantly affected by this goal. For example, three centuries ago, Thomas Jefferson maintained that an informed and educated citizenry was indispensable for the proper functioning of a democracy. He believed, as we still believe today, that our form of self-government is not possible without citizens who are enlightened decision-makers with sufficient knowledge to work effectively with one another.[1] To reach these ends, Jefferson developed a curriculum for his university in Virginia that in many ways is still the core curriculum of a university education today.

Much the same is still true today at Harvard College, the undergraduate school of Harvard University. At Harvard College, one cannot pursue a career-oriented education. Students who seek to enter medical school to train to be physicians do not major in premed sciences as they would in many institutions; they are liberal arts students who major in the history of science. Career and professional training and education are left to focused, specialized graduate programs.

In a recent report on college curriculum, *Becoming an Educated Person: Toward a Core Curriculum for College Students*, former Secretary of Education William J. Bennett offers this valuable perspective on education and training: "Education is not the same as training. Plato made the distinction between *techne* (skill) and *episteme* (knowledge). Becoming an educated person goes beyond the acquisition of a technical skill. It requires an understanding of one's place in the world—cultural as well as natural—in pursuit of a productive and meaningful life. And it requires historical perspective so that one does not just live, as Edmund Burke said, like 'the flies of a summer,' born one day and gone the next, but as part of that 'social contract' that binds our generation to those who have come before and to those who are yet to be born." Bennett goes on to say, "An education that achieves those goals must include the study of what Matthew Arnold called 'the best that has been known and said.' It must comprehend the whole—the human world and its history, our own culture and those very different from ours, the natural world and the methods of its study, quantitative and verbal skills, and the lively arts."[2]

What educational thinkers throughout the ages have always agreed upon is that education should be an end unto itself. Traditionally, a university education that was an end unto itself was called a liberal education—an education that has its own value and is not utilitarian in any direct sense. In other words, the end, goal, or use of education is not found in anything outside of the study itself. In a recent study on liberal education, Thaddeus Kozinski noted, "The liberal arts, as all arts, are tools, in a sense, but they are tools for making humans. They perfect the intellect, the highest part of man, and thus enable man to know the world, oneself, and God as these really are."[3] Thus, students would study the arts, literature, history, philosophy, law, religion, and science with the goal of attaining knowledge in these fields and preparing to be the enlightened citizenry that Jefferson envisioned. Getting a job was neither an expectation nor a real consideration of these studies until very recently.

The dilemma today for colleges and universities is to strike a balance between these objectives of advancing students to become educated citizens and providing these same students with a path to a career. Colleges and universities attempt to achieve these lofty goals for an educated person by requiring a strong core curriculum, a set of courses that all students are required to complete. This core is sometime called a liberal arts core or the common core. Regardless of what it is called, the core, through a sequence of study, ensures that every student graduates with a solid understanding of such basic subjects as English and history, mathematics and science, foreign language, the arts, literature, and the social sciences.

Many adults returning to college argue that they already have acquired these areas of knowledge and view these courses as superfluous and repetitious. As a result, some institutions evaluate life experience as equivalents to these core requirements. However, college faculty still maintain that returning adults with significant life experience can enhance their knowledge in these core areas, develop new ways of seeing the world, build problem-solving and decision-making skills that push beyond their current levels of mastery, and enhance their tolerance of new ideas and other cultures.

To reach these goals, most universities today include in all programs of study (i.e., majors) a common set of courses designed for the adult student. These courses address the global perspectives required of educated adults. As renowned education leader Ernest L. Boyer says so well, "The integrated core concerns itself with the universal experiences that are common to all people, with those shared activities without which human relationships are diminished and the quality of life reduced."[4] The core curricula of colleges and universities today have these ideals at heart.

One important realization about the core curriculum, or general education program as it is sometimes termed, is that it is the same core for all students. That is why it is sometimes called the "common core." The common core meets a set of student learning outcomes and is assessed in similar ways across all programs and formats. Additionally, core requirements adhere to the standards set for all colleges and universities by the regional accrediting associations. For example, in the New England states, the New England Association of Schools and Colleges (NEASC) establishes the requirements. Many colleges cite as a major strength their comprehensive, faculty-driven, outcomes-assessment programs for all degrees, majors, and general education programs, and many have received recognition for these assessment initiatives and their innovative core curricula.

While there are commonalities across core curricula in colleges and universities, an institution's mission drives elements of the core curriculum in ways that are specific to the institution. For example, the mission of a college that specializes in women's education may state the following: "A pioneer in innovative undergraduate programs for women and professional graduate degrees for men and women, [the institution]—through its focus on leadership, communication, and technology—educates students to become confident and resourceful contributors to our increasingly interdependent world."[5] Thus, the core curriculum of this institution provides opportunities both in the classroom and in experiences to build and strengthen technological and analytical skills and oral and written communication skills, as well as to apply and expand knowledge through internships, field placements, or focused projects in a wide variety of settings. The achievement of these skills becomes the hallmark of the graduates of that institution. Thus, reading a college or university mission statement provides a window into one of the key factors that shape the institution's curriculum.

As a result, mission-driven goals are set not only in the core requirements but also in the requirements for major programs of study, albeit the specific course requirements, the assignments and activities, and the nature of the experiences may be different in order to meet the needs of the differing demographics of students. For example, a traditional-aged student generally has far less life experience than the adult student, so she might need to engage in activities that foster growth and development, while the adult woman might need to hone her problem-solving and decision-making skills in new contexts and circumstances. One can see this in practice in this way: A program for adult women might offer a women's leadership seminar early in the degree requirements so that the adult woman can better set her personal goals and map her progress to those goals. For the traditional student, however, leadership experiences might be integrated throughout the traditional undergraduate program and become more focused toward the end of the college experience as the student grows in maturity and knowledge.

Perhaps the easiest part of the college curriculum to understand is the major program. The adult learner will view the major as being most closely related to her goals for a degree program. The major drives students to pursue a college education—both adult and traditional students. Every major program leading to a degree includes both introductory and advanced courses in the respective field, many of them required and in a sequence, with increasing rigor and depth as the program evolves toward completion. It is important for students to realize that the major program curriculum is created as a coherent set of building blocks that makes sense as the blocks are understood and placed together. A well-designed program requires transference of knowledge and skills from one course to another, and professors expect this of students as they advance through their courses. In addition, professors expect that students apply the general education knowledge and skills developed in the core curriculum. In other words, courses are not merely a requirement to tick off on a checklist, but rather an integrated building of knowledge with the goal of developing educated and skilled professionals for a global environment.

Finally, a word about electives: Adult students sometimes question the nature and use of elective courses. Generally, there are two types of electives: free or open electives, i.e., courses that may fill general elective slots in the curriculum, and electives within one's major field. Generally, the number of electives will vary greatly from program to program across institutions. In programs designed for adult women to complete the degree in the shortest amount of time, the electives may be chosen by the college—both open electives and major field electives. This ensures that courses are filled and that they are offered according to the program outlines and completion dates. Other programs allow students considerable freedom to select electives so they may explore new and interesting areas of study outside the major field focus.

In conclusion, the university curriculum may best be viewed as a symphony. A symphony is composed of individual pieces, each unique and complete in and of itself. There are musical instruments and musical notes and variations on each of these. The individual notes are capable of being arranged in almost infinite combinations, thus affording composers the opportunity to create various pieces. Each one in and of itself is complete and coherent, but different from all others in many ways. Bach and The Beatles drew upon the same reservoir of musical possibility, with vastly different results. Thus, each composition does not make use of all the possible varieties of notes, instruments, techniques, and combinations. The composer selects and edits and creates a complete, unique masterpiece.

The college curriculum is much the same. Each course, lecture, experience is unique and complete in itself. There are many possible ways to create a program of study, but no one student could reasonably be expected to complete all the possible combinations or opportunities that are available. It is the institution's and the student's respective responsibility to design the symphony—to create a coherent college experience that leads both to becoming an educated person who functions as a citizen of the world and to a meaningful profession or career. If done successfully, we have together achieved the goals of higher education.

KEY POINTS TO REMEMBER:

- Education should be an end in itself.

- Modern colleges and universities try to balance providing students with a career path and instilling values and knowledge to create educated citizens.

- Core curriculum courses can help students develop new ways of seeing the world, build problem-solving and decision-making skills, and introduce them to new ideas and other cultures.

- Electives can enhance a student's major course of study or provide the freedom for a student to explore new areas outside of her major.

ACTION STEPS:

1. Take a little time and write your goals for your college education: What do you hope to achieve, both in terms of a major field and your personal growth? Now, what courses in the curriculum do you think will help you achieve your goals?

2. Find the university's mission statement in the catalog or on the website, and see what the institution has set for goals for its students. How does this set of goals compare to your own?

3. Look at the general education or core requirements that you will need to fulfill beyond your major field courses. What courses interest you? If you have the opportunity to choose courses, what course selections would you like to make?

4. Since your education is an opportunity for personal growth, determine what courses you would like to take simply for your own enjoyment, just because they sound interesting or are in an area that intrigues you. Then, make a plan to fit some of these courses into your overall plan of study.

$\mathcal{B}$ONNIE'S STORY

For 22 years, Bonnie's life was focused on raising four children and doing the bookkeeping for her husband's construction business. Moving eight times made it difficult for her to return to school. But, she wrote, "When my youngest went to kindergarten, I decided I needed something just for me." With the encouragement of her mother, she took a course each semester while her children were in school. "As mothers usually are, she was right!" Bonnie said. She reminds women, "It is so easy to lose sight of who you are as an individual when you are busy raising a family. It is very important to do something for yourself, and for me that would be taking a class each fall and spring. This would turn out to be the highlight of my week, because it was just for me . . . My mind was challenged, and more importantly, my soul nourished!"

RESOURCES:

Bay Path University. (n.d.). Mission Statement.

Bennett, W. J. (2003). Foreword. In American Council of Trustees and Alumni of the Institute for Effective Government. *Becoming an Educated Person: Toward a Core Curriculum for College Students*. Washington, DC: American Council of Trustees and Alumni of the Institute for Effective Government. Retrieved from www.goacta.org/images/download/becoming_an_educated_person.pdf

Boyd, J. P., Cullen, C. T., Cantanzariti, J., & Oberg, B. B., et al. (Eds.). (1950). *The Papers of Thomas Jefferson*. Princeton, New Jersey: Princeton University Press.

Boyer, E. L. (1990). *Scholarship Reconsidered: Priorities of the Professorate*. Princeton, New Jersey: Carnegie Foundation for the Advancement of Teaching.

Kozinski, T. (2013, October). The Uselessness of Liberal Education: An Apology. *Articles, Education and Liberal Learning*, 1.

NOTES:

1. Boyd, J. P., Cullen, C. T., Catanzariti, J., Oberg, B. B., et al. (Eds.) (1950). *The Papers of Thomas Jefferson*. Princeton: Princeton University Press, 33 vols. Relevant quotes on education from Jefferson are numerous; following are a sample:

   1782. *(Notes on the State of Virginia)* "Every government degenerates when trusted to the rulers of the people alone. The people themselves, therefore, are its only safe depositories. And to render them safe, their minds must be improved to a certain degree."

   1786 August 13. (to George Wythe) "I think by far the most important bill in our whole code is that for the diffusion of knowledge among the people. No other sure foundation can be devised, for the preservation of freedom and happiness. . . Preach, my dear Sir, a crusade against ignorance; establish & improve the law for educating the common people. Let our countrymen know that the people alone can protect us against these evils [tyranny, oppression, etc.] and that the tax which will be paid for this purpose is not more than the thousandth part of what will be paid to kings, priests and nobles who will rise up among us if we leave the people in ignorance."

   1787 December 20. (to James Madison) "Above all things I hope the education of the common people will be attended to; convinced that on their good sense we may rely with the most security for the preservation of a due degree of liberty."

2. Bennett, W. J. (2003). Foreword. In American Council of Trustees and Alumni of the Institute for Effective Government. *Becoming an Educated Person: Toward a Core Curriculum for College Students* (n.p.). Washington, DC: American Council of Trustees and Alumni of the Institute for Effective Government. Retrieved from www.goacta.org/images/download/becoming_an_educated_person.pdf

3. Kozinski, T. (2013, October). The Uselessness of Liberal Education: An Apology. *Articles, Education & Liberal Learning*, 1.

4. Boyer, E. L. (1990). *Scholarship Reconsidered: Priorities of the Professorate*. Princeton, NJ: Carnegie Foundation for the Advancement of Teaching.

5. Bay Path University Mission Statement.

THE REGISTRAR'S OFFICE

*T*hroughout your time on campus, the registrar's office will be an important resource. This office will help you complete your degree in a timely fashion and meet the requirements for graduation.

It is important to realize the personal responsibility that completing your degree entails. No college will promise that you will obtain a degree in a certain amount of time or in the way it was outlined to you upon admission. Why? Because, again, life happens; if you need to drop out for a considerable amount of time, the requirements for the degree might have changed by the time you have returned. I point this out because too often students will accuse colleges of false advertising. But in 95% of the cases, students did not read the college catalog on a yearly basis, did not ask their advisors the right questions, or ignored notices sent to students online or in the mail because they were too busy.

I strongly caution you to review all e-mails from the registrar, your academic advisor, the provost, the deans, or the vice president for academic affairs, because they do not write to you unless it is something important that could, perhaps, affect your graduation date—a missed course, for example, or a change in offerings.

The registrar's office is also critical when students need to drop in and out of college and/or transfer to another college.

Advisors may change, but the registrar's office will always be the "go-to" place for answers.

The staff in the registrar's office is invaluable to a student. Dr. William Sipple, Provost and Vice President for Academic Affairs Emeritus at Bay Path University, is an excellent resource. The Provost and Vice President for Academic Affairs and the registrar work closely together to ensure that the curriculum is clearly outlined for students and that they know the progress they are making toward their degree. In the previous chapter, he explained the college curriculum for you. In the following pages, he will explain the role that the registrar's office will have throughout your college career.

THE OFFICE OF THE REGISTRAR, "KEEPER OF RECORDS"
BY WILLIAM L. SIPPLE, PH.D.

Once you are enrolled and on your way to a college degree, one way to help ensure your success is to understand where to get help on campus and where to go for official information related to your degree progress. The official records office on campus is the registrar's office, and the registrar (who generally works with the vice president for academic affairs) is one of the best persons on campus to give you definitive answers to your questions about your degree requirements. Of course, your advisor and your department faculty can also give you some of this advice, but the registrar's office maintains all official records, and the registrar has the most current official degree requirements for your program.

Why would you need to go to the registrar's office in the first place? Most likely when you are admitted, a very helpful admissions representative will get you enrolled and ready to start classes. All you might have to do is get your books and show up in the right room on campus or, if you will be studying online, log on to the right discussion forum. But there are a couple of reasons you might regularly seek out the registrar. First, except perhaps for your first semester, you generally will register for classes through the registrar's office. Second, if you want to drop a class, add a class, or change your schedule, the only staff members who can do that for you are in the registrar's office. And third, if you need to know the exact requirements for your degree, what courses and how many credits you have officially completed toward that degree, and what tasks still remain in order for you to complete your degree, you will find those answers in the registrar's office. The registrar maintains all these official records and is the only office authorized to give you an official transcript of your work.

It might be helpful to look more closely at what exactly a registrar is and what services that office provides. Simply stated, the registrar, "the keeper of records," is the college or university administrator who is responsible for keeping official and complete student records. Each student has an official record called a transcript, which conveys the history of the courses completed both successfully and unsuccessfully, the courses that were attempted but not completed (usually assigned a W grade, meaning "Withdrawal"), and all courses completed at another accredited institution, in the armed forces, or through another recognized and approved organization. In addition to course credit, a student's transcript might reflect credits attained through the College Level Exam Program (CLEP) or work/life experience programs such as the ones offered by the Council for Adult and Experiential Learning (CAEL); those programs are discussed in detail in Chapter 7: "Finding the Right College."

One of the issues that frequently concern adult students is getting credits for courses completed at another institution onto their current transcript and accepted toward the degree requirements. Because official transcripts are private, protected records, only you, the student, can request and obtain your transcript from a prior institution; you will need to sign a written request. After you complete the request for an official transcript, the institution may send the record directly to your new university, or a school representative may give you a transcript in a sealed envelope. Be sure that you do not open the envelope, but rather deliver it, still sealed, directly to the registrar's office so staff can add the appropriate courses to your record.

Generally, admissions representatives record transfer credits during the admission process, but often the recording of transfer credits is not completed at that time. Thus, it is important for you to look at your transcript with the registrar early on to be sure that all the courses you have completed in the past will be credited. Keep in mind that not all courses may be eligible for transfer. Specifically, only courses with a grade of C or better from an accredited or officially recognized organization will transfer; credits for some courses will "expire" if they are technology related—for example, when new technologies supersede the material you originally studied.

The transcript designates how many credits from these courses can be transferred to your college and applied toward your degree program. In many instances, these "transfer courses" may replace or fulfill required courses; they may also be used as open electives (for a detailed discussion of open electives, see Chapter 10: "The College Curriculum"); or the courses may be listed on your transcript, but no credits for them will be applied toward your degree completion. No one except the registrar can make changes to this record, and it is permanent.

Students often have questions about what goes on the transcript and how it can be changed; the easy answer is that everything is recorded on your transcript, because it is a formal record. Generally speaking, nothing can be changed, but that does not mean that everything in that record will be used to calculate your grade point average, or GPA (this number, which is based on your grades and the number of course credits you take, is used for determining class rank, eligibility for honor societies and graduation honors, eligibility for some merit-based financial aid programs, readiness for upper-level courses, and qualification for graduate programs). For example, if you start a course but withdraw, the course stays on the record, but the withdrawal will not be calculated in your grade point average. A course with an F grade, however, will remain on your record and affect your GPA. However, if you re-enroll in the course and complete it successfully, the F grade will not be calculated into your GPA; instead, the new grade will be used. While figuring out which courses will become part of your GPA may be confusing, if you are concerned about how a course withdrawal or failure will affect your transcript, you should go to the registrar's office and discuss your options. The staff will clearly explain it all to you.

Finally, with regard to transcripts and graduation requirements, the registrar does what is called a "degree audit" of every student transcript to ensure that all degree requirements are met successfully. Once the requirements are met, the transcript will state that the degree is indeed to be granted to the student. It is a good practice to check with the registrar periodically to see if you are on track to meet the degree requirements in a timely manner. You will want to be sure that you are taking your courses in the proper sequence so you can meet prerequisites for upper-level courses; you also want to be sure that the right courses will be available to you when you need them. This kind of careful planning will ensure that you successfully complete the requirements for your degree in the shortest amount of time.

The transcript is the only document that verifies degree completion. A diploma alone is not a sufficient document, even though the institution grants it. Diplomas can be forged, but it is not easy to forge an official transcript, because it is printed on paper with special watermarks and stamped with the college or university seal.

Another reason to consult the registrar's office is if you want to add or drop classes. All universities have regulations about when you can add or drop classes and what the restrictions or penalties are for doing this. Usually, there is a "drop/add period," during which time students may make changes to their schedules without penalties. This is a short window of opportunity based on the length of the term. Be aware, however, that in accelerated programs, there might not be a drop/add period at all, or it might be only a day or two long. In general, adding a class at the beginning or just after the start of a semester is usually allowed. Dropping a class at the beginning of the semester may also be allowed without penalty, generally before you begin to submit work in the class.

However, as you get further into the term, withdrawing from classes might result in other outcomes, such as losing a large percentage or all of the tuition paid for the course or becoming ineligible for grants and scholarships due to insufficient course credits. Or you might drop from full-time to part-time status, which might jeopardize financial aid and make you ineligible to enroll in subsequent courses. All of this might put your completion of the program off schedule.

From experience, we know that dropping courses is a very frequent problem for adult students. Adults return to school and are optimistic and enthusiastic, but when the work begins and life interferes, they sometimes get behind, fail to submit work in a class, and eventually need to withdraw from the course. Faculty are very attuned to this problem and may alert you if they believe you are struggling, and may even contact your advisor, especially in online programs. Keep in mind that the further you get into the term or semester, the larger the penalty becomes for withdrawing from a class. Usually, you cannot drop a course toward the end of the term just because you want to avoid an F grade. Thus, it is important that you work closely with your academic advisor to plan a realistic course load so that you will not be heading to the registrar's office to drop a course, which could result in substantial financial losses. Also, keep in mind that it is not the job of the registrar's office staff to warn you of these problems; you need to be alert and monitor your own progress.

Now, a few words about the university catalog: The catalog is kept up to date by the registrar in cooperation with the academic affairs department; it contains all the regulations, degree requirements, and relevant information related to degrees, programs, majors, minors, grade point averages, and a myriad of other information that you will need. Reading the catalog without a specific purpose is akin to studying the phone book because you know that someday you will be making calls and needing phone numbers. In other words, it is really boring to read the catalog just to peruse all the information in it without a specific purpose. However, when you want to know something specific about your program requirements—a course description, specific policies, or other academic matters—it is your chief and best source. The catalog is the "bible" of the registrar's office, and you need to know how to gain access to it, most likely in an online version, as most institutions today do not print paper copies. If you do not understand something in the catalog or cannot find certain information, you should go to the registrar's office for help. Faculty and your advisor can help you as well, but for definitive information on regulations, requirements, grade point computations, prerequisites for upper-level courses, and transcripts, you must visit the registrar.

To help ensure your success, look at the university catalog early in your educational process with these goals in mind: First, read the section of the catalog that describes your major program and pay attention to the degree requirements and the student learning outcomes (student learning outcomes, or "SLOs," outline what students are expected to know and accomplish and what skills they are expected to acquire through completing a course of study). The degree requirements may include participation in activities in addition to the completion of courses and attainment of a certain grade point average. Second, look at the recommended sequence of study for your program. Often, departments will set out a plan for you to complete your courses in a specific order so that each course builds upon the previous ones. The registrar's office uses this plan when helping you to register for classes. Third, look at the course descriptions and see if any courses have prerequisites, such as other courses that you must finish first, a minimum grade point average, or the completion of other activities such as a practicum or an observation. Finally, if you have any questions, seek out the registrar and get the answers so you know where you are headed in your program.

In order to maintain good relations with the registrar, you should respond promptly to any requests from that office. The registrar will monitor degree progress for students, and if there is a problem, someone usually will contact you. Therefore, do not ignore any e-mails or letters from advisors, faculty, or the registrar. Also, program requirements sometimes change, and the registrar will send out e-mails or letters informing you of these changes. It is your responsibility to follow up on these communications and to take action, if necessary, to stay in good standing in the process of completing your degree. Everyone at the university wants you to succeed, and the registrar's office is there to help you on your way to your degree.

As Dr. Sipple has explained, the registrar's office can assist with just about every aspect of your student life. Make yourself familiar with the services and information the registrar's office provides, both before and during your college journey. The staff can help you successfully negotiate the maze of academic paperwork and procedures and keep you on track to graduation.

KEY POINTS TO REMEMBER:

- The college catalog is a contractual agreement between you and your college; study it carefully.

- Make sure to verify any transfer credits for which you may be eligible.

- Pay close attention to registration and add/drop deadlines. Missed deadlines can delay your graduation and might cost you money.

- If you're having problems, go to the registrar's office and ask for help as soon as possible.

- Keep tabs on your degree audit to make sure you're on track for graduation.

- As you approach graduation, check in with the registrar to make sure there are no potential obstacles.

ACTION STEPS:

1. Call the registrar's office of your chosen college and ask them to send you the latest college catalog or explain how to locate it online.

2. Call your high school or the last college you attended to inquire how to request an official transcript and how much it will cost to send it to the colleges in which you're interested.

3. When you arrive on campus, locate the registrar's office and stop in. If you are transferring credits, call or e-mail to meet the staff and inquire how to obtain an audit of your transfer credits.

$\mathcal{A}$MANDA'S STORY

A young single mother, Amanda said she "didn't know if [she] could ever manage [college] financially and time-wise." But she learned about a Veterans Administration program to help disabled vets pay for college or job training. She enrolled in a weekend program for elementary education and discovered that the experience not only benefited her, but also helped her son. "I find by me being in school and doing my homework, I am also a role model for my son. I am showing him that education is important to me and should be important to him as well."

RESOURCES:

American Association of College Registrars and Admissions Officers. (n.d.). *AACRAO: Advancing Global Higher Education.* Retrieved from www.aacrao.org

American Council on Education. (2014). Credit for Prior Learning. *American Council on Education: Leadership and Advocacy.* Retrieved from www.acenet .edu/higher education/topics/Pages/Credit-for-Prior-Learning.aspx

College Board. (2014). CLEP Exams. *CLEP.* Retrieved from clep.collegeboard .org/exam

TAKING YOUR FIRST COURSE

*A*s an adult student, returning to the classroom after many years away from school can be overwhelming, particularly if your earlier school experiences were unpleasant. Not only can professors be intimidating, so can being an older student in a class full of 19- and 20-year-olds. You may ask yourself questions like: "Will I be able to keep up?" "What if I ask a stupid question?" "What if I can't follow the lecture?" It may comfort you to know that many of your classmates are probably worrying about the same things. Practicing good classroom etiquette and active listening and note-taking can go a long way toward making a good impression with your teachers and fellow students and relieving your back-to-school jitters. Making sure you're well prepared for each class will do wonders for your confidence.

Virginia Freed is professor emerita of English at Bay Path University, with two master's degrees. She began her career as a secondary school teacher and has taught English literature and writing courses. In this chapter, Professor Freed offers tips on surviving your first class.

SUCCEEDING IN THE CLASSROOM
BY VIRGINIA FREED

Given your maturity and wisdom, you may find the following practical advice for being a successful student too obvious, but we do sometimes overlook the obvious, especially when, like you, we are so busy. Professors and students are partners in a joint endeavor and need to respect each other. As a student, you will begin that process in the first class of each course with something as simple as getting to class on time, or even a little early, and sitting in the front of the room. Given your hectic life, that will not always be easy, but it will be worthwhile.

And, frankly, that seat in the front will be helpful in some classes that might require real effort for you to stay focused on the material being presented—especially in enormous classes held in lecture halls. Sitting at the back of a large auditorium is not a recipe for anything good. You will be distracted by everything from the student in front of you twirling her hair to your own compulsion to check your text messages. Even in smaller classes, some lectures can be long. Your mind can wander to worries about sitters, an impending performance review, or getting the grocery shopping done. But if you are in the front of the room, large or small, looking into your professor's eyes, dismissing that person and what he or she is saying will be next to impossible; as an adult woman, you know that is just rude. You will be more likely to listen and learn. You will also be more likely to contribute to class discussions. Face-to-face interaction is essential for building relationships between students and professors; the classroom can provide easy opportunities for you to do so and, at the same time, to engage with the material being presented.

In your first class and in subsequent classes, completing the assigned reading before the class in which it is scheduled to be discussed is another simple technique for becoming engaged with the material and the professor. When I was a beginning college student, my strategy was to go to the class first and then do the reading. My rationale was that listening to the professor would make the reading easier. I now know that the reverse is true. If you don't do the reading ahead, you won't know which portions of the reading will be difficult, and, therefore, you won't know which questions to ask. Not doing the reading will also hamper your ability to participate in class discussions. As a sidebar, let me confess that we professors love what we teach, and we are encouraged by, remember, and respect students who have obviously cared enough to do the reading and ask salient questions. These are also the students who have taken the time to study the syllabus and are always prepared to contribute to the day's agenda.

Paying attention to the course syllabus will immediately distinguish you because, quite honestly, most students don't. Preparing the syllabus takes instructors a long time. While they do have to fill certain institutional criteria, they still have the prerogative of personalizing the document. On some you will see illustrations and stylized fonts; others will be as bland as a white carpet in a room with white walls and woodwork. But all of them will provide you with ways to contact your professor, office hours and location, test dates, grading components and weights, texts to be purchased, and expectations for attendance and class participation. The syllabus provides you with a blueprint for the course and a contract between you and your professor. Syllabi are serious documents, and professors are not pleased when students do not follow them or are unaware what they contain. Studying the syllabus in each course is a good use of your precious time. It will ensure that you have prepared for any activity designated, and have completed any reading assignments for each class.

These reading assignments will sometimes be challenging and lengthy, but some critical reading strategies can help you connect with the topic and the professor. An easy way to begin is to consider what else is on the page with the reading assignment. For example, whether you have been assigned an essay, a short story, or a chapter in psychology, one obvious item to think about is the title. What does it mean? Suppose you are assigned an essay with the title "Becoming Engaged."

Your natural inclination may be to think about diamond rings and impending marriages. But it could be about becoming involved with life or learning. If you have assumed wrongly, have you wasted your time? Probably not. At the very least, you are thinking about the reading instead of what you have to pick up at the grocery store.

After thinking about the title, consider whether you are familiar with all of the words in the reading. If not, look them up. Find a way to connect personally with the text. When was it written? Is that the year you were born or the year you went to your first concert? Who is the author? Can you find a picture of him or her? Do you know anyone else his or her age? Just as humanizing the relationship between faculty and student is critical, doing so with textbooks and other reading material is also important. Inanimate words don't always intrigue us, but if we look at them as communication from another person and find creative ways to engage with the material, they can. These quick, little steps can be ways to manage difficult reading assignments successfully.

If the reading is still baffling, go to the end of the chapter and see if there are any study questions that can help you better understand the selection. Break up the reading into smaller parts. Many of us have shared the experience of "pretend reading": our eyes have floated over every word, but we get to the end and have no clue what we have read. Thinking about the title and the author, using the questions at the end or the headings in the middle, breaking up the reading, and reading with pen in hand or computer nearby to underline or take notes will maximize the value of your reading time and shorten the time you will need to prepare for tests. Your studying will have already begun, and the later stress of preparing for midterm and final exams will be greatly alleviated. Traditional students often believe that the "real studying" begins a day or two before the test is scheduled; that belief is flawed and generates the dreaded, last-minute, overrated art of cramming. While students may learn the material long enough to repeat it for an exam, that kind of learning almost always disappears as soon as they leave the testing site. Study at the college level entails more than superficially considering and memorizing facts; it means engaging in and internalizing meaningful inquiry and analysis.

Real learning spread consistently over the semester can make contributions to group projects more valuable. Not only will you have the knowledge necessary to do your part for the group, you will also be prepared to get to work in the times you meet to prepare. Group projects provide excellent opportunities for learning, but they also afford chances for frustration. (Few things are more exasperating than being assigned to a group with members who come to planning and work sessions unprepared or who don't come at all—especially when women like you have had to juggle busy schedules to get together.) Group work needs to be a collaborative endeavor, and once again, mutual engagement and honest, open communication are critical to its success. Fortunately, preparation, respect for one another, and commitment to the joint endeavor are often strengths of adult women.

Despite using these suggestions for reading, studying, and participating, students with diagnosed learning disabilities will require accommodations to succeed. Over the years, I have been impressed with students who advocate for the services they need. Because they are so highly motivated, adult students are especially adept at taking advantage of available assistance to reach their goals. While traditional-age students may be reluctant to use campus learning centers that offer advisors, tutors, workshops, and state-of-the-art technology, the returning adult learner, equipped with the advantage of age and experience, understands the importance of doing so. Why not take advantage of the support offered, usually free of charge?

The potential benefit to using these critical strategies for taking classes is that you can simultaneously engage with the teacher, other students, and the material. Adult women are "other-directed"; they thrive on the personal connections of life. The classroom provides an opportunity to capitalize on this tendency and promote real, deep learning in a community where education takes place. You have the attributes necessary for academic success. Have confidence in your strengths, your life experience, and your dedication to this new venture. And have fun. We will all benefit.

KEY POINTS TO REMEMBER:

- Face-to-face interaction is essential for building relationships between students and professors.

- Try to complete assigned reading before it will be covered in class.

- Study the syllabus carefully.

- Use end-of-chapter study questions to help remember your reading.

- Start studying well before exams; cramming isn't productive.

- Take advantage of advisors, tutors, workshops, and other tools provided by your campus learning center.

ACTION STEPS:

1. Practice actively reading and note-taking with books or other literature you're currently reading.

2. Find out what resources are available at the campus learning center of the college you're interested in attending.

3. Find out whether it's possible to sit in on a class or two at the college you're interested in attending, so you can get a feel of what it will be like to take your first class.

Maria's Story

Maria worked for a county district attorney's office for 13 years. When the D.A. decided not to run for re-election, Maria realized that a change in administration might cost her her job. "After being faced with the possibility that I could lose my employment due to an election, I realized I needed to complete what I had started many years ago: my degree," she said.

"It took 18 years away from school, a marriage, two children, my elderly father, a dog, and an election to get me here. Coming from a lower socioeconomic beginning, I never thought I would be here today—graduating with a Bachelor of Science in Criminal Justice with *Magna Cum Laude* status. They say it takes a village to raise a child; I am an example of that. Had it not been for all the encouraging words I received throughout my years from some good friends, family members, and mentors, I would have never completed this journey, and for that I will always be grateful."

Maria credited a professor with helping her build the confidence she needed to succeed. "In September 2011, I walked into my first English class…[The professor] was incredibly understanding and comforting towards us. I had lost my voice that day. I couldn't speak; I was incredibly nervous and was not my usual spontaneous and funny self. Within the next few hours, she had helped me come out of my shell. [She] encouraged me and pushed me outside my comfort zone . . . I will always remember it as my first real stepping-stone … I can't thank my professors, the academic advisors, my friends and colleagues enough."

THE FACULTY

*T*he faculty who will be your professors, advisors, and mentors play a significant role in your academic journey. They will share their knowledge on subjects that they have studied for many years. They will share personal stories about how they have used that knowledge. Most of all, they will try to inspire you to enjoy the subject matter and want to learn even more.

There are all types of faculty, and they all have different styles of teaching. Some instructors teach primarily through lectures, with some student participation in class. Others will want to have your active engagement and will lead discussions using the case-study style of teaching. In this type of teaching, the faculty member uses a real or fictitious case to involve your critical thinking skills and see how you would react to a certain situation. For example, if you are in a criminal justice class, the instructor might present a case and ask how you would have reacted as a police officer, a forensic scientist, the lawyer for the defendant, or the lawyer for the prosecution. By involving you and other members of your class, the instructor encourages you to use the information you learned in earlier classes to think critically about how you would solve the case. Case studies can be in any subject matter, from business to education to biology.

Online teaching is definitely different from classroom, or "on-ground" teaching. You never see the professor face-to-face unless you are in a hybrid class—some classroom time and some online classes. You may see the professor on a video or YouTube presentation, or you may hear her voice, but you will not be seated in a traditional classroom. You will be online and learning most of your material independently, with input from the professor and your classmates.

Although there has been considerable discussion about the effectiveness of online education, the research has shown that, in most cases, it is nearly as effective as on-ground teaching. Hybrid teaching seems to be the best method. In the end, which method is preferable depends on the student and how she learns best. As higher education is moving toward more and more online courses, you will probably have experience with online learning at some point in your educational journey.

No matter what type of learning environment, the faculty member is a critical player as the facilitator of learning. More and more faculty realize that they can no longer be the "sage on the stage"—the expert who only lectures without interacting with students. Students must be engaged in the process so that learning is deep and broad.

So who are these faculty members who will be teaching you? To teach in a community college, most faculty will have a minimum of a master's degree. At the four-year level, most faculty will usually have a doctorate. This holds true for the graduate level as well.

Faculty teach with different titles and ranks. A full-time faculty member can be an instructor (usually with a minimum credential, such as a master's degree, to teach), assistant professor, associate professor, or professor. Every college has a different way of promoting faculty through the ranks. Most often, promotion depends on research done by the instructor and years of service to the college community. Depending on other responsibilities (like chairing a department), most faculty will teach from six to eight courses per year. In large research universities, the number of courses an instructor teaches may be considerably less, depending on his or her rank, tenure, and other areas of responsibility.

Adjunct or part-time faculty members usually have other full-time jobs or may be retired professionals. They do not receive the salaries or benefits of a full-time faculty member, but often have chosen to teach because they enjoy sharing their knowledge with students. Many judges, attorneys, business professionals, and teachers love to work with college students and will take on anywhere from one to three courses a semester, depending on their personal and professional availability. In most cases, students might not even know whether or not the faculty member is full-time.

In this chapter, I am including advice from two faculty members who have taught both traditional and adult women students for many years: joining Virginia Freed (She advised you on succeeding in the classroom in Chapter 12) is Mary Lou Di Giacomo. Ms. Di Giacomo spent many years in the nursing field, rising to the Vice President of Nursing at a major hospital, where she used her nursing and her Master of Business Administration (MBA). Retired from the hospital, she now serves as an adjunct professor at Bay Path University. She will provide some insight into her work and her philosophy of teaching as an adjunct.

Enjoy these words of advice from two of the best.

FOSTERING A RESPECTFUL PROFESSOR-STUDENT RELATIONSHIP
BY VIRGINIA FREED

When I began teaching, a colleague across the hall posted a sign that I thought at the time was witty and accurate. The sign read, "Knowledge: Free Monday through Friday. Bring your own container." Now, many years of teaching and learning later, I can see the flaws in its logic. It may be glib, but it is not correct. For one thing, acquiring knowledge is expensive, literally and figuratively, especially for the adult woman returning to college. Tuitions are high, and the emotional and physical investment in real learning is arduous. Furthermore, a Monday through Friday time frame is unrealistic. Learning goes way beyond time spent listening in the classroom, and courses can now meet any day of the week, Sunday through Saturday, and for online courses, 24 hours a day.

But what I now see as most inaccurate is the sign's omission of human collaboration in the learning process. Professors are not simply dispensers of facts, and students are not just objects to be filled with them. Students and professors are people mutually engaged in the same venture. As an experienced and intuitive adult woman returning to college, you are poised to be at an advantage when you understand that the best learning takes place through the engagement of students with professors and with the material they are studying. I have so many wonderful memories of returning adult women mixed into my traditional classes. In many cases they were unaware of how much they added to the class; in others, they were unaware of what they could have added.

Because both student and professor are human, life will intervene. Some classes will be better than others; some courses will be better than others; some instructors will be better than others. But establishing a relationship with each other will make navigating the difficult times easier. You must feel comfortable approaching your professors during their office hours about topics or assignments that confuse you, grades you feel are unfair, or aspects of the course that you are interested in pursuing further. Office hours are times set aside specifically for you to speak with them on such matters; you are not interrupting them. Professors welcome this interaction. And you are not crossing any boundaries by cultivating a positive relationship centered in your desire to learn. The trick is to achieve that human interaction so that these discussions can occur. Both student and professor must be aware of each other and appreciate each other's perspective.

As an adult woman, you can use your life sensitivities and experiences to promote this mutual respect.

Like you, your instructors will be unique individuals with their own personalities. You will relate to some better than others because of your unique personality and perspective. Understanding that basic fact of the human condition will assist you in those situations that might feel uncomfortable. As you have assessed people in your other life experiences, you will assess your professors and adapt your learning strategies, just as the professors assess the individual students in their classes and adjust their teaching approaches. Even if you have some upfront knowledge about the professor and his or her class, you will come to your own conclusions, and that's wise. We all react to people differently. Remembering they are not the "other" is important; they are human like you. You just happen to be in different roles.

Your life experiences will provide you with a perspective and patience that the traditional student does not have. You know that disagreements can arise and must be handled with tact and respect. Disagree with a grade on a paper, a test or a course? Approach the professor diplomatically and courteously, expressing your goal to understand and learn. Sometimes, you may not be satisfied with the explanation. Should that happen, you are welcome to follow the chain of command and meet with your instructor's supervisor. Because you are an adult, you will recognize the wisdom and appropriateness of such a move. More likely than not, you have been in similar situations as an employee or a parent or even as a student in your former life.

In most instances, your professor will appreciate your interest in, and commitment to, his or her discipline. Use your maturity and life experiences to guide you in selecting the appropriate words, tone, and time. Your discussion will not go well if you challenge your professor at the end of the class or in an unexpected campus meeting when you have not taken the time to frame your thoughts calmly, and he or she is in a hurry trying to get to an appointment or a next class. Just as you would become defensive if someone approached you in that manner, an instructor might. Instructors are genuinely interested in working with their students in a cordial and mutually satisfying way and don't like conflict any more than you do. In the best situations, you will establish connections that extend far beyond your semester together and enhance the experience for both of you. You will have lifelong mentors; sources for letters of recommendations, internships and research opportunities; and maybe even friendships. And they will have further proof of the gratification they feel from what most of us believe is the best profession on the planet.

Many years ago, another colleague introduced me to a survey that was given to students and professors, asking them to list the 10 things that most annoyed them about each other. Occasionally, I have my students address this question in the middle of the semester, when they are beginning to feel stressed and getting a tad cranky. In groups, they generate a list of what they see as professors' most annoying behaviors, and then we discuss them. Invariably the list is the same as that generated by the study I originally read; for example, it always lists students' aggravation with professors who insist that students get their work in on time, but then the professors take weeks getting the graded work back to the students. I let the students vent and then give them the study's list of top 10 annoying student behaviors from professors' perspectives. One often mentioned is their exasperation with students who are absent without apparent good reason and then expect a re-do of the entire class. Something therapeutic always happens after that activity. Students see the other side and understand its merit.

One year I had the opportunity to present the same activity at the opening faculty meeting of the semester. First, I asked the faculty to generate a list of student behaviors they found most exasperating; then I provided them with the list from the study that established the universality of their complaints. Next, I showed them the study's list of top 10 annoying professor behaviors from students' points of view. As with my students, something cathartic happened after the activity, generating an understanding and appreciation of the other's perspective. To return to the sign referred to at the beginning—"Knowledge: Free Monday through Friday. Bring your own container"— you are not a container and the professor is not a PEZ dispenser. You are two people connected by a shared goal. The importance of faculty and student engagement in the shared pursuit of learning is critical. As an adult, you have the wisdom and experience to understand this basic truth.

DEVELOPING A POSITIVE RELATIONSHIP WITH FACULTY
by Mary Lou Di Giacomo

A positive relationship between faculty and students can affect the educational outcome of student experiences. My role as an instructor includes, but is not limited to, serving as an educator, advisor, coach, advocate, and evaluator. I believe that setting realistic goals, establishing objectives, and developing an achievable workload at the onset of a course also affects the faculty/student relationship. In addition, it is important that the instructor set the stage for approachability. Students need to feel comfortable to discuss with their instructor course-related issues as well as personal situations that may have an impact on their performance and grades.

Keep in mind that not all instructors are equal. Some may not present themselves as approachable, and students may feel intimidated and reluctant to approach an instructor with an issue. Students must remember they are paying for an education and have the right to question or clarify situations. I would suggest that the student request a meeting with the instructor and discuss her concerns in a respectful manner. If a student is still not satisfied or is uncomfortable, a meeting with her advisor should be the next step, in which case most issues are resolved.

If you experience a conflict with your professor, research the college policy on grievances and appeals. Be sure that the college provides advisors to assist students in choosing the most appropriate courses as you move through the educational system, and that an advisor will be available if issues arise. Examine the college manual, read the course descriptions, and review the schedules and course offerings.

As a woman returning to college today, you should carefully research a variety of colleges to be sure that the choice you make is best for you. Should you consider continuing with your education online, the key is to research programs that offer diverse methods of teaching. You should be looking for exposure to a variety of learning experiences. Today, educational excitement is gained through the use of modern technology: the Internet, webcam, videos, online or in-class group projects, class debates, and the like. Sitting in a classroom for any length of time simply listening to a lecture that can more than likely be read from a book is no longer producing tomorrow's scholars. The last thing you want to do is to get locked into a situation that will not meet your educational and personal goals.

I will share my personal experience with obtaining college degrees as an adult and the impact that professors had on my personal and professional life. It was during my college years that the importance of faculty/student relationships impressed me. However, thinking back to my high school days, I recall doing much better in classes where teachers showed support, kindness, and understanding.

Teaching at the college level is a second career for me, and I have enjoyed every minute of it. I was a vice president of nursing and patient care service at a large acute and rehabilitation hospital, a position that I enjoyed and in which I experienced emotional and intellectual satisfaction. I mention this only so that women realize that, whether we love our work or not, or are simply looking for a lifestyle change, it's never too late to explore alternative careers.

Let me go back and share a little bit of my personal history with you. I graduated from a diploma school of nursing, which is probably not familiar to many of you. Not so long ago, baccalaureate nursing programs were few and far between, especially in Western Massachusetts, so nurses were educated in hospitals. The nursing programs were three years in length, without summer breaks, and students lived in dorms located on hospital grounds. Upon completing three years of education, students were granted a diploma and went on to take state board exams. After passing the exam, students were then granted a license as a registered nurse. After graduation I worked in the operating room—another job I loved. However, after about nine years, I reluctantly accepted the position of Acting Director of Nursing. Once into the job, I began to enjoy the challenge. Just about a year later, the state required that I hold a minimum of a bachelor's degree if I planned to remain in that position. To make matters worse, they gave me two years to complete my studies. So once again, I found myself in uncharted waters—back to college, the books, and studying.

I was not as fortunate as women who return to college today and have a variety of options. Women can enroll as full- or part-time students; they can choose to attend hybrid courses or decide to complete their education fully online. The choice is theirs, and whatever best fits their lifestyle is the way to go.

So here I was, 31 years old, returning to school and having to take three and four courses a semester in order to meet the state's deadline. I did so while holding down the Director of Nursing position at a 360-bed acute care and rehabilitation hospital. Having graduated from a hospital program, I was licensed as a registered nurse, but I did not have a bachelor's degree or college credits. It wasn't easy, but I accomplished the task.

I share this bit of my history with you because without that degree, my 30-year career in healthcare and hospital administration would not have come to fruition. Today, more than ever before, a college education is the ultimate reward that will open doors one never expected. So never say never. It's simply a matter of "How badly do you want it?" Just sit back, think, and consider the long-term benefits versus the short-term sacrifices. If I could do it, believe me, anyone out there can do it!

Although college was a struggle for me, as it may be for you, I encountered a few professors who exposed me to the fundamentals of wisdom that have carried me through some difficult times and have helped me grow both professionally and personally. Aside from learning, I was most impressed with how much they valued relationships with their students. They were professors so dedicated to education and committed to helping students succeed that they went that extra mile to meet student needs.

On the other hand, I recall one professor's comments on the first day of statistics class, when he announced, "To be sure, the majority of you will fail this course." Obviously, the students, including me, did not admire him. As I previously mentioned, all instructors are not equal, so when you come across that type of professor, you, as the student, need to create a mind-set that you will succeed at any cost. Don't allow yourself to be intimidated. If you share your concerns with fellow students, chances are you will find that the professor intends to intimidate students in every class, and it's probably meaningless. However, I never forgot that, and promised myself in my new role as adjunct faculty that I would always start off teaching every course on a positive note, so that students would be encouraged to be successful. In any class that I took in college as an adult, when the professor impressed me and I respected him or her, I would try as best I could to excel in the class. It's the same in life. If we really like and respect someone, we want to do the best we can for that person and look as good as we can in their eyes. I guess that's why I place great value on my relationships with students. All too often I hear the old cliché: "I don't care if they like me as long as they respect me." Yet in my mind, I can't separate the two. I don't expect faculty to become friends with their students, but kindness, respect, and tact are critical. Simply stated, treat people the same way you would like to be treated; it goes a long way. As faculty, we sometimes fail to recognize the struggles adult women face while working toward a degree. However, the student needs to be cognizant that, while studying and preparing for tests and papers may be difficult, it's her responsibility to meet all course requirements. Here we are once again: "How badly do you want it?" Remember that long-term benefit versus that short-term sacrifice.

Women at any age should not fear returning to school. Adult and lifelong learning is an enriching experience and can offer unexpected options.

Your life experience gives you an advantage over traditional students in dealing with faculty, because you've probably already had experience dealing with a variety of personalities and work styles. While you may encounter some difficult personalities, most of your professors want you to succeed.

Fostering a positive relationship with faculty is the responsibility of both student and professor. In most cases, respectful communication and trust will go a long way toward that goal. Think of faculty as your allies in your college journey. Some of your teachers may even become lifelong mentors and supporters.

KEY POINTS TO REMEMBER:

- Take advantage of your professors' office hours to ask questions and resolve problems.

- Don't wait until the end of the semester to discuss problems with your professors.

- Mutual respect between instructors and students is the key to a good classroom experience.

ACTION STEPS:

1. Use your college's online directory to find out a little bit about the faculty who will be teaching your courses.

2. Once you've begun your college work, set up a meeting with your advisor as soon as possible to discuss your goals and concerns.

$\mathcal{A}$NDREA'S STORY

Encouragement from a supportive faculty member helped Andrea to move toward her dream of becoming a lawyer. Andrea had become a single parent at the age of 17. "I never had the opportunity to advance," she said, "because juggling full-time employment and taking care of a child was much too stressful." She eventually enrolled in a paralegal associate's degree program. Through the encouragement of a professor, Andrea then began working toward a legal degree. "All it took was one professor to believe in me. She said, 'You're going to be a lawyer, right?' She then explained to me [that] my research and writing abilities were [those] of a successful lawyer. From that day forward, I felt deep inside that this was what I was destined to be. That professor gave me the confidence to believe in myself and what I can become." A Saturday college program helped her work toward her goal while maintaining a job.

RESOURCES:

Academic Partnerships. (n.d.). *Research on the Effectiveness of Online Learning: A Compilation of Research on Online Learning*. Retrieved from www.immagic.com /eLibrary/ARCHIVES/GENERAL/ACPTR_US/A110923F.pdf

Ya Ni, A. (2013). Comparing the Effectiveness of Classroom and Online Learning: Teaching Research Methods. *Journal of Public Affairs Education, 19*(2), 199-215. Retrieved from www.naspaa.org/jpaemessenger/Article/VOL19-2/03_Ni.pdf

14

FINDING THE ACADEMIC HELP
YOU NEED TO SUCCEED

*O*nce you have chosen a program, we can't stress enough the importance of establishing key relationships with specific people in your academic circles. The most fundamental relationship you need to cultivate is the one with your faculty advisor. Find out who this person is as soon as he or she is assigned to you, then set up a phone, online, or in-person meeting as quickly as possible. Share with this person who you are, why you entered this program, what you are thinking about for career directions, your concerns, your questions, and your current situation (learning disabilities, financial issues, family, work outside of school, etc.).

Good academic programs have specialists to guide you along the way in a variety of areas. Your faculty advisor will be able to refer you to the right people to get help with your unique needs. Remember, your advisor cannot read your mind and knows little or nothing about you when you first join a program. It is your responsibility to create and develop a relationship with your advisor as soon as possible and keep her or him informed of your progress, changes in your situation, and your needs. In some schools, adult women students can rely on dedicated staff who understand that the challenges adults face may be far different from those faced by 18- to

22-year-olds who are entering college right out of high school. Make sure that your program offers dedicated staff who can help you with your entire life circumstances, including your financial, educational, emotional, social, career, and physical challenges and well-being. We strongly encourage you to seek the assistance you need, because it is part of the services you pay for with your tuition. You are entitled to these services as part of your education, and taking advantage of them (whether on-ground or online) is in your best interest. Reaching out to your faculty advisor can make the difference between failing and succeeding.

Sometimes reaching out is difficult for a variety of reasons. You might think you need to handle an issue yourself. You might think someone is not approachable. You might feel you have not tried hard enough, or you might not know what to say. Whatever the barrier, put it aside. Take the risk of asking for help, because people who are in a position to help do not know what you are faced with unless you take the leap, and leap early. The sooner you tell someone that you are feeling overwhelmed, overchallenged, or whatever the issue, the better the chances are that you'll work things out with a little help. **Don't wait!**

Students are sometimes paralyzed about talking to a faculty member about difficulty in a course. The very first step I would recommend is to share your concerns and anxieties with the faculty member in a timely manner. If you don't understand why you received a certain grade, meet with the faculty member as soon as possible. If you are confused about a lecture or an assignment, make an appointment or send an e-mail right away. Faculty members have office hours. If you can't meet in person, ask if you can chat online. In most cases, the instructor will welcome your comments and will help you navigate the course in a different way, give you insight into what she or he values when grading, or offer you the contact information for a tutor. The key to solving problems is to take action early and often to get help.

We all have different learning styles. Your experience in high school will probably be different from your experience in an undergraduate program. As a high-achieving high school student who worked very hard to get good grades, I had a difficult time with my first-year English courses. I struggled to receive a C in my first semester. I was crushed, but I vowed that I would never have another C. When I had difficulties, I would see my professors or seek the assistance of a peer tutor, a student who had mastered the subject matter. It made all the difference in my educational journey, and I never received a C in any course from that time forward. It's important to take that first step and admit that you don't always understand what is expected or how you might improve to achieve a good grade.

Working with adult women students, I have found that they tend to want to excel in every course. Grades are important to them for all kinds of reasons. One that was important for me was validation that I was good at something. Sometimes when our confidence is not as strong as it should be, we mistakenly believe that our grades reflect our self-worth. This attitude can be counterproductive, however. Instructors are grading on our mastery of the subject matter and have no idea how strong or weak our egos are. So I offer a word of advice: Do your best to achieve the highest grade you can, and be satisfied that you have done your best. You are responsible for your grade, not your instructor.

Now, as with most rules, there are exceptions. There may be a time when you do deserve a higher grade. Take the time to discuss your concerns with the instructor in order to get an explanation for your grade. Ask if you may revise the assignment to improve it. Every program has an appeal process for cases when the student disagrees with an instructor's decision. In the end, if you have communicated, listened, revised, and tried your best, and you still disagree with the grade, use the appeal process. Your faculty advisor or the registrar's office can help you with this process.

Some adults feel that if they seek help it is a signal that they are weak or cannot do the work. I assure you, as one who needed a tutor in statistics while working on my Ph.D., everyone can use a little help along the way to achieve a sometimes complicated set of requirements leading to a degree.

Laureen Cirillo is the Executive Director of the Sullivan Career and Life Planning Center at Bay Path University and has more than 20 years of experience in human resources development and career counseling. In this chapter, she offers more details about the importance of your advisor, and provides a list of resources to help you face almost any dilemma that involves skills to be learned, course work, assignments, and fears.

GETTING THE HELP YOU NEED
By Laureen Cirillo

Congratulations! Your college career is now underway and you've been assigned an advisor. Now what?

Here is some important information and a few easy steps that you can take right away to be confident and comfortable. Many times we are nervous or anxious because we are dealing with unknowns and a lack of information, so it's important to be proactive in helping yourself relax and discover how to take charge of your academic success. This section introduces you to people with whom you will want to build relationships immediately, and discusses resources that can help you master your challenges and overcome obstacles.

- **Your Advisor: A New Holistic Approach**
  Your advisor is one person you will want to get to know and, more important, with whom you will want to share your educational, academic, and personal circumstances in order to design a program that fits you and provides you with the support you need to complete your program successfully. Every student has different interests, challenges, and needs. Your advisor's job is to help you

understand how you can structure your academic goals, to integrate these goals with your professional and personal goals, and to give you the tools to get help to accomplish these goals.

Advisors in some programs may use a holistic approach by taking on more of a coaching role with you. "Holistic" means that, instead of telling you what to do, automatically assigning you to courses, and making assumptions about what you want, your advisor will consider how to help the academic, professional, and personal aspects of your life work in harmony with one another so you can identify and achieve your dreams. When an advisor uses a holistic approach, she or he knows that you are in the driver's seat, and she or he supports you in making your own decisions. You are empowered to make choices that work for you. You will be asked to think deeply about how your academic goals, career goals, and personal goals are tied together to help you succeed. You will be asked many questions to guide you in reflecting on the direction of your life's path. In short, your advisor will be a guide who is both a sounding board and an expert resource finder with whom you can partner during your academic experience.

One of the basic tools an advisor uses is your degree audit. (Your degree audit is explained in Chapter 11: "The Registrar's Office.") The audit lists your core courses, courses required for your major and minor, elective courses, and transfer credits. It also lays out the requirements for your degree. Your advisor can explain these and give you all the information you need to make good choices regarding courses, credits, and other options to fulfill degree requirements. Ask lots of questions! You can only lead yourself well if you have the knowledge to do so.

Your advisor can also help you change your schedule around (dropping and adding courses) to work in concert with your life changes, work out questions related to grading, help you if you need to take a leave of absence, and assist you in communicating with your instructors. If you are assigned to an advisor and you feel that the two of you don't "click," don't be afraid to contact your program chair or the registrar's office to see if there is an option for another advisor to work with you. In the meantime, maintain a professional and courteous relationship with your existing advisor.

- **Your Career Coach**
  A quality educational experience includes opportunities to meet with a career coach. This role is explained later in the career services section (Chapter 20: "Career Development"). Make sure you meet with your career coach as soon as you are accepted into the program, because he or she can help you integrate your career plans with your academic plan. Gain the benefits of working with your career coach and advisor right from the start, including cultivating a great resource for a professional reference from your career coach.

- **Faculty**
  Building healthy relationships with faculty is invaluable for several significant reasons. Faculty members get to know you, see your academic accomplishments, and can help you navigate your journey if you communicate appropriately with them on a consistent and professional basis. What does communicating professionally mean? Composing thoughtful, clear, and polite e-mails or voice mails to faculty when you have questions or would like to share information is important. Let them know what is going on with you, especially if you need to be late for a class, miss a class, or need to hand in an assignment after the due date. It is essential to communicate as soon as possible, and preferably before you are late, before you are absent, or in advance of an assignment's due date. When faculty members know what is going on with you, they can better assist you to reach your learning goals.

- **Peer Mentors**

  Many programs have developed a dedicated group of seasoned students who enjoy helping other students adjust to the college environment, get answers to questions, find help with homework, and provide a host of other support. Your college may assign you a mentor or may publish a list of mentors whom you can contact whenever you need some support or an answer to a question. Mentors know how to navigate the system and are personally invested in helping you be a successful student. If your school offers a mentoring program, be proactive and reach out for help as soon as you need it.

- **Sister Students**

  We love to listen to students share with us the reasons they achieve the goal of graduating from college. High up on this list of reasons, right alongside support from family and friends, are sister students who have accomplished this mountainous feat alongside one another. Bond with your sister students. Get cell phone numbers and e-mail addresses of women you meet in your first class, and form study groups online or by telephone to help each other. Arrive at school early to meet with friends and work together. Share rides, share babysitters, share listening, and share encouragement. Many women who encounter difficult personal circumstances while in school are tempted to quit or take a leave of absence; sister students often can encourage these women to stay in school. We find that the students who stay in school actually manage their personal crises more effectively by keeping on track and relying on support from sister students. One of the best personal strategies for healthy living is to surround yourself with functional, healthy people who have the positive drive to live their passion, purpose, and potential. Having a common bond helps you build and keep your foundation strong.

Brother students may also be strong mentors and support you along the way. Though they may not face the same challenges that women face, they can offer valuable advice to help you navigate your education.

Start by asking yourself who the healthy people are in your life who you want to have as part of your support system. Some people find coworkers, others find family members, and still others find people at the school they attend. If you need a support system and don't have anyone, try your faculty advisor or subject tutor, or get a mentor through your school's director of alumni relations.

- **Academic Support**
  Students often need extra help to achieve positive academic outcomes. Quality college programs offer a wealth of resources by providing support in all academic areas. These services are designed to give you peace of mind in knowing that you have places to go outside of the classroom to get the extra help you need. We all have struggles and fears about our own intelligence and abilities, and many of us may have unsettling memories from our early school experiences that cause us to doubt ourselves. It is a sign of strength and courage to figure out that you need help and go after it for yourself. We want to help you empower yourself to identify and fix academic problems, because, in reality, these problems can provide your opportunities to succeed.

  Find out about academic resources on campus. Some educators call these "tutoring resources." Schools organize these resources in different ways. Sometimes faculty are listed as experts in subjects and welcome students to come to them for extra help. Many schools have students who are equipped to work with other students in a variety of subject areas. Online academic support services are available via the Internet through numerous educational programs. Academic support can be obtained via telephone, in person, via e-mail, or by "virtual" (Internet) contact.

Common fears students encounter relate to reading, writing, and math. These are foundational skills required to be successful in any degree program. If you struggle with reading speed, reading comprehension, or with taking notes while reading, talk with your advisor about these concerns, because your advisor can connect you with the right support for your needs. Maybe you don't feel confident with your writing skills. Maybe when you sit down to start writing assignments you draw a blank. Maybe you are not sure what it means to write a good introduction or a good conclusion. Maybe you have no clue about footnotes and bibliographies. Rest assured that a good advisor can share with you exactly who the resident experts are to help you work on these challenges. Some of us think our math skills are hopeless. You are not alone! We work with women all the time who turn their math challenges into successes and are able to develop confidence in their abilities to work with numbers. Faculty, student, and online academic support systems are ways for you to get the help you need.

Finally, if you have a learning disability, talk it over with your advisor and let your instructors know. Advisors can work with faculty members to help implement any accommodations you might need in order to achieve your learning goals. There are many technological advancements that can help with a variety of disabilities, so please don't let this concern get in your way.

The value of your education, in part, is a result of the proactive ways you use the resources presented to you. We hope that this chapter has helped you fully understand that your outreach to the available resources is your responsibility. Making it a point to cultivate your relationships with advisors and instructors from the start will help you gain immeasurable value from your program, and will help minimize any obstacles along the way.

KEY POINTS TO REMEMBER:

- Don't hesitate to ask for help if you're struggling.

- Your academic advisor can be a powerful resource to help you in your academic journey.

- Many colleges have career coaches who can assist with academic and career planning.

- Many colleges have peer-mentoring programs to assist students who need help.

- Sister students can be an important source of support, encouragement, and advice.

- Many types of tutoring and academic support are available to struggling students.

ACTION STEPS:

1. Ask the admissions officer if the college has a career coach for students or a separate career advising department for adult women. This may be an important resource as you progress through your course of study.

2. Ask a college-educated friend or colleague how she or he handled a failing grade or communicated with a faculty member that he or she couldn't understand.

3. Check the college guidebook that was either mailed to you or is online. Does it list offices for academic support, academic development, or career coaching?

4. Does the college in which you are interested offer free tutoring for adult students? Is it in person or online? Ask

the admissions office or registrar. Many colleges realize that adults as well as traditional students (aged 18–22) need help, and will offer assistance free of charge. Be wary of colleges that charge for tutoring. That could add to your expenses.

STACEY'S STORY

Stacey spent seven years juggling work and school on her road to college. Fortunately, her employer offered a tuition reimbursement program, though for only one class a semester. With the encouragement of her husband, she enrolled in an accelerated one-day-a-week program at Bay Path University to finish her degree. For Stacey, peer mentoring was essential to overcome the challenges of returning to school. "I remember one class in particular, Algebra I, that gave me a lot of trouble," she said. "The dreaded day was when I received an F on my first test. Tears came streaming down my face as all my classmates were getting their tests back. During the break, one of my classmates came over to ask why I was so upset. I told her, and she comforted me by telling me it was OK, and that she could help me. Wow, this was a woman. . .I did not know [who was] offering her assistance to me in a class where I thought I'd never succeed. Eight weeks passed by, and I passed that class with a B. Thanks to my determination and her help, I did something I didn't think was possible: I passed Algebra! The same experience also made me a better woman. This one person, [who] was just as busy as myself, helped me because 'we were all in this together.' She taught me to be there for someone else, even though life at the moment is crazy." The women Stacey met through her one-day program did more than help each other through their studies. "We shared family stories, work stories, past stories, and future goals," Stacey said. "In the classroom, each woman shared professional stories, which everybody listened to and practiced in our own jobs." For Stacey, it was a wonderful experience to hear one woman share something she did at work, then later hear another one say, "I tried what you did, and I got this response." According to Stacey, "We were all eager to learn from one another, and together we achieved greatness." Stacey wrote that in the year and a half she spent in the one-day college program, "Not only did I become a better student, I became a better woman, professionally and personally. As a student and a woman, I proved to myself that when I put my mind to something, I can—and will—achieve greatness."

15

Study Skills and Learning Styles

*B*eing successful as a student is not only based on knowing the major you want and selecting the right courses, but it also involves a true understanding of how you learn best and the study skills you adopt throughout your educational journey. Many theories of learning form the basis of an understanding of facts, figures, and the accumulation of knowledge. As children, how we learn best is, in many ways, a function of how we study material presented in class and which we read and absorb on our own time.

In the previous chapter, Laureen Cirillo, Executive Director of the Sullivan Career and Life Planning Center at Bay Path University, wrote about the importance of getting help when you need it. In this chapter, she will explain how to determine your own learning style, and she will introduce five essential study skills a student should master to achieve success.

UNDERSTANDING YOUR LEARNING STYLE AND MASTERING STUDY SKILLS
BY LAUREEN CIRILLO

Everyone learns differently. One of the first steps in successfully navigating your higher education journey is to understand how you learn best, and then analyze the skill sets you need to cultivate. There are tools that can help you understand and reflect on your learning style. Having a good sense of your learning style helps you find ways to learn more efficiently, minimizes your frustration, and makes your academic experience more enjoyable. Some of our favorite learning-style tools are listed below. Go ahead! Jump on these websites and explore your particular learning style.

- **The Study Guides and Strategies Website**— www.studygs.net/metacognition.htm—can help you identify your own learning style and determine how to use it effectively.

- **VARK Learning Styles Inventory**: www.vark -learn.com. VARK is a questionnaire that helps users identify and understand their learning preferences. Users complete the questionnaire and can then use a learning guide to develop strategies for optimizing their particular learning style.

- **Study Skills**
  In addition to becoming familiar with your learning style and developing a strategy for using this information to optimize your learning process, we recommend that you think about the following essential skills for your academic journey. You'll need a similar set of skills to be successful on your career path. After all, a quality educational experience prepares you well for career success. These are the five essential skills that you should develop:

1. Time management

2. Critical thinking skills

3. Group collaboration skills

4. Finding your voice in discussions and presentations

5. Test taking

Each skill can provide you with distinct advantages and confidence when you learn how to incorporate them into your schoolwork—and beyond. A closer look offers suggestions for successful strategies and some resources that can help make the skills work for you.

• **Study skill #1: Time management.** Many of us thought that if we found the magic formula, we could achieve perfect balance in our family, academic, career, and personal lives. Some women think these are four distinct areas that we need to take care of separately. Many of us are so focused on balancing family, school, and career that we forget about our personal life. Maybe it's time to think differently. But how?

One approach might be to view our daily life as an opportunity to make good decisions about what is important in any given moment—a skill called "triage." You can become good at prioritizing what you want to do instead of pursuing the impossible quest of achieving perfect balance.

One key way to prioritize is to view yourself as a whole person, with needs, desires, and responsibilities in the family, academic, career, and personal aspects of your life—all of which are no doubt important to you. By working to choose priorities from these areas every day, you might be better able to navigate your journey. Managing time by triaging priorities is an effective approach. When it comes to school, make sure you know your priorities every day, every week, by writing them down in a notebook or on your laptop. Work to accomplish your highest school priorities every day, every week. Seek the help of a peer, mentor, advisor, coach, or other experienced person to help you learn this art.

Time management starts with recognizing that you are in control of how you spend your time. Realize that you call the shots here! Once you understand this simple truth, you can empower yourself to use your time in a way that reflects your priorities. Strategies that can help you develop good time management habits include: effective use of class time, effective use of study time, good scheduling habits, and removing obstacles like procrastination.

- *Effective use of class time means:*

  - Attend each class and ask questions in class when you need help.

  - Record a lecture on a small device, with your instructor's permission.

  - Record specifically what you need to do for the next class, as well as for longer-term assignments.

  - Review your learning as soon as possible after each class. Your brain likes repetition, and review increases the chances of your retaining each lesson.

  - Estimate the time you'll need to work during the week.

  - Share contact information with another student from the class in order to have someone with whom to ask questions, study, or work on assignments.

  - Reach out to your instructor as soon as you have questions about the material or an assignment.

- Submit all work on time (or early!) as much as humanly possible.

- *Effective use of study time includes having:*

  - A scheduled study routine that includes a block of time daily or every other day.

  - An established study place, such as the town or school library.

  - A checklist of everything you need with you to study.

  - A study partner or partners, especially if you learn well by processing information with others.

  - Chances to teach what you learn to others, as you'll help both yourself and the other person to learn.

Good scheduling habits can make all the difference for you! Use the calendar available with your school e-mail system or the calendar on your cell phone, if you have one. Make sure you set aside 30 minutes every Sunday to schedule your time for the upcoming week. Keep track of your personal, work, and school schedules on the same calendar. Enter all of your commitments as soon as you make them, in order to keep your calendar up to date. Booking time to study and complete assignments is essential. Treat this time as you would any other appointment.

Procrastination is a human habit with which many of us wrestle. This habit often gets in the way of our learning. If you want to be a successful student, and if you have this habit, you need to discipline yourself to break it, or you will have a hard time. Think about how you can break down your assignments into smaller pieces and make yourself do a piece every day. If you have questions, ask them in class or e-mail someone (professor or classmate) the first day you discover the question. Form a support group of a few students from your class, promise each other that you won't procrastinate, and take steps together to dig in a little every day in between classes. If you procrastinate, your work might suffer beyond repair. Students often fail classes because they procrastinate to the point where it is simply too late to catch up. Make "Do it today" your motto. (Some useful web-based resources for time management are listed at the end of this chapter.)

- **Study skill #2: Critical thinking**. Critical thinking is a way of using your curious and creative thoughts to learn to think like an explorer or a researcher. Instead of taking something at face value, you learn to ask questions to understand the statement more fully. When you read information, you learn to think more objectively without judging or assuming things, and you learn to ask questions to dig more deeply. In learning to use critical thinking skills, you realize the importance of checking assumptions that might not be true, you learn how to find more data, and you learn that there may be more than one right answer. By taking the time to question your assumptions, to dig for more information, and to accept that there may be more than one way to reach a result, you learn to think differently and accept others for thinking differently. Instructors will teach you how to think critically and help each other be creative in learning activities. You will bring this refreshing skill set into other areas of your life.

    For example, you might use your critical thinking skills to choose an educational program. Instead of taking someone's opinion or believing an advertisement that a program is good or bad, use your critical thinking skills to make your own list of questions about the program; research that program through Internet sources, personal interviews with people who have graduated from that program, and data you gather from admissions and faculty. Once you have a comprehensive dataset, you can develop a more objective picture of how this program might meet your needs. (Resources at the end of this chapter include helpful websites on critical thinking.)

- **Study skill #3: Group collaboration.** A quality college experience involves learning to build effective relationships with a variety of people. You may work in teams in the classroom and be assigned group projects outside of class; you may need to collaborate with people in your classes; you will need to be cooperative. Being a good group member involves great listening skills, considerate and polite manners, being willing to share your thoughts and ideas, and being a responsible and dependable member of the group. These relationship skills are important in many aspects of life. Some of us like to talk more than listen. Some of us feel too shy to speak up in a group. Others like to be leaders instead of followers. You can learn about your natural personality and how you are most comfortable being with people. Then you can take steps to develop in areas that might not come easily for you. By practicing with students in a safe educational setting, it is easier to prepare yourself for using these skills in your career. Your faculty, advisors, and coaches can help you master these skills.

  So what are some things you can do to be a collaborative group member? Here is a good start:

  - *Be reliable.* Show up on time for scheduled meetings. Come prepared and follow through by doing what you say you will do, when you say you will do it.

  - *Be an active listener.* Active listening means giving group members your complete attention and listening to understand the words and feelings that someone is trying to convey. An active listener might repeat or paraphrase what the member says to ensure that she has heard the message in the way the member intended it. Active listening also means not interrupting. Instead, concentrate on the message rather than what you want to say next. Active listening means listening to many aspects of what the speaker is saying, including context, tone of voice, delivery, and the message alongside the words. It also means making eye contact with the speaker, giving nonverbal indications that you are listening, and asking questions or making comments related to the message being delivered. Active listening helps you engage in what the speaker is communicating and increases your comprehension in class.

• *Talk about roles in your group, if appropriate.* Who is leading the process? Who is taking notes? Who is making sure everyone has the appropriate assigned parts? Who is helping to see that everyone is sharing the floor by making sure each member has a turn to speak?

• *Pull your own weight.* Group discussions and group projects have the best results when everyone shares her thinking and hard work. The best results happen when each member takes her share of the work, does it well, and does it on time. Make sure you use these steps to be the kind of group member with whom everyone wants to work!

• **Study skill #4: Finding your voice in discussions and presentations.** Whether you are in a physical classroom or participating in a class taught online, you have a great opportunity to learn to be comfortable giving individual presentations and participating in class discussions. You will learn that you have something of value to share, that your opinion matters, and that you can think in ways that you never believed possible through sharing your ideas with others. Well, how in the world will you do this?

There are many reasons people have anxiety about speaking in a group or giving a presentation. One reason relates to fear of the unknown and/or a lack of confidence in contributing. Generally, people want to know what they are talking about before using their voices. If this is true for you, one strategy that will help you present information confidently and participate in discussions is to always be prepared. When you do your homework, read the assignments, and review course materials, you feel more comfortable that you know what you are talking about, and are more likely to share.

If you are presenting, it will help your confidence to rehearse your presentation with a friend and practice on your own, because you'll know that material much better. Your friend might even give you pointers on how to make your presentation more effective. You are calmer when you know you are presenting to friends who want to help you. In group discussions, you can let people know that you are on the quieter side and can then ask them to draw you into the conversation when you are quiet.

Finally, when you have done your homework, read the materials, and reviewed the course material, you will find it easier to ask questions of the group. Asking questions is an effective way of participating and guiding learning. Asking good questions also builds your confidence.

You will have many chances to practice and learn the skills that go into making good presentations. You will learn what makes a good contribution in discussion. You will learn to ask helpful questions, summarize information, bring new material to the discussion, and think about the subject matter in different ways. When you graduate, you will be confident in your ability to present information in the workplace, and you will take an active role in the meetings you attend and the teams on which you may serve in your career.

- **Study skill #5: Test taking**. Exams are part of your learning experience, so you may as well be as comfortable as possible with the process. You can start preparing right from the first day of class by connecting with the instructor, reading and understanding the entire syllabus, and noting the exam schedule. Build review time for exams into your homework schedule rather than waiting until just before the test to start studying. Make sure you review text highlights and other supplemental materials provided. Study groups can also help, depending on your learning style and logistics. If you are interested in reducing test anxiety, being well prepared builds confidence. Combine being well prepared with a good night's sleep, a little exercise, and some healthy food, and you will be set.

  Here are some steps to consider when preparing for and taking exams:

  - *Take notes in your own words in class and when reading.* Taking your own notes helps you learn the material. Review your notes after each class and after reading assignments.

  - *Use tools like flash cards to help memorize key concepts.*

  - *Study with other students; you learn your material better when teaching it to someone else.*

  - *Check in with your instructor with your list of questions before each exam.*

  - *Be sure to study any material your instructor tells you will be on the exam.*

- *Do practice quizzes if they are available.* Otherwise, quiz other students and ask them to quiz you.

- *Try to eat protein, exercise, and get a good night's sleep before any exam.*

Mastering time management, critical thinking, group collaboration, presentation skills, and test taking can be a challenge, but developing these skills will help you get the most out of your college experience.

KEY POINTS TO REMEMBER:

- Fully participate in each class. You can fully participate only if you are fully prepared. Show up on time. Your best gift to yourself is to take total advantage of every assignment and every class in order to fully benefit from your investment.

- Write down thoughts and questions to share and ask in class. Sharing your comments and questions will allow you to communicate what you think about what you are learning and to understand how you can apply what you are learning in a practical way.

- Initiate and maintain contact with your instructor. Review your assignments at least a few days before class to make sure you are able to complete assignments properly. If you have questions about an assignment, e-mail your instructor or another student with these questions in a timely manner so that you can complete the assignments on time.

- Develop contacts with one or two other students with whom you can talk outside of class. Exchange phone numbers and e-mail addresses at the first class, and keep in touch between classes.

- You might find yourself working with partners and in small groups to complete assignments and conduct discussions. Be an active and reliable contributor! (Refer to the section on "Group collaboration skills.")

- Frequently, you might discover that there is more than one way to solve a problem and sometimes more than one "right" answer. It's helpful to keep an open mind and be able to brainstorm many options. Many aspects of learning are not linear and clear-cut.

- Bring your best interpersonal skills into the classroom! Expect to show respect and consideration for others, use great listening skills, and don't forget your appropriate sense of humor with your classroom group.

- Get and be comfortable with technology. Whether it be e-mail, online research, online classes, or navigating college resources, it's critical to your success as a student and an employee to jump headfirst into technology. Avidly use your student technology resources to help you get started and get comfortable!

- Discover and use your resources. Find out about the people, places, and tools that are available to support you as a student and USE THEM. Once you identify what you need, whether it is a discussion with your instructor, a meeting with your advisor, an appointment with a career coach or mentor, or a visit to the library, move forward quickly and judiciously to receive the support you need.

ACTION STEPS:

1. Get to know your learning style and develop some strategies to maximize your learning.

2. Explore the resources related to time management and create an organized calendar.

3. Do critical thinking exercises such as the ones provided in the critical thinking resource section.

4. Think about the groups you have worked with and about what kind of group member you are. Take the Team Style Inventory listed in the "Resources" section of this chapter to gain some insight about your role. Write down a few things you can do to be a great team member. When you are assigned to a group, share these resources with your group members.

5. Practice using your voice to speak with others about your thoughts and opinions to help get used to sharing what's on your mind. Take every opportunity to talk in front of small groups. It's easier once you dive in and do it.

6. Use opportunities to take quizzes and tests to start practicing these activities. (Refer to the "Test Taking" section of the "Resources" portion of this chapter to find practice sites.)

Heather's Story

"Going back to school has been something I have wanted to do ever since I can remember. Getting my degree is actually on my 'bucket list,'" Heather said, "and it happens to be right up there with skydiving!" Although she'd started college right out of high school, she acknowledged that she was not ready for the experience and dropped out. Years later, with a full-time job and two children, she wasn't sure how she would manage going back to school. Her husband alerted her to a one-day-a-week college program. "I knew right away that this would be the beginning of my incredible journey," she said. An advisor from the school's admissions office told her that she would meet "some amazing, inspiring women from all walks of life. She told me I would actually look forward to coming to school, and [that] this support system of soon-to-be friends would help me get through the tough times. She was absolutely right. She also mentioned that I would learn a lot about myself along the way. Yes, of course you learn the textbook 'stuff' that apparently you need to graduate . . . but nothing could have prepared me for what I have realized about myself and what I can accomplish."

RESOURCES:

Time Management:

University of Guelph. (n.d.). A Guide for Time Management. *University of Guelph: You and Your Library.* Retrieved from www.learningcommons.uoguelph.ca /guides/time_management/

> This is a comprehensive time-management resource geared toward students in a college or university environment. You will find resources on many aspects of time management, including study skills, procrastination, scheduling, goal setting, and establishing priorities.

Virginia Polytechnic Institute and State University. (2014). Where Does Time Go? *VirginiaTech: Invent the Future.* Retrieved from www.ucc.vt.edu/academic _support_students/study_skills_information/where_does_time_go

> This website, maintained by Virginia Tech University's Cook Counseling Center, helps students analyze how much time they spend on various activities, and guides them toward creating effective study schedules. The site also includes guides on effective study skills, note-taking, and more.

Critical Thinking:

Critical Thinking. (n.d.). *Study Guides and Strategies.* Retrieved from www.studygs .net/crtthk.htm

> This Study Guides and Strategies website offers strategies for critical thinking in learning and project management.

Group Collaboration Skills:

Cooperative and Collaborative Learning. (n.d.). *Study Guides and Strategies.* Retrieved from www.studygs.net/cooplearn.htm

> This Study Guide and Strategies website has a section on collaborative learning that discusses the role of a good team member and defines the team process.

Sarkisian, E. (2010). Working in Groups: A Note to Faculty and a Quick Guide for Students. *Derek Bok Center for Teaching and Learning, Harvard University.* Retrieved from isites.harvard.edu/fs/html/icb.topic58474/wigintro.html

> Harvard's "Quick Guide for Students" discusses getting started, including everyone, leading groups, focusing on a direction, how teams function, and solutions to common problems.

McGraw-Hill Companies. (2004).Team Style Inventory. *Human Relations Strategies for Success.* Retrieved from www.mhhe.com/ps/hrelations/general /teaminventory.html

> This self-assessment questionnaire helps you determine what role you'd best play in a group or team setting: director, supporter, analyzer, or creator.

Test Taking:

College Board. (2014). SAT Practice. *SAT*. Retrieved from sat.collegeboard.org
    /practice

> This website features many practice test questions and answers in the areas of
> reading, math, and writing. It offers a helpful way to ease into the test-taking
> process.

Dickson, K. (2014, February 4). Mastering Exam Anxiety. *Athabasca University*.
    Retrieved from counselling.athabascau.ca/exam_anxiety.php

> This resource helps you explore test anxiety and learn how to take steps to
> reduce yours.

General Test Preparation. (n.d.). *Study Guides and Strategies*. Retrieved from
    studygs.net/tstprp1.htm

> This Study Guide and Strategies article includes comprehensive information
> on how to prepare for tests and how to take tests.

General Resources:

Study Guides and Strategies. (n.d.). Retrieved from www.studygs.net

VARK-LEARN Limited. (2014). *VARK: A Guide to Learning Styles*. Retrieved from
    www.vark-learn.com

16

THE LIBRARY

*A*s is evident from Chapter 14: "Finding the Academic Help You Need to Succeed," there are several ways you can ensure academic success by using the resources at your fingertips. Often in today's technology age, we don't consider going to a library to actually talk to a librarian and seek out original materials. But I can assure you, today's college and university libraries are incredible sources of assistance and guidance. They have not only materials in print and online, but also professionals who can help you quickly find the information you need.

Michael Moran, currently Director of Library and Information Services at Bay Path University, has served a wide range of students in different types of institutions, including state community colleges and private universities. His words of advice may be just what you need when you receive your first assignment to write a paper or do some serious research.

UNLOCK YOUR COLLEGE LIBRARY:
THE KEY TO YOUR ACADEMIC SUCCESS
BY MICHAEL MORAN

"How can I find scholarly journal articles about the psychology of feminism?"

"Where should I look for information about the collapse of Lehman Brothers?"

"Could you show me how to insert a YouTube video into my PowerPoint presentation?"

These are a few of the many questions that college reference librarians are asked every day by the students who use their campus libraries, a key to their academic success. There are three very good reasons why you should spend as much time as possible in your college library:

- **To Become Information Literate**

- **To Enrich and Deepen Your College Experience**

- **To Get Good Grades That Will Give You an Advantage in the 21st-Century Workplace**

Let's take a closer look at each of these reasons.

- **To Become Information Literate**
  The Association of College and Research Libraries (ACRL), a division of the American Library Association, defines information literacy as "the set of skills needed to find, retrieve, analyze, and use information." ACRL notes that "[t]he beginning of the 21st century has been called the Information Age because of the explosion of information output and information sources. It has become increasingly clear that students cannot learn everything they need to know in their field of study in a few years of college. Information literacy equips them with the critical skills necessary to become independent lifelong learners."

According to ACRL, "Information literacy forms the basis for lifelong learning. It is common to all disciplines, to all learning environments, and to all levels of education. It enables learners to master content and extend their investigations, become more self-directed, and assume greater control over their own learning. An information literate individual is able to:

- Determine the extent of information needed

- Access the needed information effectively and efficiently

- Evaluate information and its sources critically

- Incorporate selected information into one's knowledge base

- Use information effectively to accomplish a specific purpose

- Understand the economic, legal, and social issues surrounding the use of information, and access and use information ethically and legally."[1]

All college libraries have reference and instruction librarians who will not only teach you information literacy skills one-on-one in the library, but who will also visit your classrooms to provide group instruction and will host class visits to the library. They will show you the best ways to find information in the most appropriate sources for your needs, so that you can gradually develop your own information literacy skills through regular use.

As more students enroll in online courses and programs, college librarians are creating new tools to teach information literacy skills. These may include online tutorials about specific research needs and self-paced instructional modules for students to learn or review information literacy skills at their convenience. Librarians at Bay Path University, for example, have created an online course in five modules: (1) Overview; (2) Getting Started on a Research Project; (3) Finding Information;

(4) Evaluating Information; and (5) Citing Information. Any of these modules can also be accessed separately. Check with your college library to see whether it offers a similar tutorial.

- **To Enrich and Deepen Your College Experience**
  Now that you know a little more about becoming information literate, we can take a closer look at the second reason you should be a frequent user of your college library: to enrich and deepen your college experience. For most of your courses you will need to purchase or rent one or more textbooks, which your professors will require you to read chapter by chapter throughout the semester and to which they will often refer in class lectures and discussions. But most professors will also assign work beyond the course textbooks, for which they will often expect you to do additional research using library materials.

  Every college library builds its collection of materials primarily to support the curriculum or the degree and certificate programs offered at that institution. For example, at a college that offers a Bachelor of Arts degree leading to elementary education licensure, the library will purchase or acquire access to materials that students in this program can use for research projects assigned by their professors. At Bay Path University, these materials include a collection of the kinds of children's books that students might later use as teachers in their elementary classrooms.

  College library materials now come in a wide variety of formats, including:

  - **Books**—printed books, which are still the core of most college library collections;

  - **E-books**—electronic books, which can be read entirely online or downloaded onto mobile devices, and which make up a growing percentage of most college library book collections;

- **Periodical subscriptions**—newspapers, popular magazines, and scholarly journals, in print or online format;

- **Multimedia materials**—DVDs and streaming film and video, which can be found and viewed online;

- **Research databases**—online indexes to articles, often including the full text of those articles, in thousands of periodicals; ready reference tools like encyclopedias; and handbooks in various academic disciplines.

In addition, many college libraries offer materials such as:

- **Archives of specialized resources**—publications, photographs, and other primary source materials that document the history of the college or its association with public figures who might have donated personal records;

- **Microfilm of publications**—materials that have not been preserved in electronic form, including older editions of local newspapers;

- **Maps and image collections**—visual resources that might reflect specific areas of the college's curriculum;

- **Special collections of primary sources**—personal, corporate, or organizational papers of people, businesses, or organizations relevant to the college's mission or degree programs, or pertaining to special study topics.

In addition to materials that support the curriculum, most college libraries collect materials to support students' extracurricular needs. After all, every student needs a little downtime, when she might welcome the chance to read a popular novel (or listen to it on CD) or watch a recent movie on DVD.

All these materials are indexed in the library's online catalog (readers of a certain age might recall the catalog as a series of index cards in drawers), which is one of the first links you will want to find on your college library's website. The online catalog is also where you will find most e-books in your library's collection, as well as streaming versions of any films the library owns.

Most of the above materials can be borrowed by currently enrolled students for several weeks at a time with some renewal options, depending on the library's regulations. While anyone can view the online catalog and the library website over the Internet, only students, faculty, and staff can gain access to the content of the library's e-books, streaming videos, or databases, using a college username and password to log in, whether on or off campus.

You will find that some materials can't be borrowed but can only be used in the library itself. These are typically classified as either reference or reserve items. Reference collections are stored and labeled separately from items that circulate, but they are usually accessible on open shelves. Reserve materials are generally stored behind a circulation desk; you need to request a specific item. These are most often materials that professors have asked librarians to make available only to students in specific classes. The library might own some reserve materials; the professor might own—and loan— other items.

Since you may not be able to visit your campus library if you are an online student, many college libraries offer online access to e-book versions of reference materials through their website; you can reserve the materials in electronic form (also called e-reserves) through the college's learning management software (LMS).

With the cost of textbooks continuing to rise, some college faculty may place copies of required course textbooks on library reserve, either on the shelves as print books, or through the college's LMS as e-textbooks.

Using these resources for assignments from your professors—and exploring more of them to pursue your own developing interests as you progress through your course work—are two of the biggest steps you can take in college toward becoming a well-rounded and educated person for the rest of your life.

- **To Get Good Grades That Will Give You an Advantage in the 21st-Century Workplace**
Now that you have a better understanding of the second reason you should become a regular user of your college library, we can take a closer look at the third reason: to get good grades that will give you an advantage in the 21st-century workplace.

It should be obvious by now that college librarians are pretty smart people who can help you become an efficient, self-directed researcher and learner; in other words, they are a powerful campus resource that you would be foolish to overlook. Not only can they answer the questions at the beginning of this chapter, but they have designed the library's website to bring a wealth of information to your fingertips in a user-friendly format.

Most college libraries' websites include separate and clearly visible links to key research tools: the online catalog, as we have seen; a list of periodicals that the library subscribes to in print or online form; and a list of available databases arranged by academic discipline, often in a series of research guides. These sites usually include interactive options like reference services by e-mail or chat, and an evolving range of social media tools.

Other useful links on most college library websites are tutorials on doing particular kinds of research, and links to authoritative websites, which have usually been selected by librarians in collaboration with faculty experts in specific disciplines. That's why you will generally get better results for your academic needs by starting your research on any project at the library's website than you would if you started with Google or another Internet search engine. The improved quality of your completed research assignments will lead to higher grades, which will give you a competitive edge in the 21st-century job market.

Although library materials are always becoming more accessible online, there may still be times when you will need a book or a journal article that is not available in your campus library collection or virtually through the online catalog on its website. That is why college libraries offer interlibrary loan service, through which you can request an item from another library and have it delivered to your own campus library, where you can pick it up and return it as needed, or have it sent to you electronically. Most interlibrary loan service is provided free, but some libraries may charge a modest fee for certain types of materials.

One advantage of the growth of online library collections is that it reduces the need for more library space to store print books and periodicals; makes more space available for students to do group and individual work; and enables librarians to have room to host workshops and teach information literacy skills. Many college libraries have created spaces they call "learning commons" or "information commons," where a number of computers in an open area are often located next to smaller enclosed rooms that are used for group work. Librarians— and often other teachers, learning professionals, and tutors— oversee these areas and offer personalized assistance to students.

Other technology found in many college libraries includes printers for photocopying, scanners for electronic transmission of documents, and wireless access so that students can use their own laptops, tablets, and other mobile devices in any convenient location. Some group study rooms may include audio, video, and projection equipment where students can collaborate on group projects.

Students returning to college after being away from school for a few years may find some current library technology a little intimidating at first, but college librarians are well-trained to be patient and persistent with students who need extra support. In this era of rapid change, it can be a challenge for faculty and even librarians to keep current. Never be afraid to ask for the help you need; you have paid the tuition and fees for your education; you are entitled to get your money's worth.

Research consistently indicates that college students who use their campus library facilities on a regular basis get better grades than their library-shy peers. So make it a habit early on to visit your college library and get to know the librarians. They may turn out to be the key to your academic success in college.[2]

KEY POINTS TO REMEMBER:

- Information literacy is crucial to career success in the 21st century.

- Studies show that students who regularly use the library tend to get better grades than their peers.

- College libraries offer many nonprint and online resources in addition to print books and periodicals.

- Don't hesitate to ask your librarians for assistance.

ACTION STEPS:

1. Visit a local library or college library. Check out the collection and ask the librarian if she or he has any online databases you could use on a favorite subject—Shakespeare or the space program, for example.

2. Request a tour of a college library in your area to familiarize yourself with the resources and services you'll need when you begin your own studies.

3. When asking your selected college about library resources, find out if there is a free interlibrary loan service available to students.

4. Thoroughly explore the library website of your selected college for special resources or services related to the field in which you'd like to major.

*S*HANNA'S STORY

A financial executive, Shanna quit work to start a family. But she said, "I had also given up a huge part of what made me, me. I no longer had anything that was just for me. After my second child and two years of feeling as though the walls of my house were closing in on me, I knew that something had to give." But Shanna didn't want to sacrifice time with her children to return to her life as a busy executive. "A happy middle was teaching," she said. She found a program that allowed her to arrange her school schedule around her husband's job and the time she needed to spend with her children. As she neared graduation, she realized she had gained much more than an education from her time in college. "I have a priceless network of friends whom I will remain connected to for many years to come," she said. "The ladies that I have spent the past two years with are amazing and smart, each with [her] own unique stor[y] that made learning an incredible experience."

RESOURCES:

Association of College and Research Libraries. (2000). *Information Literacy Competency Standards for Higher Education*. Chicago: American Library Association.

Bell, S. J., & Shank, J. D. (2007). *Academic Librarianship by Design: A Blended Librarian's Guide to the Tools and Techniques*. Chicago: American Library Association.

Davidson, K. S., Rollins, S. H., & Cherry, E. (2013). Demonstrating Our Value: Tying Use of Electronic Resources to Academic Success. *Serials Librarian*, *65*(1), 74–79.

Samson, S. (2010). Information Literacy Learning Outcomes and Student Success. *Journal of Academic Librarianship*, *36*(3), 202–210.

Weaver, M. (2013). Student Journey Work: A Review of Academic Library Contributions to Student Transition and Success. *New Review of Academic Librarianship*, *19*(2), 101–124.

NOTES:

1. Association of College and Research Libraries (2000). *Information Literacy Competency Standards for Higher Education* (p. 2). Chicago: American Library Association.

2. Davidson, K. S., Rollins, S. H. & Cherry, E. (2013). Demonstrating Our Value: Tying Use of Electronic Resources to Academic Success. *Serials Librarian*, *65*(1), 74–79. Samson, S. (2010). Information Literacy Learning Outcomes and Student Success. *Journal of Academic Librarianship*, *36*(3), 202–210. Weaver, M. (2013). Student Journey Work: A Review of Academic Library Contributions to Student Transition and Success. *New Review of Academic Librarianship*, *19*(2), 101–124.

17

TECHNOLOGY

*T*oday, the world of education has changed drastically, and it will continue to change for one major reason: technology. A world of information is now literally at our fingertips. Yet there are many women who have not had the opportunity to use technology in any significant way, or who do not believe they have the ability to use technology or to study online.

Today, colleges offer students many options that use technology. For adults, courses may be offered totally online or totally on-ground, or in a mix of the two called the hybrid model. In Chapter 7: "Finding the Right College," we provided an outline for how to determine the type of learning environment you want. You may decide that you would like to be in a classroom, face-to-face with a professor and peers. As you progress in your education and feel more comfortable, you may enjoy the flexibility that online learning provides.

The use of technology will not be limited to the manner in which you take your courses. You will also be expected to use technology when doing research for papers, when completing homework assignments, when registering for classes, and when using the library. You will definitely need to have a comfort level with technology when working on a degree.

You might say that it is not worth it; you can't afford a computer; you will never be good at using technology. To that,

I offer one key piece of advice: There is no way in our lifetime, now and in the future, that we can avoid technology. From paying bills, taking money out of a bank, doing your taxes, and even accepting an entry-level job in almost every single profession, you will need some experience and some expertise in technology.

This chapter will give you an overview of the key words and concepts you will need to understand to be knowledgeable about technology on a college campus. Dr. David Demers, currently the Chief Information Officer at SUNY Buffalo and former Vice President for Academic and Administrative Technology at Bay Path University, has a rich background in working with students at community colleges and public and private universities, both as a professor and as an administrator overseeing the purchase and delivery of technology on campuses. His words of wisdom will give you the tools you need to appreciate the power of technology and use it effectively.

TIPS ON TECHNOLOGY
BY DAVID DEMERS, PH.D.

There is no doubt that the infusion of technology into our daily lives has significantly influenced the landscape of education. With the emergence of mobile technologies such as smartphones and tablets, the demand from consumers for information and content—anywhere and anytime—has increased dramatically. Much has been written over the past decade about the millennial generation[1] and how millennials' upbringing as "digital natives"[2] has resulted in a shift in students' expectations regarding how technology should be used to obtain educational content. Web-based, on-demand access to instructional content has become mainstream in higher education with the ubiquity of learning management systems (LMS) such as Blackboard, Canvas, Moodle, or

Desire2Learn. The use of these systems to provide anytime, anywhere access to course content is no longer an option for colleges and universities—it is a requirement.

The development and emergence of the Internet has made access to content and media easier than ever. Robust search engines, such as Google (www.google.com), Bing (www.bing.com), and Yahoo (www.yahoo.com), have made locating information as simple as typing a search term or query, in plain English, into your web browser. Information repositories, such as Wikipedia (www.wikipedia.org), are also popular with students,[3] while gaining acceptance as viable research and educational tools.[4] The simplicity and usability of these resources has led college and university libraries to demand streamlined interfaces that mimic the capabilities of these search engines for use in their own library catalogs, and the software vendors who provide these tools have begun to respond. This has resulted in streamlined use of research databases, making it easier for patrons to gain access to material online, including electronic journals and e-books, all with the click of a mouse. It will not be long before smartphones and e-book readers, such as Amazon Kindle, Barnes & Noble NOOK, and even the Apple iPad, will be able to tap directly into library catalogs to provide on-demand access and delivery of materials on the go for today's mobile student.

Navigating the multitude of new technologies and services available to learners today can present quite a challenge, particularly for those students who may be considered "digital immigrants."[5] If you did not grow up using Facebook or Twitter, you may well be a digital immigrant. To meet this challenge, there are a multitude of support services available to all college and university students navigating this technology landscape. The following section will provide some guidelines and direction for seeking out the information and support services you may need when undertaking a new higher education goal.

- **Hardware and Software**

  As you begin a new educational program, you may be considering upgrading or updating your personal computing devices and software to support your course-related activities. If you will be purchasing a new computer, you will want to obtain the recommended technical requirements for student computers at your selected institution before shopping. Some schools may provide incoming students with new computing devices, such as laptops, as part of their curriculum, or might offer significant discounts on the purchase of preconfigured laptop or desktop computers through special arrangements with hardware vendors such as Dell, HP, or Lenovo. Many schools offer significant discounts on productivity software (e.g., Microsoft Office) or offer this software free of charge for students. Additionally, some institutions may recommend or provide ancillary devices, such as an Apple iPad or iPod touch, to download recorded lectures, instructor podcasts, or electronic textbooks (e-books). Be sure to ask your admissions counselor for any information that may assist you in the selection of a new computer or mobile device prior to making such an investment. In most instances, this information will be available on your school's website.

  If you are planning to use a personal computer or mobile device you already own to support your new educational venture, be sure to carefully review the technical requirements made available by your institution. These guidelines will typically be available on the school's website. The technical requirements will outline the necessary hardware and software configuration required to ensure access to all school resources, such as the Learning Management System (LMS). The LMS serves as the electronic repository for all course-related content, providing students with 24/7 access to these materials. Your institution may use one of several LMS systems that are popular today (e.g., Blackboard, Moodle, or Desire2Learn), and each system will have its own set of minimum requirements and plugins. You will want to make sure your computer meets all of these requirements to ensure a smooth and seamless learning experience. Some typical system requirements include: operating system, memory, processor speed, hard drive space, network connection, etc. Your institution should be able to provide you with specifications for preferred hardware and software.

If circumstances limit your access to a home computer that meets the minimum specifications provided by your school, you will want to identify computing resources available on your campus. Most schools will have dedicated computer facilities available to students, with workstations that provide all of the software and resources required for all courses and programs. You may find these facilities are used more heavily during certain times of the day or during certain weeks in a given term (such as finals week); therefore, if you are planning on taking advantage of these resources, be sure to plan ahead. For facilities that are used heavily, institutions may have a reservation system. In addition, the school library will typically provide computing workstations for student use. These workstations will have access to the school's research databases and may also have the same software that would be available in the dedicated computer facilities on campus.

- **Printing**
  In addition to the computer resources available on campus, you will want to learn how your school provides printing services for students. Your institution may provide dedicated network-connected printers in each computer facility, classroom, and/or the library. Network-based printers allow students to print from any workstation within the facility or location. Some institutions may charge a nominal per-page fee for printing privileges, which may be managed in several ways. For example, your

school may provide students with an initial quota of free prints that might be included in your tuition or school fees; once this limit has been reached, you will then need to pay a fee for each print thereafter. Be sure to review the printing policies set forth by your school, or ask your information technology (IT) department for assistance in using the printers available on your campus.

Today the cost of printers is low, but ink cartridges are expensive. It may be worth your while to buy your own printer and cartridges.

- **Wireless**
  If you plan on bringing your own laptop or mobile device to campus, chances are good that you will be able to connect your device to your school's high-speed wireless network. This service will typically be free for students and may require you to provide your login or account credentials (assigned username and password) to verify that you are a member of the institution. If you are successful in connecting to your campus's Wi-Fi network, you will have access to all of the network resources, including library research databases and e-book systems, if available. Your IT department will have information that will assist you in connecting your personal computing devices to the wireless network, so be sure to check the school's website to locate this information prior to visiting the campus.

- **Training and Support Services**
  Most of your IT training and support information will be covered as part of your initial orientation program. Specifics should include:

  - **Acceptable computer use policy:** guidelines and policies for how campus computing resources may and may not be used;

  - **Available IT training programs/workshops:** a schedule showing training programs available to students on a variety of topics, and training that might be available as on-demand video tutorials from your school's website;

• **Support services:** information on how to obtain help, including where the IT help desk is located, the hours of operation, and how to contact them by phone or e-mail.

Perhaps the most important IT topic covered during the orientation program will be how to seek assistance with technology-related issues. All schools will have a technology support department, such as an IT help desk. The help desk will assist students in troubleshooting and resolving any technical issues the users might be experiencing, such as:

• **Network access trouble** (including wireless Internet access);

• **Account issues** (network accounts, passwords, etc.);

• **Trouble gaining access to or using a particular service or application;**

• **General hardware troubleshooting and support.**

In most cases, information about the IT help desk will be available on your school's website. When locating this information, be sure to make note of the following information:

• **Location and phone number for the help desk;**

• **Help desk hours of operation;**

• **Additional means for reporting issues** (e-mail, on-line form, instant messaging/chat).

The help desk will typically use a "ticket" system for recording and managing requests for technical support. These systems will chronicle all interactions and communications regarding your issue, from initial report through final resolution. When you report an issue, a support ticket will be assigned to a member of the help desk staff who will assist you with the issue and update the ticket as progress is made. You will receive an e-mail each time the ticket is updated. The e-mail will provide you with a detailed record on the status and progress of your reported issue.

- **Online Learning**
An emerging trend in higher education is the expanded availability of flexible learning environments, such as online learning, where classes meet virtually in cyberspace. Online learning opportunities, in particular, cater to the busy adult student who needs scheduling flexibility due to time constraints at home or work. Before considering the benefits of these programs, you should first consider the drawbacks or potential pitfalls the uninitiated online learner might experience.

  For example, success in an online course or program requires a tremendous amount of discipline, time management, and self-motivation. Since the online learner is solely responsible for the amount of time spent working with course material, he or she must develop and adhere to a regularly set schedule where time is set aside to devote to course work. This requires effective time-management strategies and the discipline to maintain a regular schedule. As a cautionary statement, consider a historical report that indicates that the completion rate for traditional face-to-face courses attended by an adult student typically falls in the 65–73% range, while the same course offered online might see a completion rate as low as 33% for the same population.[6] More recent reports have shown that this gap has closed significantly where on-ground course completion rates are only 3–5% higher than online counterparts.[7] The reasons for lower online course completion rates fall into several categories:

- **Time**. Many colleges and universities with online programs indicate that online courses may, in fact, require a greater amount of time than a traditional face-to-face course to achieve the same learning outcomes.[8]

- **Outside pressures.** Commitments at home and at work may supersede the commitment to the online course.

- **Lack of support/guidance.** Lack of direct guidance from the instructor may lead to decreased engagement from the student.

- **Technology**. If a new online learner struggles with the technology used to gain access to course material, increased frustration and disengagement will likely result.

Despite the drawbacks listed above, online courses are at least as effective as traditional face-to-face courses in supporting student learning.[9] In fact, the growth and increased acceptance of online learning is rapidly transforming the face of higher education across the globe and helping to eliminate the personal, cultural, and situational barriers that have traditionally impeded adults in the pursuit of a college degree. Before embarking on a new educational journey as an online learner, here are a few strategies for success to consider:

- **Find the right program.** If you are a first-time online learner or are a novice with technology, it will be important to find a school or program that provides the best fit for your situation. Find a program that provides personalized support and assistance throughout the educational experience. Ask your admissions counselor about the technology support services and programs offered by your prospective school and the hours that support is available. Inquire if there is telephone support on the weekends, when you will likely have more time available to work on your course content and assignments. Find out if your school offers training or guidance on effective time-management skills for online learners.

- **Take advantage of online tutorials and workshops.** Most schools that offer online programs or courses will provide new students with online resources designed to orient students to the LMS. These resources can be available in several forms, including:

  - *Self-paced interactive tutorials,*

  - *A mandatory "Introduction to Online Learning" course,*

  - *Series of video tutorials.*

  These training opportunities are very important, as your goal is to find out how best to learn online before you begin your first online course. A typical orientation or training program may cover topics such as how to navigate the institution's LMS, how to locate your course materials within the LMS, how to complete and submit assignments, how to participate in online discussions, and how to obtain help. By working through these exercises, you will resolve any potential technological barriers before you start your first course, thereby ensuring that your ability to focus is exclusively set on your course content rather than on struggling with technical issues. With mastery of the LMS completed up front, you will enjoy a smooth transition into the world of online learning.

- **Get acquainted with your distance learning office.** Most schools that offer online programs or degrees will have an office or department dedicated to providing support to the online student. This office may be a part of the continuing education office, the IT department, academic affairs, or the library. Find out how to contact this office and inquire about the services available to online students. The distance learning office may provide additional training opportunities or virtual workshops that will prove useful throughout your online learning experience. This office's mission is to ensure you have the greatest opportunity for success in your online course or program; it is up to you to take advantage of these opportunities and services.

- **Check out your school's library.** The library may be the most overlooked resource available to you in your online learning endeavor. Library professionals are experts in retrieving, organizing, and cataloging information. You will find that the library is staffed with knowledgeable professionals eager to assist you in navigating and leveraging the wealth of information available to you in the institution's catalog as well as on the Internet. Review your library's website or call the reference desk to ask a librarian about the support services available to you. Your library may offer training in the form of face-to-face or online courses or individual training sessions on important topics such as information literacy. Information literacy is a skill that will prove useful throughout your academic career in seeking, harvesting, and evaluating information sources for your research and assignments. In addition, you will learn about the abundance of electronic materials available to you as a student, including electronic journals, databases, and e-books. (See Chapter 16: "The Library" for more details.)

In summary, the technology tools that are available to students today are more advanced, more powerful, and more user-friendly than ever. These tools have enhanced the learning environment and provide today's classroom with streamlined access to an ever-expanding pool of knowledge. The success you will have as a returning college student may depend on your ability to use these technological tools and resources effectively. The good news for you is that today's campuses are filled with knowledgeable professionals whose primary responsibility is to assist you in learning how to use these tools and to ultimately succeed. It is up to you, however, to take advantage of these opportunities and learn how to use today's technology as a powerful ally in your quest to become a true lifelong learner.

KEY POINTS TO REMEMBER:

• Technology is an inescapable part of a 21st-century education.

• Some schools provide free or discounted computer hardware and software for their students.

• If purchasing a computer for school use, make sure it meets the institution's technical specifications.

• Your school's information technology (IT) department can be an important source of training and support.

• Online learning is becoming a larger part of today's college experience.

ACTION STEPS:

1. When discussing your program of study with the admissions department, ask them how you might be successful with online, on-ground, or hybrid learning. This will give you a sense of whether you are ready to tackle the technological skills necessary for online learning. Note: Once you have started a program and are comfortable with your environment as a student, you can always try online classes and determine how you wish to finish your degree.

2. Take a thorough inventory of your own computer equipment. If you have a computer and printer, write down the specifications. Call the IT department of the college you are interested in attending and ask what their requirements will be for your computer hardware and software packages, printing options, learning management system, etc.

3. If you do not have a computer or printer, call the IT department and ask how many computer workstations are available for general student use.

4. Remember: Technology is here to stay. It may be in your best interest to obtain your own computing device to be successful with your studies and be effective in your workplace. Call your local computer store or check with the IT department to see what discounts might be available to you as a college student.

5. When talking to the admissions staff, ask if you will need to own a computer or mobile learning device (tablet, smartphone, etc.). Ask for information on how to purchase a computer compatible with what will be used in the classrooms.

6. Ask about online courses and what percentage of the school's courses is offered on line.

7. Ask if there are tutorials offered for credit or no credit on how to use the most important software packages necessary for success: for example, MS Word to create a paper; Excel to manage a spreadsheet in business or math courses; or PowerPoint to learn how to create a document for an oral presentation with graphics, charts, pictures, photos, or simply words.

MICHELE'S STORY

Her father's heart attack brought Michele's world "to a screeching halt" and ended her first attempt to attend college. As caretaker for her father, and then as a wife and mother, she found herself drifting further and further from her college dreams. Volunteering at her sons' school inspired her to become a special education assistant and then an applied behavioral analysis technician, but Michele worked in the field for more than a decade before she eventually knew that she wanted to be more than a paraprofessional. "I wanted the pay and title that went along with my 'expected' job duties," she said. While she wanted to return to school, difficulties with childcare and her demanding work schedule made that goal seem impossible. Then she learned about a one-day-a-week program at a local college. According to Michele, an advisor for the program was "wonderful, inspiring; she tolerated my tears and was so incredibly supportive....

"Without the support of my fellow students, faculty, and professors," she added, "I really do not know how I would have done it . . . I am such a stronger person for my struggles, and I owe a lot of it to my experience here . . . I cannot even articulate the magnitude of my emotions and gratitude."

RESOURCES:

Calhoun, C. (2014). Using Wikipedia in Information Literacy Instruction: Tips for Developing Research Skills. *College & Research Libraries News, 75*(1), 32–33.

Canning, R. (2002, February 1). Distance or Dis-stancing Education? A Case Study in Technology-Based Learning. *Journal of Further and Higher Education, 26*(1), 29–42. Retrieved from www.researchgate.net/publication/248979334 _Distance_or_Dis-stancing_Education_A_case_study_in_technology-based _learning

Hoover, E. (2009, October 11). The Millennial Muddle. *The Chronicle of Higher Education.* Retrieved from chronicle.com/article/The-Millennial-Muddle -How/48772

Howe, N., & Strauss, W. (2000). *Millennials Rising: The Next Great Generation.* New York: Random House.

Larson, D. K., & Sung, C.-H. (2009). Comparing Student Performance: Online Versus Blended Versus Face-to-Face. *Journal of Asynchronous Learning Networks, 13*(1), 31-42.

Miller, M. H. (2010, March 16). Wiredcampus. *The Chronicle of Higher Education.* Retrieved from chronicle.com/blogs/wiredcampus/students-use-wikipedia -earlyoften/21850

Pennsylvania State University. (2014). How Online Learning Works. *Penn State Online.* Retrieved from www.worldcampus.psu.edu/how-online-learning -works/how-it-works-faqs

Prensky, M. (2001, October). Digital Natives, Digital Immigrants. *On the Horizon, 9*(5), 1-6.

University of Maryland. (2011). Is an Online Course Right for You? Several Caveats about Online Learning Before You Take the Plunge. *University of Maryland Graduate School.* Retrieved from www.graduate.umaryland.edu/thanatology /Academics/Is-an-Online-Course-Right-for-You

University of Oklahoma. (n.d.). *Successful Strategies in Online Education.* Retrieved from ocipresources.pbworks.com/w/file/fetch/64098241/Successful%20Strategies %20in%20Online%20Education.pdf

WICHE Cooperative for Educational Technologies. (n.d.). *Managing Online Education 2013: Practices in Ensuring Quality.* Boulder, CO: WICHE Cooperative for Educational Technologies. Retrieved from wcet.wiche.edu /sites/default/files/2013ManagingOnlineEducationSurveyFinalResults.pdf

NOTES:

1.   Hoover, E. (2009, October 11). The Millennial Muddle. *The Chronicle of Higher Education.* Retrieved from chronicle.com/article/The-Millennial -Muddle-How/48772 . Howe, N. & Strauss, W. (2000). *Millennials Rising: The Next Great Generation.* New York: Random House.

2.   Prensky, M. (2001). Digital Natives, Digital Immigrants. *On the Horizon, 9*(5), 1-6.

3. Miller, M. H. (2010, March 26). Wiredcampus. *The Chronicle of Higher Education*. Retrieved from chronicle.com/blogs/wiredcampus/students-use -wikipedia-earlyoften/21850

4. Calhoun, C. (2014). Using Wikipedia in Information Literacy Instruction: Tips for Developing Research Skills. *College & Research Libraries News*, 75(1), 32–33.

5. Prensky, 2001.

6. Canning, R. (2002, February). Distance or Dis-stancing Education? A Case Study in Technology-Based Learning. *Journal of Further and Higher Education*, 26(1), 29–42. Retrieved from www.researchgate.net/publication/248979334 _Distance_or_Dis-stancing_Education_A_case_study_in_technology-based _learning

7. WICHE Cooperative for Educational Technologies. (n.d.). *Managing Online Education 2013: Practices in Ensuring Quality*. Boulder, CO: WICHE Cooperative for Educational Technologies. Retrieved from wcet.wiche.edu/ wcet/docs/moe/2013ManagingOnlineEducationSurveyFinalResults.pdf

8. Pennsylvania State University (2014). How Online Learning Works. *Penn State Online*. Retrieved from www.worldcampus.psu.edu/how-online -learning-works/how-it-works-faqs . University of Maryland (2011). Is an Online Course Right for You? Several Caveats about Online Learning Before You Take the Plunge. *University of Maryland Graduate School*. Retrieved from www.graduate.umaryland.edu/thanatology/Academics/Is-an-Online-Course -Right-for-You . University of Oklahoma (n.d.). *Succesful Strategies in Online Education*. Retrieved from ocipresources.pbworks.com/w/file/fetch/64098241 /Successful%20Strategies%20in%20Online%20Education.pdf

9. Larson, D. K. & Sung, C.-H. (2009). Comparing Student Performance: Online Versus Blended Versus Face-to-Face. *Journal of Asynchronous Learning Networks*, 13(1), 31–42.

18

WRITING: TIPS FOR SUCCESS

*Y*ou cannot achieve academic success without being a good writer. This is a skill that is developed over time. You may fear that your previous educational experiences have not prepared you. Even if you have been prepared, the writing style your professor prefers may not be the style in which you write. I strongly advise you not to take the criticism you receive on your writing personally, but to view it as an incentive to practice, practice, and practice until you become more adept at writing and understanding the assignments and your professor's preferences.

Writing is also a top skill required by employers. When I receive a cover letter with a grammatical or spelling error in it, I am not inclined to interview the candidate. Why? Because if you are working in an environment where you must communicate via e-mails, letters, or reports, you must be a good writer. When we ask employers what skills they look for in an employee, they start with communication skills; writing is critical to being a good communicator. Consider your writing assignments as practice toward excelling and advancing in your career. Professors require you to share your knowledge in writing because it gives you a chance to prove you understand what you have heard or read about the subject you are studying, and it gives you the chance to practice expressing your thoughts clearly and concisely.

Just a caution regarding plagiarism, which is mentioned later in this chapter: If you attempt to pass off someone else's work as your own, or if you fail to properly credit sources you have used in your research, you are committing plagiarism. Check your institution's policies on academic integrity, plagiarism, and ethical behavior in an academic setting. Faculty members will assume your assignments are your original work, unless you otherwise cite your sources. For example, if you quote a passage from a journal article or book, you must give proper attribution to the source and author. Many times, such citations add strength to an argument in a paper or provide color or context for your thoughts or opinions. In all cases, however, the faculty member will assume that any uncited work is yours. If there are doubts by the faculty member, or if the faculty member finds your material is not original, she or he may report his or her concerns to the academic administration. Every college and university has its own procedures about how to handle plagiarism and academic integrity. Committing plagiarism could lead to loss of credit for a course or even expulsion from the college. If you are not sure whether you are properly crediting sources in your assignments, discuss your concerns and questions with your instructor.

Suzanne Strempek Shea is an author by profession and has taught all types of writing courses at many colleges and universities throughout the country. She has written six novels and five nonfiction books and has an extraordinary following of readers throughout the world. She also has been a teacher of budding writers and a mentor to many. In addition, she is the Director of Creative Writing and Writer in Residence at Bay Path University and has just established a creative writing MFA curriculum. Her words of advice for adult women starting or returning to college are priceless and humorous; her easy style of discussing the art and science of writing will be just what you need to get in the right frame of mind before responding to your first writing assignments.

WRITING YOUR WAY TO SUCCESS
by Suzanne Strempek Shea

"Tell me about yourself."

This question, innocent enough, has been known to strike fear when followed by the direction: "In 500 words."

It might be easy enough to give a quick verbal reply like "I'm 48, have three dogs." But being asked to sit down and multiply that a hundred times—and on paper—is a whole different thing. Putting into words something about who you are, who's in your life, what your interests are, what matters to you, what riles you, how you came to this point in your schooling, what your goals might be and how you might achieve them—all that can be daunting for those who don't first and foremost consider themselves writers. But I think it's a vital exercise for the start of any class, whatever the subject. And I love to assign it.

The answers to some of these questions might never have been fully pondered by the person leaning over her notebook. "I'm Kathy" might have been one person's verbal answer, but that blank page before her gives her the space and the often magical opportunity to expound on the truth as she adds in pen, "and I never, ever, thought I'd be back to finish my schooling. But here I am."

Similarly, the reasons for Kathy's incredulity might never make their way into a quick and casual answer to "Tell me about yourself," especially in a room full of strangers on the harrowing first day of a new semester. But in writing she might tell the story of dropping out to get married, or her family's running out of tuition money, or the addiction that sent her life onto a whole different track and kept it there until just a few years ago. When the 15 or 20 minutes I allot for this exercise are over, more often than not a few sets of eyes remain focused on the lines written. The stories are not done being told. In most cases, they've only just begun to be shared.

And that's usually a shock to the participants. One of the wonders of writing is that it can crack open parts of our hearts and souls we thought had been long sealed, or maybe we never knew existed. The piece of paper isn't staring at us critically as we reveal our shortcomings, our shyest hopes, our big plans for a new career, or even just for getting through the next four months of classes—or this first day. There's something safe about writing that allows a voice for even the most closed personality. When informed that time is up, students might be surprised how quickly the minutes have passed, how much they put down, how many tangents they began, each of which could benefit from another 15 or 20 minutes of writing. When I invite the students to read from their pages, there's additional surprise. "I've never done this before, but what the hey," one might start. "I've never told anyone about this" is how another student, still mystified as to what just happened in a simple writing exercise, might conclude her reading. Listeners sit rapt, shaking their heads, so amazed that a woman who just signed up for my writing class because she had a humanities space to fill can almost immediately turn out such a vivid, candid, brave, and fascinating work. I don't shake my head. I know that, as my mother long ago told me, "You don't know what you can do until you try." Which is why I love to start my classes in this way. Through writing—even through such a brief and instant exercise—I might learn a lot about my students, and they might learn more about themselves.

Easy for me to say, maybe, because I think writing is fun. Even when it's hard, it's still fun. It's what I've done for a living for the past 34 years, first as a newspaper reporter and then as the author of novels, nonfiction books, and freelance pieces for newspapers and magazines. I can sit down at my keyboard and create a world from thin air or tell the truth of an experience that the subject of a story or I have gone through. What could be cooler? And think about it—what are your friends doing for a living? Too many people hate their nine-to-five existence. I feel fortunate and blessed to have found this thing I do for a living, and a big goal when I teach is to foster and share that excitement—the idea that the process of writing, and the writing life, can be a blast.

But the fact is that few of my students are aiming for a version of a writing life. They're in school to study forensics or law or education, and they wonder why the heck they're being told to write even before we get to talking about the syllabus or the textbook or what time we'll take a break. The answer is simple. First, I want them to write. I do that because it's my base in the world, and also because I want to stress to them its importance, no matter where they might be headed.

That's because wherever they head, whatever they do after the graduation ceremony is over, they're going to have to write something: a daily plan, a meeting report, a project assessment, a suggestion to the boss, a memo to coworkers, a proposal for a grant. And that's for starters. In life in general, they might want to pen a gripe to the middle school principal, an idea-filled letter to the editor, a blog to connect the neighborhood. In none of this do they want to come off as less than professional, to be dismissed or ignored because their work is unclear or sloppy. But, sadly, unclear and sloppy is too often the case with student writing.

Blame cuts in school funding, a society in which video games take up the free time reading once did, or electronic messaging that makes acronyms of every word. Whatever the reason, more and more students enter college with deplorable writing skills—which is one reason students balk at my first class assignment. To me, there's a difference between being able to write, as in telling a story well, and being able to write, as in correctly using spelling, grammar, and syntax. I encourage those in that first early exercise not to think about what they might be doing incorrectly. "Just tell your story," I say. "We'll figure out the rest later."

I say that because we certainly will. It's my job as a writing teacher to help students with any basic writing skills that might need to be improved or honed. It's become very hard for me to read anything—from a few pages of students' writing to a book I've taken out of the library—without underlining a sentence I think could be clearer, a word that's misspelled, a comma that's out of place, or commas that are all over the place when they needn't be. I do that religiously with my students' work. But a student in another classroom shouldn't expect her instructor in Strategies for Network Security or in Advanced Criminalistics and Crime Scene Investigation and Reconstruction to be guiding her in the proper uses of subject, verb, and adverb. A student might receive a lesser grade for the quality of her writing and that will be that— that, and the student eventually coming up short against peers in the job market, in the workplace, and in any portion of society where the written word is used. Which, again, is pretty much everywhere.

So what's a student to do if she's made her way into a college program but still needs to work on her basic writing skills?

The first thing is the same advice given to anyone with any kind of problem: acknowledge that you have one. I've worked with too many students who turn a deaf ear to my constant reminders about something as basic as putting a period within the quotation marks. They shrug, they grin, they don't see the point of the fuss. "But I'm going into social work," one argues, as if in social work, there won't be many, many, many pages of reports to write, problems and solutions to suss out on paper, cases to argue as best as can be argued. Clearly and effectively. In writing. Whatever your course of study, vow to use as much care with your writing as you do with the preparation— the reading, the listening, the researching—that goes into a paragraph or an entire project.

When you acknowledge you have a problem, you get help. Ask your professor for a meeting to outline your major writing challenges. He or she might not be able to tutor you at length or at all outside of class, but writing tutors are available free of charge on most campuses. Make use of them. These are folks who want to make your work better. Even an hour with them once a week could enlighten you on something you might have missed while being just one in a classroom full of students.

Ask both your professor and your tutor for helpful books. Though I make my living as a writer, I had no formal training. Most of what I've learned about my craft has come from the daily habit of sitting down to do the work and from the daily habit of reading what others have written in newspapers, magazines, and books. Here are a few of my many favorites:

- ***Bird by Bird: Some Instructions on Writing and Life* by Anne Lamott**
  I absolutely love this book and have given it to people who'll never care to write more than their name. The subtitle is the reason; the advice and anecdotes that bestselling novelist, memoirist, and essayist Lamott offers can apply to anyone in any profession. We all need to get off our duffs and do our work; we all need to realize that the first version of anything won't be perfect; we all need to turn off the self-defeating negativity in our head (which Lamott likens to a radio station with call letters that can't be printed in a family publication); we all need to stop being afraid and do something with our lives. The title alone is a slogan I lean on often, taken from a story Lamott tells about her brother, who had three months to complete a grade school project on birds but only started it the night before it was due. Their father, himself a writer, sat down with his son and gave the advice to just take the project bird by bird. Word by word is how to build a story. Day by day is how to build a life.

- ***Eats, Shoots & Leaves: The Zero Tolerance Approach to Punctuation* by Lynne Truss**
  Born as a British radio show titled *Cutting a Dash* (yes, there are countries in which punctuation is so regarded as to merit a program on a national radio network), *Eats, Shoots & Leaves* is a surprisingly fun book for those who are only semi-sure when to use a semicolon. Truss has made her living as a book critic, columnist, and sportswriter for *The Times of London*, has published 11 books, and has written television sitcoms and dramas. So don't expect an academic tone to this tome that became an international bestseller. Do expect, once you're done reading, to spot improper

punctuation all around you—including (shockingly often) in your own writing.

- *The Elements of Style* **(Fourth Edition) by William Strunk, Jr. and E.B. White**
  This is a classic general guide to writing well, and, at 105 pages, deceptively brief in all it has to offer both the novice and the veteran writer. Penned way back in 1918 by Strunk for use at Cornell University, where he was teaching English, it enlightened and aided then-student White, who went on to become a legendary writer at *The New Yorker* and author of books, including *Charlotte's Web*. White was also eventually commissioned to revise the book, which offers its advice via lists of rules, principles, and approaches that remain solid nearly a century on.

- *A Piece of Work: Five Writers Discuss Their Revisions* **edited by Jay Woodruff**
  This book was first printed in 1993, but the fact that a writer or poet always needs to revise hasn't changed in the past 20 years, and probably won't in the next 1,500. Reproductions of handwritten and typed drafts in various stages hit home the fact that even such big shots as Tobias Wolff, Tess Gallagher, Robert Coles, Joyce Carol Oates, and Donald Hall don't deliver pristine copy the first time around. They had to revise, revise, revise. Interviews with each author further dissect the process regarding specific pieces and provide enlightenment as to what went on inside the heads of some of our country's most acclaimed literary figures as they crafted the pieces.

- *Write from the Heart: Inspiration and Exercises for Women Who Want to Write* **by Lesléa Newman**
  With apologies to the author, I ignore the word "Women" in the title. I have used this book while leading writing groups that have included both genders. I think a fish could benefit from reading this, if that fish wanted to

learn how to write more effectively. Answering that old self-tripping question of "What do I have to write about?" Newman answers, "Nothing much. Absolutely everything . . . Everyone's life is mysterious, beautiful, stunning magic. It doesn't matter if you've lived in the same town your whole life or traveled around the world seven times. What matters is your ability to open up to the breathtaking and spectacular adventure that happens to be your life. Your job is to experience it, see it, feel it, live it and write it down."

From there, she leads readers down aisle after aisle of exercises that get them completing pages of work before they realize it.

- *They Say, I Say: The Moves That Matter in Academic Writing* (Third Edition) by Gerald Graff and Cathy Birkenstein
  If you need to know what will make your academic writing sing, this book should be on your list. The authors, who teach English at the University of Illinois, know their subject and present it in user/writer-friendly ways that guide and encourage. Templates for framing arguments are nice plusses, but the biggest might be the interest this book can instill (or revitalize) in a component of higher learning too often presented in a dry manner.

Read these books and anything else you can get your hands on. If you were studying cake baking and never ate a slice, how would you know what a good cake tasted like? Read to find out what good writing is and to observe how it's done. Ask your professors for some examples of highly effective term papers, reports, reviews, whatever it is they regularly assign during the semester, and read them to find what makes the piece work. Is it structure? Approach? Seamless sentences? If you can't determine this, ask the professors why they liked the example so much. Then read the piece again. Writers probably read as frequently as they write. It's how the great ones got that way, and how the rest of them try to get better. Follow their example.

Does your favorite writer use an outline? Never, ever, use one? You might try writing both with and without this form of a plan. Does that writer sit down and pour out all that's in her brain, or does she take pages of notes before she goes near her keyboard? Try the sitting and pouring out, but also try that time-trusted and so-rich practice of taking notes. Keep a pad in your pocket—or, as did prolific poet Emily Dickinson, use the backs of envelopes and other bits of paper. What you write on doesn't matter. The point is that you must write. Do that writing daily. Even a few sentences. Practice brings results, and with daily work you'll soon have a first draft begging to be tweaked into shape.

Use Anne Lamott's idea of the small assignment to move through your work bit by bit, both in the writing stage and in the key revising period. Say that for the next two days you'll look at the piece in general, to see if it makes sense, if the theme is clear, if there's a strong beginning, middle, and end. Schedule a few more days after that to go back and work on what you've marked that needs further tending. And then go back a few days after that to put the microscope to grammar, spelling, punctuation. Don't have a week to work on it? Then schedule accordingly, but break up the task over the days, or even hours, to lessen stress and make sure you cover all the bases. And, perhaps, to lessen any eleventh-hour temptation to do what can be all too easy today: highlight something online and paste it into a document bearing your name.

If a piece of writing is not yours, don't say it is. Cite sources, quote authors, note that this line or that paragraph is from a certain publication. It's fine to paraphrase, but only if the result is your own writing. And, again, try to credit where the info came from in the first place. Make sure to cover these bases if you are using work by another. That's all A-OK. What's not is to slap it on the page and act as if some (or even all—yes, it's been done) of your homework or report is your own, and then turn it in. Plagiarism is not only misrepresentation; it's stealing. As easy as technology makes it to cut and paste, it's also pretty easy for your instructor to determine what's yours and what's not. Not only might she or he have that instructor's built-in detector for writing that's way beyond your current ability, but also she or he definitely has a myriad of computer programs that can determine plagiarism to the letter, and quickly can produce the document from which work was cribbed. If there's an offense to report, the next step could be the scary prospect of a date with powers-that-be, and, beyond that, possible expulsion. It's not worth risking all the work you've done to get to this point. If you want to write, why not use your own voice, intelligence, talent? Make your schedule and get to it. Get writing, and then get revising.

I know many writers who say that revision is when the real fun begins. They have a basic story and then can make all sorts of large or small changes to make it more effective, sharp, compelling, whatever. I see it as making a bed. You pull on the sheet, the blanket, the cover, and then you have to keep pulling and smoothing before it all looks nice and neat and is recognizable as a well-made bed. I'm always smoothing my work; with each pass I make, I usually can find another thing to tweak. For the student, revision can be when the real work begins, too. Slapping an essay onto the page and handing it in isn't the way to go. Or to learn. Take the time to make your work better by going over it to look at different components.

You might not have read aloud since you last cared for a toddler, but if you want to do your best writing, you'll have to start reading aloud again—this time to yourself. You'll be amazed how hearing your piece will alert you to problems you didn't see with your eyes. Missing words, sentences that go on for ages, the same word used over and over again, verbs and subjects that don't match, misspellings, tenses that change several times in a single paragraph—any or all of those finds might await you when you sit down and read your work aloud. I know this because they await me when I read mine. I might think a struggled-over essay is finally complete and ready for enshrinement in some writing hall of fame, and then I read it aloud again. What in the world does that sentence mean? That's not what I meant to say. And didn't I have a comma there—it's certainly needed. I circle the spots that need work, and sit down yet again. And the next time I read, it might indeed be ready. It wouldn't have been, if I hadn't checked.

I have used the revision section of *Writing Fiction: A Guide to Narrative Craft* by Janet Burroway and Elizabeth Stuckey-French with writers of all prose genres. *Writing Fiction* is the most widely assigned standard text in creative writing classes nationwide, but it's far from stuffy and scholarly, making it a fine fit for the serious at-home writer who wants to grow and learn—again, as I've noted, in a variety of prose genres. Burroway, an acclaimed novelist, poet, playwright, and author of craft books, and Stuckey-French, a respected short story writer and novelist, examine the writing process and elements including story structure, characterization, place, point of view, and theme. Each chapter is crammed with excerpts, complete short stories, author interviews, and assignments and exercises. The revision section includes a list of helpful questions, including: "Why should the reader turn from the first page to the second?" "Where is (the piece) too general?" and "Is there unnecessary summary?" The section also offers suggestions on the revision process, examples of how several writers have revised a piece, and exercises to hone your work further. A favorite of mine: Take one of your stories that isn't quite working, and explore the main character by writing from that character's point of view. You might have her write out a diary entry, e-mail, dream, letter, or even a short autobiography. Don't worry about whether or not what you write will actually fit into the story. It might, but it might not. In either case, you'll probably learn something important about your character and her story.

But you can only do that, you can only have something to revise, if you've written in the first place. If you don't already, try keeping a journal just for the heck of it. There is no lack of cool notebooks and journals in any store you enter these days. Pick up one of those—or just break barely a buck for the black-and-white composition book you used back when you were learning the penmanship part of writing. It's like anything:

The more you do it, the more comfortable you'll be. This doesn't have to be for anyone else—just for you. Whatever you're feeling, write it out: your apprehension about returning to school, the excitement of selecting your courses, the range of reactions from family and friends when you told them you were once again going to be a student. As busy as we are, we can always find a spare ten minutes in our day. Cull some time for this very important act of writing your own story, and while doing that, you will write better and better with every line.

So pick up your pen. Open that notebook. Tell yourself about yourself. You never know what you can do until you try.

KEY POINTS TO REMEMBER:

- Writing is an essential communication skill for success in a professional career.

- Most colleges offer tutoring or writing clinics for students who have difficulties with writing.

- Books that approach the craft and practice of writing in fresh and friendly ways can invigorate.

- You're not finished after the first draft; revision is essential for effective writing.

- Plagiarism is academic suicide; you could be failed or even expelled for doing it.

ACTION STEPS:

1. Why not use Suzanne's first assignment in her writing classes as your first attempt at writing? In 500 words or less, write something about who you are. You might want to include your dreams for your college education.

2. Purchase or borrow from the library one of the resources listed below and read it. Most include writing prompts or exercises. Try doing a few of them as a way to get going.

3. Assume you are in your first class and you need to prepare for your first writing assignment. What resources will you need to have at your fingertips?

4. Do you know how to format and make citations in a research paper? If you don't know the answer to this, check out the standard text, *The MLA Handbook for Writers of Research Papers* (online version available for a fee at www.mlahandbook.org). Other style guides for professional and academic writing include the *Chicago Manual of Style* (online version available for a fee at www. chicagomanualofstyle.org), the *Publication Manual of the American Psychological Association* (used in the social and behavioral sciences—available online for a fee at apastyle .org), and the *Associated Press Stylebook* (used by journalists— online version available for a fee at www.apstylebook.com). Always ask your professors which style guide they prefer.

CHRISTINE'S STORY

Christine's college experience literally came as the result of a dream. When Christine graduated high school, her mother opposed her plans to go to college and refused to help her with school expenses. So Christine worked full-time and went to school at night. Then in the middle of Christine's second semester, her mother became terminally ill; Christine had to quit school to take care of her. After her mother's death, Christine couldn't afford to return to college. She worked many jobs as an administrative assistant, but was unable to advance further in her career because she didn't have a degree. Ironically, a dream about her mother gave her the push she needed to return to school. "I was frustrated and angry that I had worked for so many years and was unable to move forward career-wise. One night I went to sleep in tears and asked my mom, 'What should I do?' That night my mom came to me in my dream, and we had a conversation. She kept telling me over and over, 'Christine, you need to go back to school.'" Shortly after that, Christine received a brochure in the mail from a local college. "I glanced at the brochure and threw it out. A few days later, another brochure came in the mail. I threw that brochure out also. When the third brochure arrived, I remembered what my mom had said to me about going back to school. I said to myself, 'I got the hint, Mom; I need to go back to school.'" Christine started college in 2008, received an associate's degree in business administration in 2010, then went on to receive a bachelor's in executive management. She concluded, "I can honestly say it was a gift from heaven above."

RESOURCES:

American Psychological Association (2010). *Publication Manual of the American Psychological Association* (6th ed.). Washington, DC: American Psychological Association. Online version available for a fee at apastyle.org

Burroway, J., & Stuckey-French, E. (2000). *Writing Fiction: A Guide to Narrative Craft* (5th ed.). New York: Longman.

Gibaldi, J. (2009). *MLA Handbook for Writers of Research Papers*. New York: Modern Language Association of America. Online version available for a fee at www.mlahandbook.org

Graff, G., & Birkenstein, C. (2010). *They Say/I Say: The Moves that Matter in Academic Writing*. New York: W.W. Norton & Co.

Lamott, A. (1994). *Bird by Bird: Some Instructions on Writing and Life*. New York: Pantheon Books.

Minthorn, D., Jacobsen, S., & Froke, P. (Eds.). (2015). *The Associated Press Stylebook and Briefing on Media Law*. New York: Basic Books. Online version available for a fee at www.apstylebook.com

Newman, L. (2003). *Write from the Heart: Inspiration and Exercises for Women Who Want to Write*. Berkeley: Ten Speed Press.

Strunk, W. J., & White, E. B. (1979). *The Elements of Style* (3rd ed.). New York: Macmillan.

Truss, L. (2006). *Eats, Shoots & Leaves: The Zero Tolerance Approach to Punctuation*. New York: Gotham Books.

University of Chicago. (2010). *Chicago Manual of Style* (16th ed.). Chicago: University of Chicago Press. Online version available for a fee at www.chicagomanualofstyle.org

Woodruff, J. (1993). *A Piece of Work: Five Writers Discuss Their Revisions*. Iowa City: University of Iowa Press.

19

Mathematics

*V*ery few subjects can stir fear in the hearts of students the way mathematics can. Math anxiety is particularly prevalent among female students, often because they've been discouraged from excelling in technical courses like math and science. It's one factor leading to the underrepresentation of women in STEM (science, technology, engineering, and mathematics) careers. According to the U.S. Department of Commerce, women have a low share of STEM undergraduate degrees compared to men and hold less than 25% of all STEM jobs. Yet choosing a STEM-related major can open the door to higher-paying jobs. Women in STEM jobs can earn up to 33% more than college-educated women in non-STEM jobs.[1]

You might have grown up hearing the myth that girls are naturally bad at math and science, so you believed you weren't capable. Perhaps it's been so long since you've taken a math course that you're afraid you've forgotten everything. Or perhaps you're afraid that you're too old to learn something as complicated as math.

And yet mathematical ability is an essential part of daily life—you probably have better math skills than you think. If you're pursuing a scientific or technological career, math can be as important to your academic life as reading and writing.

Jane Weyant is Mathematics Department chair at Bay Path University and a former engineer with Digital Equipment Corporation. Her straightforward look at math in everyday life will provide you with a number of strategies for conquering math anxiety.

MATH IN EVERYDAY LIFE
BY JANE WEYANT

Let's be honest here. What are you thinking before you take your first college mathematics course? If you are like most people, you're probably wondering why you need to take the class in the first place. After accepting that it is most likely a required course, you are now wondering where you will possibly use these concepts in your everyday life. Listed below are several examples in which you need math skills during a typical day:

- **Shopping**

  - What should I leave for a tip for my excellent waiter when the bill is $63.00?

  - Should I buy those paper towels in bulk at the warehouse store, or is it better to wait until they go on sale at the supermarket, and buy smaller packages?

  - Am I going to have enough money to pay for all of these things in my grocery cart, or am I going to be embarrassed at the checkout line?

- **Gambling**

  - Which is the best horse to bet on at the racetrack, and what is my payout if I actually win?

  - Should I spend $20 on that lottery ticket that has a potential payoff of $20 million?

- Do I really want a player on my fantasy baseball team who is currently hitting .222 with an on-base percentage of .250?

- **Driving**

  - Is it worth it to buy a hybrid Prius and get 52 miles per gallon versus 21 miles per gallon with my old clunker?

  - If I get caught going 20 mph over the speed limit in a school zone, what is my fine going to be?

  - If I drive five miles per hour faster to get to school, will I get there in time for my 7:30 a.m. class, or is it not worth it?

- **Employment**

  - What is the ratio of bleach I should put in the customer's hair dye to lighten her hair but not turn it stark white?

  - At what angle should I approach a patient with this needle to maximize the amount of blood drawn from her arm?

  - What should I charge for cupcakes at my bakery so that I can realize a 20% profit?

- **Cooking**

  - How much flour do I need to make a half recipe of chocolate cookies if the full recipe calls for 5/6 cups of flour?

  - How many 2" × 2" brownies can I bake if my pan is 8" × 8"?

  - How many cupcakes do I have to make for my daughter's four classes of 21 students each in order to have one for each student?

- **Home and Garden**

  - Do I have enough space to fit this sleeper sofa in my small living room?

  - How many plants should I buy to fill my 8' × 4' flower bed?

  - How many square feet of carpet do I need to carpet this room?

- **Traveling**

  - Is it more economical for me to fly to Florida and rent a car, or should I drive and pay for gas and put wear and tear on my own car?

  - If I want to visit Paris, how many euros can I get for each American dollar?

  - How fast am I really going in miles per hour when I am driving 88 kilometers per hour when visiting Canada?

You get the picture. The possibilities are endless. Math is a part of your everyday life, whether you like it or not. Maybe now you can see the importance of that math class that you have to pass in order to get your college degree. It is no longer "Why do I have to take this?" Now it should be "Gee, I really need this!"

- **Women and Math Anxiety**
  Studies show that there is a direct correlation between your proficiency at math and your perception of that proficiency. If you think that you are terrible at math, you will most likely turn out to be just that. This is especially true for women. According to research done by the American Association of University Women, negative stereotypes about girls' abilities in mathematics measurably lower their mathematics test performance. However, if girls are

told that they are just as capable as boys, the difference in test performance essentially disappears.[2]

Research published in *Science* showed that the difference between the performance of boys and girls on a standardized math test suggested that cultural biases rather than biology explained the difference in test scores. For instance, girls in countries such as Norway and Sweden performed at a level equal to boys. These countries are considered to be mathematically-emancipated, meaning that perceptions of gender-based differences in math abilities do not exist in these countries.[3]

Some of women's perceived inadequacies in math may start in the home and be passed down through generations. For example, a conversation with Lois Ostrander, high school mathematics teacher at Longmeadow High School in Longmeadow, Massachusetts, brought to light another aspect of the math phobia dilemma. Think of how many times in your life you have heard somebody remark that she is terrible in math. However, how many times have you heard someone remark that she is terrible in reading? Ostrander believes that this is because it is not socially acceptable to admit that you can't read very well, but it's perfectly fine to admit that you can't do math, especially if you're a woman. In fact, Ostrander has heard from parents who don't believe their children are capable of doing well in math because they themselves did poorly. Ostrander believes that parents sometimes unknowingly impress this upon their children, especially girls, and give them a free pass not to try to succeed in mathematics. This is another example of how social and cultural standards can influence women's perception of their abilities, or lack thereof, in math.

Another perception in our society is that men do not like women who are good at math. As an example, next time you are looking for a DVD to watch, try *Mean Girls*. In this movie, Lindsay Lohan plays a high school student named Cady, who is excellent in math. Cady excels in her calculus class, but she deliberately fails the exams in order to attract the guy she likes. Sadly, this is probably happening all over America. However, keep watching until the end of the movie; Cady ends up winning a math competition for her school's Mathletes team and still gets the guy in the end. This happy ending might get through to a few young women out there!

Your own attitude about your mathematical abilities can be a self-fulfilling prophecy. If you tell yourself or let others tell you that you can't do it, it will most likely turn out to be true. Maybe you are better in writing or reading, but that does not automatically mean that you are bad in math. Don't let society dictate your confidence in mathematics. As with reading and writing, practice and patience will aid you in your journey through the wonderful world of mathematics!

- **Tips on Succeeding in a College Mathematics Course**

  So now that you agree that you have to take this really useful math class in college, exactly how are you going to succeed? Follow these tips to make your life a little easier:

  - **Get lots of rest before class.** Coming to class tired is going to doom you from the start. Try to get class times when you think you perform best, if possible (i.e. "I'm a morning person," or "I can't function before 10:00 a.m.").

  - **Take complete notes.** Don't be afraid to ask your professor to slow down or to go over a problem again. Ask the professor to post some version of the notes online. If that is not possible, ask if the professor can provide physical copies of the notes, or ask if you may snap a picture of the board before s/he erases it. You can use the pictures to go back over your notes and make sure you got everything.

- **Most colleges will have you take a math placement exam.** Do the best you can on this exam. If you take it lightly and don't put any effort into it, you may be placed in a course that is beneath your skill level. Being bored in class is just about the worst situation you can put yourself in, so perform to the best of your ability on these placement exams. If the exam seems difficult for you, try not to get stressed out. You aren't getting graded on this exam! The institution just wants to know what course is appropriate for you. The correct placement will help you succeed in your subsequent courses.

- **Try not to rely heavily on calculators.** Sure, they are great tools, and you should use them. A lot of times, however, you can quickly figure out simple calculations in your head or on paper. You might not always have a calculator handy, so it is important for you to build your skill level and confidence to do simple calculations. You can sometimes use mental math to make calculations that you never thought you could do without a calculator or long, drawn-out calculations. Also, be aware that a calculator is a tool that can be used incorrectly. It only works if the person using it knows how to manipulate it and follows the rules of mathematics.

- **Use your institution's available tutoring resources, which are almost always free.** Sometimes the tutors are other students, just like you. You might feel more comfortable with a peer; if not, institutions often hire professional tutors. See what is available and choose the option that is most appropriate for you. In some cases, tutoring is offered online.

- **Ask questions in class.** Let your professor know if you have any concerns or problems with the material covered. If you don't say anything, the professor will assume that all is well, and then s/he will move on to new material. If you are having a problem understanding, there is likely to be someone else in the class in the same predicament as you are, but who is either too scared or frustrated to voice concerns. Try not to worry about whether classmates or the professor are going to look down on you for asking questions. You are paying for the course and deserve to get the most out of it that you can. If you still can't get yourself to ask questions in class, try asking the professor before or after class, through an e-mail, or with a phone call.

- **Take advantage of your professor's office hours.** Meeting with your professor provides important one-on-one time and gives more time for both of you to get to know each other. In addition, meeting with your professor lets him/her know that you are serious about the course work and that you really want to learn the material.

- **Keep up on assignments!** This is extremely important because not only does late submission affect your grade in the course, it also will affect your ability to keep up with the concepts covered throughout the course. Once you get behind, it is extremely difficult to catch up. Math is cumulative. If you miss a concept at the beginning, it may greatly affect your chances of comprehending the next concept.

- **Try to use outside resources when appropriate.** It is often true that you can learn anything about life from the Internet! If you are having a problem with a certain math concept, try Googling it. You would be surprised how much help you can get. Just be aware that not everything on the Internet is fact, so you must evaluate the source of the information. You can always ask your professor to suggest websites such as Khan Academy that might help you out.

- **Use the resources that the course provides.** Sometimes this may be a textbook. Try reading it before you assume you don't understand a concept. Most math texts have examples and demonstration problems. Some math courses use e-books or learning software like MyMathLab or WebAssign. Both of these programs provide an array of learning tools like sample problems and solutions, lecture videos, or direct links to the text in which the material is covered. These tools can greatly enhance the learning experience.

- **Form relationships with other students and take part in study pairs or groups.** You are in this together and can help each other a great deal. Even if you feel that you know the material, it can be helpful to explain it to someone else. This can deepen your understanding and allow you to help a fellow student in need.

- **If you have school-aged children at home (or maybe even nieces or nephews), ask for their help.** Sometimes they are covering the same material in school that you are reviewing. It makes them feel pretty good if they can help Mom or their aunt in her college-level course!

- **If for some reason you don't connect well with your current professor or s/he is not available to help, seek help from previous professors or other professors in the math department.** They can be a good resource when you most need help.

- **If you have done all the assignments and still do not feel confident with a concept, ask the professor to go over more examples in class, or ask if s/he could provide you with supplemental problems.**

- **Take your time with exams.** Ask the professor ahead of time if you may have more time if you don't complete the exam. Some may be willing; some won't. It doesn't hurt to ask.

- **Don't overdo it!** Remember the Alcoholics Anonymous definition of insanity: doing the same thing over and over again and expecting different results. If you have tried a problem over and over and keep getting it wrong and expect to suddenly get it right, it probably will drive you insane. That is when it is time to take a step back and call in the troops. Take a break and contact your professor or another student in class for help.

- **Relax!** If you go to class stressed out, your ability to learn new concepts is going to be impaired. The mind is a powerful thing, and walking into class with an air of confidence may help with the learning process.

After reading through this chapter, we hope you feel a little more confident about tackling that required college mathematics course. We hope that you now understand the need for math in your everyday life and that you have some confidence and strategies that will help you succeed. The key point to remember is that if you believe in yourself and put in the required time and effort, you will be able to succeed in a college math course.

KEY POINTS TO REMEMBER:

- Your proficiency at math is directly related to your perception of that proficiency; telling yourself you're bad at math can be a self-fulfilling prophecy.

- Don't hesitate to seek help from your professor, tutors, and/or fellow students.

- Special software and online learning resources can supplement the information you get in class and your textbooks.

- Studying in groups can help reduce math anxiety.

- Try not to stress yourself over math; having confidence can help with your learning process.

ACTION STEPS:

1. Make a list of all the ways you use math in your daily life.

2. If you have math anxiety, find out what resources are available at your college for helping you overcome it: online tutorials, personal tutoring, etc.

3. Talk to your fellow students and try to find someone who has overcome math anxiety. Ask her how she succeeded.

4. Talk to your fellow students about forming a study group for your mathematics course.

5. If you are very anxious about your math courses before you start a program in college, consider taking a math refresher course either online or in your community. Many communities offer math courses for adults.

$\mathscr{E}$LLA'S STORY

Ella returned to school when she realized that a college degree could improve her opportunities for promotion and career advancement. She wrote, ". . . [I]n today's society there seems to be a greater demand for [degrees], including in the clerical fields." She also wanted to fulfill a promise to her mother. "Before my mother died, she made me promise that I would go back to school and finish what I had started . . . My mother said that I spent most of my life taking care of others, and now is the time to take care of me."

RESOURCES:

Advanced Instructional Systems, Inc. (2014). *WebAssign*. Retrieved from www .webassign.net/

Beede, D., Julian, T., Langdon, D., McKittrick, G., Khan, B., & Doms, M. (2011). *Women in STEM: A Gender Gap to Innovation*. Washington, DC: U.S. Department of Commerce. Retrieved from www.esa.doc.gov/sites/default /files/womeninstemagaptoinnovation8311.pdf

Bohannon, J. (2014, March). Both Genders Think Women Are Bad at Basic Math. *Science*. Retrieved from news.sciencemag.org/math/2014/03/both-genders -think-women-are-bad-basic-math

Corbett, C., Hill, C., & St. Rose, A. (2010). *Why So Few? Women in Science, Technology, Engineering and Mathematics*. Washington, DC: American Association of University Women. Retrieved from www.aauw.org/research/why-so-few

Khan Academy. (2015). Retrieved from www.khanacademy.org

Oswego City School District Regents Exam Prep Center. (1999-2011). Retrieved from regentsprep.org

Pearson Education, Inc. (2014). *MyMathLab*. Retrieved from www .pearsonmylabandmastering.com/northamerica/mymathlab

NOTES:

1. Beede, D., Julian, T., Langdon, D., McKittrick, G., Khan, B., & Doms, M. (2011). *Women in STEM: A Gender Gap to Innovation*. Washington, DC: U.S. Department of Commerce. Retrieved from www.esa.doc.gov/sites/default /files/womeninstemagaptoinnovation8311.pdf

2. Corbett, C., Hill, C., & St. Rose, A. (2010). *Why So Few? Women in Science, Technology, Engineering and Mathematics*. Washington, DC: American Association of University Women. Retrieved from www.aauw.org/research /why-so-few

3. Bohannon, J. (2014, March). Both Genders Think Women Are Bad at Basic Math. *Science*. Retrieved from news.sciencemag.org/math/2014/03/both -genders-think-women-are-bad-basic-math

20

CAREER DEVELOPMENT

*C*areer development is a critical part of your educational journey. At many colleges and universities, a career services or development officer can work with you as you explore your major or as you search for a job. The mistake students often make is to wait until they're about to graduate to visit that office and meet with the staff, and then expect the staff to find the students' dream job. Your contact with career services should take place well before your final semester, when everyone else is seeking help to find a job. If you introduce yourself early in your college career, you will ensure more attention and a lasting relationship with the staff. They will get to know you as an individual with all your dreams and aspirations, your talents, and your passions. They can be incredible partners with you on your educational and career journey.

Let's start with career exploration. Often we do not have any idea what we wish to do or even what our desired profession entails. For example, suppose you are choosing between occupational therapy and accounting. How do you really know which career you'd prefer? For fields like occupational therapy, nursing, or teaching, there are usually practicums or observations that will give you some sense of the field. But what if you're considering accounting, management, or working in the criminal justice field? How do you know it is something that you would enjoy?

In an earlier chapter, we discussed how important it is that you select a major that will lead you to the career for which you have an interest or passion. College campuses have many resources to assist you as you begin to determine your career choice. There are instruments and books that will lead you to a deeper understanding of the field(s) you'd like to explore. One student may know in her heart that she has always wanted to be a teacher. For another, the career search is a mix-and-match journey in which she may delve into several areas of interest before finding a true passion. No matter what your career discovery path will entail, there are advisors who can help along the way.

This chapter will provide some of the resources you can use to begin the selection process. From a faculty advisor to a registrar to an assistant dean or dean, help is available if you know where to find it. Sometimes it may be the career development director or the academic development director who will help you discover your inner passions for a certain line of work.

Questions students often ask themselves before they enter college and while pursuing their degree include:

- **I have so many things I enjoy doing, how do I know what career is best for me?**

- **I know what I want to do, but how can I complete the necessary degree in the most efficient way?**

- **I thought I knew what my career choice would be, but I have changed my mind. What do I do now?**

- **I need help finding a job that will give me great security and is in demand. I also want it to be something that I enjoy. How can I pursue these goals?**

- **What are the best resources to help me determine my strengths and my interests?**

You will face all these questions as you work toward your degree. One office that can assist (in addition to your faculty advisor) is the career center.

We met Laureen Cirillo in "Chapter 15: Study Skills and Learning Styles." She is the Executive Director of the Sullivan Career and Life Planning Center at Bay Path University, and has been advising students for years about career choices. Prior to working in academia, she was in the human resources field, so she is the ideal person to share her excellent perspectives on what to consider and how to make the most of your career center's resources.

CAREER PLANNING
BY LAUREEN CIRILLO

You enter college as your own unique self, having traveled your own unique path. A good college experience offers career coaches who are interested in getting to know you and in understanding your academic history, your job experience, your family life, and your personal hopes and dreams. One of the best steps you can take as soon as you become a student is to make an appointment with a career coach. Do this within the first few weeks of starting a new program. This way, your career coach can help you integrate your major field of study and course work with your professional path right from the start. You can begin to gather and create important documents that you'll work on as you progress through your program, such as a personal branding statement, résumés and cover letters, work samples, and other documents that make up a collection of papers called a portfolio; and you can start thinking about how your college education can significantly enhance your career.

Career coaches consider it our role to understand where you are in your career track, help you discover your future course, and assist you in developing strategies to get from where you are to where you want to be. We are invested in providing a framework for you to integrate all aspects of your life into your own unique journey. You may have grown up thinking that work is something you have to do to pay the bills, and that you save what you really love to do for your free time. Many women have sat with me, describing the dreariness and sheer boredom of their duties at work, describing feelings of disconnection, futility, and a sense of being misunderstood or undervalued. These same women proceed to discuss a hobby or family activity or book they have read that excites, fascinates, and revitalizes them. Their faces change; their eyes become bright. The energy in the room shifts when people talk about what they love to do. There is a misconception that if you do what you love, it must not be work. A good career coach can assist you in determining how to transform what you love to do—and what you are good at doing—into a professional career.

Take a moment and list everything you love to do in one column on a page, and everything you are really good at in a column next to the first one. Then circle the things that are common to both lists. You might have the beginnings of your ideal job description. You might realize that you can do what you love to do for a living, especially if you are good at it. You might learn something about your passion (what you love to do) and your purpose (the difference you can make in the world). A good college experience adds the third ingredient by giving you the resources to develop your potential (your untapped knowledge, intellect, and talent).

Now what do you do with the ideal job description you just created? Instead of searching the Internet for jobs that remotely resemble something you can stuff yourself into, take your ideal job description and go shopping in the world. Find the organizations and opportunities that need your talents. We can help you identify and market your unique combination of personal qualities, education, experience, and skills. Career coaches can help you learn to create and control your own career destiny and learn a strategic approach to your professional journey that will serve you for life. Speaking of serving for life, a good college education experience invites you to use career services for free for the rest of your life!

Your college career service office can offer the following services to help with your search:

- **Personality Assessment Tools**

  You were introduced to personality assessment tools in Chapter 6: "Choosing a Career Path and a Major." These tools help you to discover and validate your natural personality preferences and to learn what you think your world wants from you; how to adapt to these expectations in healthy ways; and how to use this information to assess job fit, management relationship fit, team fit, and organizational culture fit. Assessment tools also can help you validate your strengths in order to capitalize on them rather than putting all of your energy into fixing your weaknesses.

- **Networking and Résumé Building**

  Career coaches pave the way for you to build strategic relationships with professionals who can help you build knowledge in your career field and enhance your qualifications, create a strong network, and create customized, strategic résumés that demonstrate how you uniquely fit the desired position.

- **Creating an Inventory of Your Talents and Skills**

  Career coaches can help you discover and communicate about experiences, talents, and skills from your past in ways that significantly relate to and support your future career goals. A talent and skills inventory is especially valuable when you are changing careers or advancing in your present career as a result of your college education.

One way that you can create such an inventory is to work with a coach to identify and list past activities and accomplishments. Once you have this written list, you can take an inventory of which experiences and accomplishments relate to different career roles you are considering. When you prepare for your new career, you will be prepared to write and talk about what you have done in the past in a way that can matter for your future.

- **Assistance With Developing Communication Skills**
  Career coaches can help you develop assertive and pro-active communication skills in your professional relationships. You learn how to establish yourself as a strong contributor and become comfortable participating in discussions, sharing ideas, and giving opinions. A career coach can help you process experiences, such as when you have had challenges being assertive or proactive; the coach can brainstorm with you about different ways you can experiment to be assertive or proactive. Some career coaches will work with you individually to develop these skills; others will refer you to resources (books, seminars, mentors) that can further assist you.

- **Interview Preparation**
  Career coaches can help you build your confidence and personal presentation skills for phone interviews, team interviews, informational interviews, and similar opportunities for which you may want to feel more prepared and comfortable.

There are a couple of different ways that you can test-drive potential career paths. Three of the main methods are career story interviews, career shadowing, and internships. Oh, and here's a hint for you: Have a set of business cards made up for yourself. Our career center gives students and alumni free business cards; perhaps yours does the same. You can also find business cards available for free on the Internet (you pay only the shipping costs) through, for example, www.vistaprint.com.

What's on a business card when you are a student?

- **Your full name**

- **Your cell phone number**

- **Your school e-mail address** (your school e-mail address may be more professional than your personal e-mail address, although you can certainly use your personal address if it is something like your full name with a standard e-mail carrier instead of princesspat@gmail.com)

- **Your mailing address**

- **Your major/minor/program name**

- **Social media icons** representing any professional profiles you maintain, such as LinkedIn or a professional Facebook page

You can share your card with professionals you meet during your career story interviews, career shadows, and internship experiences.

Once you have selected a career or two (or three!) that you would like to explore, using career story interviews and career shadowing can help you research potential internships. A career story interview involves finding a professional who works in a role that relates to what you would like to explore, and spending 30–45 minutes interviewing that person. For example, if you are interested in working with children who have special needs, you could interview a special education teacher. Your career center or faculty advisor can help you identify and approach a person who fits your interest; you can also receive help to create a list of questions to ask during this interview. Some questions students enjoy asking include:

- **Describe your career path. How did you decide on the work you do today?**

- As you reflect on your career, would you have done anything differently, based on what you know now? Do you have suggestions for me to consider as I contemplate this career path?

- What are the greatest rewards for you in this work? What are the greatest challenges?

- What types of personality, competencies, skills, and education would you recommend for someone just entering the field?

- What is the landscape like for women in this field? What have you learned about being an effective woman leader while doing this work?

The list of questions you can prepare is endless, so make sure you boil down about five very important questions based upon your interests. You want to have enough questions that specifically get to the heart of what you want to learn without having too many. Generally, you want to keep your interview to less than 45 minutes, and more likely 30 minutes. Remember to bring a notebook and take notes on what you learn. Always send a personal, handwritten note to thank this person for her time and share a brief summary of what struck you the most. The great thing about career story interviews is that you can do as many as you like, and you can interview people in person, via Skype, or via telephone. Gathering information about your career path in this manner also helps you build relationships that can become part of your career network.

The second tool we want to share is that of career shadow. A career shadow involves going on-site to follow or "shadow" a professional who works in the role to which you aspire. Your career center or your faculty advisor can help you brainstorm what types of organizations might fit your interests and career exploration, as well as how to best approach these organizations. A career shadow takes a bit more work than a career story interview; you'll need to find a professional who is working in your career path and who is willing to have you visit the organization in which she works. Ideally, you'll want to spend a half day or a whole day following your professional around, experiencing a bit of what it's like to spend time in her role. Your professional should arrange in advance for your visit to her organization, so those involved will know that you'll be there. Your visit might include attending meetings with your professional, at which you should be a silent observer. You might meet a team of people with whom your professional works, and be part of a project-planning session. You might observe a training session for new employees or watch other activities related to the role. Your visit should also include time to ask questions, so prepare your list of questions in advance. After your career shadow experience, write down what you learned and how this experience affects your desire to do this type of work. Don't forget to send handwritten and thoughtful notes expressing your appreciation for the things you learned to each person with whom you spent any time.

We can't be more excited about the third great career exploration tool: your internship experience. Your faculty advisor and/or your career center can help you locate and plan an excellent internship adventure. We think so highly of internships as a learning tool that most of our traditional undergraduates are required to complete them as part of their program experience. It is a little trickier for adult women to complete internships while in school, as many of them work full-time in addition to attending classes. Therefore, it's challenging to fit an internship into their schedule. Still, we want to encourage you to try to work one into your educational plan. Start with your faculty advisor and your career center. Check both avenues: Your advisor may know a professional who is working in a field about which you are interested in learning; your career center is sure to have a list of people and organizations related to your career interests and academic program.

An internship typically consists of working in an organization in a learning role for a specific number of hours per week over several months, in a paid or unpaid capacity, with the goal of applying your classroom learning to this role and test-driving what it's like to perform this type of job. Your internship work can earn college credits or be noncredit.

The first step in planning your internship is to decide what career path you would like to learn about. (Typically, this conversation has already taken place with your faculty advisor or career center staff.) After you've identified possible career paths, you also need to decide what your essential criteria are, such as:

- **The geographic area in which you can perform your internship;**

- **If you need an internship for which you will be paid;**

- **If you need an internship for which you will earn credit;**

- **What kind of transportation will be available for you;**

- **What your time frame to start and complete your internship will need to be.**

Geography can be challenging. If you have family responsibilities and need to limit your geographic location, that's essential. If the location is not limited due to family constraints, open your mind to the possibility of stepping outside of your comfort zone. Pay is a significant issue for many students. Although we understand the need for many students to have paying jobs while in school, it is important to realize that, depending on your field, you might not be able to get a paid internship. But because the career experience is invaluable in securing employment down the road, don't rule out unpaid internships. Explore this issue fully with your faculty advisor or career center staff.

Most internships are unpaid, but you earn credits, which means you will be paying for the work experience. The internship is a course; if you are lucky enough to find one in your field, your academic advisor must approve it to ensure it qualifies for credit. Your advisor or an internship coordinator will help you plan and structure your internship experience with the person in the organization with whom you'll work most closely, and usually will supervise the internship. S/he will also be available during your internship in case you need a sounding board or assistance in any way.

On-site, you will have an internship supervisor who will help you with your training, give you assignments, and grade you at the end of the experience. This person might help with setting learning goals for your experience to ensure that everyone understands what your focus will be in this position. Once you start your work, someone from the school might call your supervisor to check in and/or visit you when you are working, to see how things are going for everyone. During your work experience, you may be asked to keep time/ activity logs that summarize the hours you work and what you accomplish; these documents will probably need to include your supervisor's signature. At the end of your work experience, you may be asked to write a paper that explains what you have learned and how the experience relates to your future career decisions. You may also be asked to do a presentation on what you learned. Many schools require that the supervisor write a performance evaluation and share it with the student. Students are often asked to write an evaluation of the organization as an internship site and to assess their own performance.

As mentioned earlier, internships are not always possible because of the student's work schedule; they are usually scheduled during the day, when adult students may be working. But you should ask if there is an option of getting course credit for doing an internship, or whether you can have the experience of one without the credit. It will provide a learning experience that may prove either to excite you about your chosen profession, or show you that this is not the field you want after all.

If it is the latter, you will need to redirect your journey so that you do not waste time and energy. If internships are not available, the career story interviews and career shadows discussed earlier in this chapter are helpful alternatives.

If you want to gain the most from your academic experience, keep this essential message in mind:

> Use your career center early and often,
> throughout your program experience
> and for the rest of your life!

So many times, we discover a student who has never visited the career center. Sometimes, we find a student who does not know that the career center even exists! Your career center may well be the most underused benefit that you pay for with your tuition and fees while you are a student. Many higher education institutions offer their graduates access to career services for life, free of charge. Find out the services for which you are eligible, both as a student and as an alumna, and use these services in the ways that help you the most. The following major services you might find at your career center are, too often, a well-kept secret:

- **Career Assessment Tools**

  Career assessment tools are available in many different areas related to your personality, skills/competencies, interests, and specialty topics, such as leadership, change, time management, learning styles, and financial, physical, emotional, social, intellectual, and spiritual health. Find out what kinds of assessments are offered and take advantage of the ones that interest you. Personality assessments can help almost everyone, especially when it comes to exploring the relationship between personality and career path. Usually, you make arrangements to take an assessment and have a follow-up meeting with a career coach to sort through the results and reflect on applying what you have learned.

- **Career Story Interviews and Career Shadow Programs**
  The benefits of career interviews and career shadow programs can't be emphasized enough!

- **Career Research Tools**
  Career centers have a virtual library of computer-based career research tools, such as salary calculators that project how much the average compensation may be for a specific career path in a particular geographic area. Other tools include the U.S. Department of Labor's *Occupational Outlook Handbook* and state resources that provide information on whether certain career paths are growing or declining in demand; the education and certification requirements for specific career paths; related career paths; and the general position/role descriptions for different kinds of careers.

- **Mentor Connections**
  Career centers can often connect you with graduates who serve as mentors for students to help with career decisions and contacts.

- **Career and Networking Events**
  Career centers often provide opportunities for professionals to meet with students at different events in which professionals are part of a panel or provide keynote speeches on various aspects of their professions. These events also provide students with practice in learning how to introduce themselves effectively and build relationships with professionals in their career choice. Career fairs are often advertised by career centers, both on campus and off; they are gatherings of employers who are seeking new employees. Typically, employers sit at tables and represent their organizations; students visit those who work in the field they are considering, and talk with them one-on-one. This is a great chance for you to show up in your

best interview outfit with your business card and résumé! In a single day, you can often meet many employers who are hiring in your career path; it's a terrific opportunity to circulate your résumé to lots of people. The best ways to capitalize on these career and networking events include: wearing your best professional clothes, carrying a business card, updating your résumé and having copies to share, and getting business cards from people you meet. After the event, follow up with a brief, handwritten note of thanks and connect with professionals you've met who are on LinkedIn, Facebook, or other social media.

- **Virtual Resources for Employment, Internship, and Volunteer Opportunities**
  Most career centers operate some type of virtual resource for students searching for internships, employment, and volunteer opportunities. These resources vary widely. We recommend that you contact your career center to find out what virtual resources are offered, and learn the most effective ways to take advantage of these opportunities. Some typical virtual resources are www.idealist.org, which can be helpful to students in search of that awesome dream job; www.internhere.com or www.internhub.com, which provide information about internships; and www.volunteermatch.org, which can point the way to a fulfilling volunteer experience.

- **Career Coaching**
  Most career centers offer individual career coaching appointments in person, via telephone, or through virtual services such as Skype and webinars.

You are ready to start searching for your dream job . . . you will manage the process more easily if you follow the ideas and suggestions that have been offered here!

KEY POINTS TO REMEMBER:

- Contact your college's career center early in your college career; don't wait until your senior year.

- Your college's career center can help you with personality assessment tools, networking, résumé building, and interview preparation.

- Take advantage of opportunities for career story interviewing, career shadowing, and internships.

- Your college's career center can provide assistance to you after graduation and throughout your career.

ACTION STEPS:

1. When visiting colleges, check the career development or career services department on the Internet or in person. See how it is organized and ask about services. Ask if they provide services to their alumnae for life.

2. Ask the career development office about jobs in your field of interest. Where have recent graduates been placed for employment? What have the salary ranges been?

3. Ask if your prospective college offers any internships or shadowing experiences for adult women in your field.

4. Call your local library or the career center of the colleges you are investigating to see if they have aptitude tests and career choice tests that you can take for free.

5. Call someone who works in the career of your choice and ask for an informational interview. An informational interview involves about 30 minutes of talking with someone who is in a career you want to pursue and who is willing to share information about her own career path. Ask what she majored in and if she can offer you advice on local colleges or universities who offer that field of study.

6. Read the book *What Color is Your Parachute?* by Richard Nelson Bolles. It will give you a good sense of how to make a decision about your career path.

SHARON'S STORY

"In 2011 I decided to go back to school," Sharon said. "That decision wasn't easy, only because at that point of my life I [had been] out of school for about nine years and was terrified of [the] thought of sitting in a classroom . . . I was working at a job that was getting me nowhere; I was a single mother of two young girls.

" . . . [M]y parents didn't talk to me or my siblings about the importance of education. I am the oldest of four [children]; I am the only [one] in the family that has graduated [from] high school, and [now I am] about to graduate [from] college. My mother only had a fifth-grade education, she speaks little to no English, and I don't know much about my father. Before entering [college], I felt lost and didn't know exactly what to do with my life. I had little confidence and never really felt empowered to stand up for what I believed in.

"After the first criminal justice class that I took . . . I felt so empowered and good about myself that I could do anything that I wanted to. [T]he...program was the best thing that ever happened to me. I started seeing little changes in myself. I started feeling more confident and started voicing my opinion in class and even at work . . .

"I always wanted to be a police officer, so when the civil service exam was open, . . . I decided to take it. After waiting several weeks for the test results, I got an e-mail letting me know that I [had] scored a 98.6, and I was going to be placed on the waiting list for any upcoming openings . . . [I] received an opportunity of a lifetime with a chance to work in the criminal justice field."

RESOURCES:

Action Without Borders. (2014). *Idealist*. Retrieved from www.idealist.org

Bolles, R. N. (2013). *What Color Is Your Parachute? A Practical Manual for Job-Hunters and Career-Changers*. Berkeley, California: Ten Speed Press.

InternHere. (2011). *InternHere*. Retrieved from www.internhere.com

Internship Collaborative. (2014). *Intern Hub*. Retrieved from internhub.internships.com/join

United States Department of Labor. Bureau of Labor Statistics. (2014, January 8). *Occupational Outlook Handbook*. Retrieved from www.bls.gov/ooh

VolunteerMatch. (2014). *VolunteerMatch.org*. Retrieved from www.volunteermatch.org

21

Getting the Most Out of Your College Experience

For many students, taking courses is their sole objective when attending college. But there are many opportunities for professional and leadership development, enriching lectures to augment your classroom experience, and events and trips that can be the break you need to recharge. Today, colleges provide a wide range of extracurricular and cocurricular activities that can enhance both your academic and your personal life.

Caron Hobin is Chief of Strategy Officer for The American Women's College Online at Bay Path University, and previously served as Vice President for Planning and Student Development. Her experience spans 25 years at women's colleges, both at Bay Path and at Simmons College in Boston. She has special expertise in the kinds of services and programs that can enrich your college experience.

COCURRICULAR OPTIONS
FOR ADULT STUDENTS
BY CARON HOBIN

Even those of us who have been in the higher education field for many years find today's tuition costs remarkable. As you evaluate your education purchase, it is important that you put into the equation *all* of the hidden resources you are getting with your tuition dollars. You probably know you are purchasing access to a great faculty, a beautiful campus setting, extraordinary facilities, and the latest technology. But your tuition dollars can also:

- **Support a healthy lifestyle**

- **Prepare you to be a student again**

- **Help you learn important life skills**

- **Give you entrée to world leaders**

- **Offer the chance to see the world**

- **Provide entertainment for you and your family**

- **Help you serve your community**

- **Help you attain the job of your dreams**

A closer look will show you how to accomplish the above and help you get the most "bang" from your higher education investment.

- **Health and Fitness**
  As student expectations of campus life mount, colleges and universities have started to offer amenities that rival those at high-end resorts. Today, campus dining facilities serve

world cuisine, often prepared with fresh, local ingredients before your eyes and to your specifications. Most campuses have elaborate fitness complexes with ropes courses, state-of-the-art cardio- and strength-training equipment, access to personal trainers, pools, running tracks, racquet courts, dance studios, intramural sports, and classes in everything from kickboxing to yoga. These amenities are either included in your tuition or student activities fees, or are available at a modest cost (look carefully at your tuition bill to assess additional out-of-pocket expenses). Consider how much you currently pay for a gym membership or a personal trainer. Eliminating these costs while you are a student could be significant. Some colleges even have lifelong access to fitness centers available to alumni for free or at a low cost.

The daily routine of a college student runs counter to what most would consider a healthy and active lifestyle. You usually sit during classes and while studying or writing and reading, and probably while you are meeting with a study group. Combine this sedentary lifestyle with unhealthy eating and no exercise, and you probably will not operate at peak performance. A plan to use your campus's facilities and incorporate physical fitness into your week will help keep your energy up, stress down, and the calories off.

Some colleges offer a student health plan. If you already have a health plan through an employer or spouse, the college plan may not be appealing. However, if you are not insured or find you are underinsured, a college plan usually includes on- and off-site healthcare providers and mental health counseling centers. Even if you elect not to purchase a college health plan, there may be discounted prices offered to students for immunizations and flu shots, smoking cessation, weight management programs, and other health education programs.

- **Academic Development**
  Academic support professionals can help reintroduce you
  to the world of research papers and exam preparation.
  Your college will have an academic development center or
  a learning lab that provides tutors trained in every major
  course of study offered by your institution. These tutors
  can teach you the most efficient way to read a text, study
  for an exam, or write a term paper. Writing tutors can
  coach you in the writing style adopted by your campus and
  can serve as proofreaders. Some campuses also subscribe
  to online tutoring programs to serve their student body in
  a 24/7 capacity.

- **Life Skills**
  Beyond academic support, campuses are prepared to offer
  a range of life-skill coaching delivered by administrators
  and peer leaders. Life-skill workshops and one-on-one
  sessions are typically provided in areas such as goal setting,
  stress management, time management, organization,
  nutrition, and emotional intelligence. Critical life-skill
  classes, such as Cardiopulmonary Resuscitation (CPR) and
  Rape Aggression Defense (RAD), are probably also taught
  through your campus student life or athletics department.

  Employers state that strong oral communication
  skills top the list of qualifications they are seeking in their
  prospective employees. Therefore, almost every campus
  will offer public speaking classes for credit, but many will
  also offer lots of opportunities to practice public speaking
  in more informal ways, such as Toastmaster chapters,
  debate teams, contests, and so on.

- **Leadership Initiatives**
  Some colleges excel in offering leadership development
  initiatives for women. Women's colleges, like Bay Path
  University, are excellent examples of such special resources.
  For example, Bay Path coordinates a large annual spring
  Women's Leadership Conference that draws nationally

and internationally known keynote and breakout session speakers. An emphasis is placed on showcasing women speakers at this event. Speakers are asked to trace their life path and share advice with the audience. We find that women can never get enough of learning from other women's experiences. A small army of student volunteers helps orchestrate this event and gains hands-on experience in event planning. Other students from our campus are offered a complimentary option to attend this conference, hear inspiring life stories, learn skills they can apply on the job immediately, and network with the other professionals in the audience. Most colleges offer similar programs highlighting professionals by field or gender. This kind of information can assist women on their career journeys.

- **Travel**
  While it may be challenging as a working parent and student to fit travel into your schedule, consider exploring options that can broaden your college experience. Most campuses have credit or noncredit short-term trips available at a significant discount to students over semester breaks. Trips might range in length from several weeks to a day. For example, most campuses have sponsored group trips during January semesters for domestic or international travel.

  In addition, day-trips into a neighboring city might include enrichment opportunities such as theater performances, museums, music venues, gardens, and art galleries. And spring break weeks may offer an opportunity to combine travel and community service in what are called Alternative Spring Break (ASB) programs. Gone are the days when students' goals for vacation consisted of travel to exotic beaches for sun-and-surf activities. Today, with increased interest in community service, students demand a broad selection of service programs for their free time. Volunteer vacations are very popular. There is great appeal to working for a week or so, for example, on a Habitat for Humanity building project in an area of the United States that was hit by a natural disaster, or to learn a new skill at a nonprofit organization like Heifer International. Adult students would be wise to follow the lead of younger students and view these experiences as résumé-enhancing opportunities as well as a chance to give back to the community.

Whether or not you are affiliated with a higher-education institution, a college campus might become part of your travel plans. If you and your family are planning nonacademic travel, do not overlook the option of staying on college campuses for relatively inexpensive overnight accommodations. Do an online search under the term "overnight accommodations on college campuses"; it will yield a plethora of options.

- **Entertainment and Family Services**
  When we orient adult students to our campus, we highly recommend that they look for an opportunity to bring their immediate family for a visit. We feel it is important, especially for mothers, to bring their children to see where Mommy disappears to when she leaves home to attend class. The power of role-modeling cannot be overemphasized.

  Once the immediate family is on campus, they will see and hear about a vast assortment of activities that colleges offer for the entire family. Campuses have phenomenal performance spaces for theater productions, dance performances, holiday programming, lectures, and movies that are generally open to the public and available at a discount (or free) to students, alumni, children, and elderly parents. Some in your immediate family may be old enough to take advantage of noncredit class offerings in a wide array of topics, from the arts to financial literacy to wellness.

Campuses are generally quieter during the summer months, so many colleges open their doors and fields to summer camps for sports, the arts, or academic enrichment. Summer programs tend to be open to the general public, but typically are offered at a reduced rate for current students or alumni. In this age of high-priced professional athletes and exorbitant ticket prices for professional sporting events, there is something refreshing about watching a free or moderately priced sporting event with amateur athletes competing with all their hearts for a division title. What better way to inspire your budding athletes than to take them to watch a college game?

Often, businesses surrounding college campuses offer students a wide range of coupons for discounted services and products that include computers, meals, dry cleaning, gift items, and entertainment.

If you are a parent and childcare is an issue while you are enrolled, you should know that some campuses offer on-site day care for a fee. Undergraduate institutions, in particular, are always a good source of students who are available for babysitting opportunities within your home. If you have elderly parents or are dealing with health issues, you should also know that campuses with large adult student populations usually develop peer support groups to weather the challenges that can impede progress toward graduation. On some campuses, adult students sometimes organize fundraisers to support their fellow classmates and their families through difficult times.

- **Community Service**
  In working with adult students in their job searches, we often discover that they tend to participate in more community service projects than younger students do, and yet they are more likely to forget to mention these valuable experiences in their cover letters, on résumés, or at job interviews. If you already teach Sunday-school classes, volunteer at your child's school, or work at a soup

kitchen, do not forget to tell prospective employers about the work-related skills you have been living, learning, and using.

For students looking to add service options on-campus, opportunities abound. You might want to consider being a mentor, a life coach, or a sports coach. If you are proficient in a certain subject, you could consider becoming a tutor. If you have a special interest or passion, think about the possibility of serving as an advisor to a special interest group or club on campus. Or, if you want to spearhead a fundraising campaign for your favorite charity or cause, campus communities tend to be very generous in their support. Again, do not forget to include this type of on-campus community service on your résumé.

- **Career Services**
  You may be comfortably ensconced in your career and returning to college only to fulfill a personal goal. If so, know that you are in the minority of returning college students. The majority of students say they need to complete a bachelor's degree in order to be considered for a promotion, for the flexibility to transition from one industry to another, or to advance to graduate study. College career offices provide guidance in locating internships, co-ops, part-time and full-time employment, and graduate programs. Career office administrators routinely offer networking opportunities, assemble peer support groups for unemployed and underemployed students, refer students to self-assessment tools, counsel students on career options, and serve as a clearinghouse for job postings. Many of these offices offer free career services multiple times over the lives of their alumni. In so doing, campus employees are always gratified to help; they love to celebrate jobs landed and graduate school acceptances.

Campus administrators and faculty want you to have the richest college experience possible. Taking full advantage of this stage in your life will add to your knowledge base, help you develop new skill sets, expand your network of contacts, provide new experiences, and increase your overall satisfaction level.

I have attempted to provide a broad, but certainly not an exhaustive, listing of the resources and benefits included in your tuition or room-and-board costs beyond the classroom. To learn more about the specific offerings at the institution of your choice, read the campus student handbook. This handbook is usually located on the college or university website under Campus or Student Services or is available in hard copy through the Student Life division. For additional information, every campus has some mechanism for "What's Happening on Campus" postings via e-mail, Internet event calendars, or on-campus displays. Check these announcements weekly so you will not miss a single opportunity.

Carpe Diem!

KEY POINTS TO REMEMBER:

- Many colleges have fitness programs and facilities and health plans for students.

- Colleges often provide life-skill coaching and workshops to help students with life management issues.

- Your college may provide the opportunity to meet leaders in your prospective field.

- Travel and community service opportunities can enrich your college experience.

- Your family can find many opportunities for entertainment and leisure activities at your college.

ACTION STEPS:

1. Does your prospective campus have a fitness center? Find out what programs are available to help you keep active.

2. If you are uninsured, find out whether your college offers a student health plan.

3. Make yourself familiar with your prospective college's tutoring and other academic support services.

4. When you visit a college campus, pay attention to postings for conferences and other special programs taking place on campus; attending such programs can supplement your educational experience.

5. Find out whether your prospective college offers theatrical performances, holiday programming, movies, or other activities that you can attend as a family.

6. Find out whether your prospective college has opportunities for community service that can complement your academic work or provide you with personal fulfillment.

7. Find out whether your student ID makes you eligible for discounts at local businesses.

8. Find out if your prospective college offers travel programs and determine how you might be able to fit travel into your schedule as a student.

CHERYL'S STORY

Cheryl dreamed of studying in San Francisco. "It was never my intention to attend college locally and stay in Massachusetts. I wanted out of this state with a burning desire that could melt tungsten." She was accepted into the Academy of Art University in San Francisco. But financial difficulties, a pregnancy, and a "toxic relationship nailed down the doors and windows of opportunity. I began to think it was utterly hopeless," she wrote. In December 2010, Cheryl "mustered the internal strength to free myself and my children from any barriers. . . My emotions were in overdrive, ecstatic to learn, disappointed to still dwell in M[assachusetts], and unsure of myself. After all, it [had] been an entire decade since my high school experience. What if I couldn't do it? What if I didn't have what it takes? What if I am stupid, [as] I was told?" She overcame her fears and blossomed at college. Reflecting on her journey, she wrote, "I have evolved from an insecure, uncertain girl to a confident, self-assured, bold woman. [College] has provided me knowledge [and] confidence, and [it] let me recognize on my terms that I am a natural-born leader. However, I am most grateful for the friends I have made on this incredible journey, and the bond of sisterhood all of us alumnae share. My personal journey . . . has given me more than I could have asked: . . . a family of amazing women who constantly inspire. Who could ask for a better journey?"

22

GRADUATION AND NEXT STEPS

*C*hapter 11: "The Registrar's Office" explained how critical it is to keep a record of your progress toward degree completion requirements. If you have done that and find that you are within 30 credits of an associate's degree or within the last 45–60 credits of your bachelor's degree, you have many things to consider.

First, what will you do with your degree? Will you seek career advancement in your present job? Will you look for a new job? Will you attend graduate school?

- **For Career Advancement**
  In some cases you may have been required by your employer to seek higher education just to keep the job you have. Or you may need a degree to obtain a promotion in your current organization.

  On the other hand, career advancement may not be possible in the company where you are currently employed. Some supervisors will always see you in the job you are currently doing. They are comfortable with where you are; you are fulfilling an important role, and they worry about what may happen if you leave. Inertia sets in.

  Or there might not be any jobs available for advancement within your company. Perhaps the company is on hold, there is a freeze on promotions and hirings, or there are no higher-level jobs that appeal to you within your company.

With a new degree, it is a natural time to consider moving on for that higher-level position. There is a biblical verse that says, "No prophet is accepted in his own country" (Luke 4:24). We don't tend to listen to the prophet in our midst. Your company might think they need an outsider to come in and share words of wisdom or a particular talent to advance the organization, so you might not have a chance for promotion, even with your degree.

But many times, employers are looking for the eager individual who takes the initiative to get a new degree, and they are willing to consider that individual for a new job. You can start by talking to the human resources office at companies that interest you. They will know of potential openings. They might suggest that you meet with department or division directors in an informational interview. This will give you and the hiring employer the opportunity to meet without all the issues around a formal job interview. I suggest that you start this process before you have received your degree. Getting an early start on informational interviewing will show organizations that you are about to have a new credential and therefore will be eligible for new opportunities. Refer back to Chapter 20: "Career Development" for more information on networking and informational interviews.

As we mentioned in the chapter on selecting a career path, you shouldn't wait until graduation day is near to take the first step. Set up informational interviews to get started; you will be glad you did not wait until you had your diploma in hand. Remember, the job market is very competitive. If you have taken advantage of networking, shadowing, an internship, or a practicum, you have a ready-made group of individuals to contact for assistance.

(Keep in mind, however, that if your current employer has paid for your tuition, you'll need to find out whether you will need to repay them, should you leave for another job as soon as you graduate. Check with the human resources office before making any steps to take another job outside of your company. Don't start your job search until you know whether or not you have a commitment to your current employer.)

- **Attending Graduate School**
  Whether you decide to attend graduate school immediately after receiving your bachelor's degree or a few years from now, it's important to consider whether or not you will need a graduate degree as an entry point for your desired career. Depending on your career aspirations, there may be very specific requirements for post-baccalaureate experience.

  For example, today a position as an occupational or physical therapist requires a minimum of a master's degree. Entering the teaching profession also requires obtaining a master's degree in most states. My advice is to find out what type of master's will qualify you to teach. There are often strict state education mandates and minimum qualifications for this type of degree.

  Some professions require training beyond the master's level. To be a college professor, a medical doctor, or a research scientist, a doctoral degree may be required.

  Depending on the type of degree, students might begin a graduate program in their freshman year, after the third year of undergraduate education, or once they finish a bachelor's degree. It's a good idea to ask your admissions counselor about advanced degree requirements early in your college career.

  In some cases, a graduate degree requires pertinent work experience prior to enrolling. For example, many graduate business schools will require one to three years of relevant work experience. But there are programs that will allow adult students to use previous life experience or relevant professional experience to meet this requirement.

Using the Internet to assist you in finding answers is excellent, but there are always staff and resources in your college's career development offices and library that can give you a sense of whether or not you'll need a graduate degree for your chosen field. If you need one, finding the best college or university is the next step.

- **Selecting a Graduate School**
  The circle has truly been complete when you enter this point in your graduate degree search, because you will go back to the initial advice at the beginning of this book about choosing a college and a major.

Dr. Melissa Morriss-Olson has been in the field of education for more than 30 years and has held almost every type of senior administrative position. She has been Provost and Vice President for Academic Affairs at Bay Path University since 2010, previously served as Dean of the Graduate School, and is a founding director of the graduate programs in nonprofit management and strategic fundraising. She has established a number of new graduate programs at Bay Path and is well qualified to offer the following advice about post-graduate education.

PURSUING A GRADUATE DEGREE: NOW THAT YOU HAVE YOUR BACHELOR'S DEGREE, WHAT'S NEXT?
BY MELISSA MORRISS-OLSON, PH.D.

After completing your bachelor's degree, you have many options to consider, including pursuing an advanced degree. In general, a master's degree in a field such as business or psychology requires approximately two more years of study after the bachelor's degree. Earning a professional degree means completing the academic requirements to become licensed in a recognized profession. For example, if you want to be a doctor, lawyer, physician assistant, or pharmacist, you'll need a professional degree, which typically requires several years of additional study.

Many students pursue full-time employment after getting a bachelor's degree and then return to college later to obtain an advanced degree, often in a different subject area from their first degree. When undergraduate students ask me if they should get a job first or go right to graduate school, I always tell them that there is no right answer. I urge them not to take this decision lightly, but rather spend some time talking to people who know them well, including professors, friends, and family members who have obtained advanced degrees, and professionals in the career fields in which they are interested. I also encourage them to do some personal soul searching, to think deeply about their interests and abilities as well as their dreams, and to consider several important issues:

- **Why do you want to go to graduate school? Is it for the right reasons?**
  In my experience, students pursue an advanced degree for many reasons. Some simply want to learn more about a particular field of study, while others pursue a graduate degree primarily for professional advancement. Some career fields, such as medicine, occupational therapy, or law require an advanced degree for job entry. Other students apply to graduate school because they have not decided what to do next after completing the bachelor's degree; considering the commitment of time and money required, this is generally not a good reason to go to graduate school. As a first step, I encourage students to clarify their goals; if they have an interest in pursuing a profession that requires licensure or certification, it is important to become familiar with the professional association that accredits or licenses in their field. Most have wonderful resource information on their websites for prospective students. Here are a few examples:

- **Occupational Therapy**: www.aota.org/Education -Careers/Considering-OT-Career.aspx

- **Law:** www.americanbar.org/aba.html and www.lsac .org/JD/LSAT/about-the-LSAT.asp

- **Medicine:** www.aamc.org/students/applying

- **Physician Assistant:** www.aapa.org

- **What field(s) of study should you consider?**
  As an undergraduate, you typically take a variety of courses as general education requirements in addition to a major. The course work in your major is usually broad and de-signed to introduce you to the major concepts, definitions, and issues in your area of study. In graduate school, you complete an in-depth study of one field that is typically narrow and specialized. For example, if you pursue grad-uate study in psychology, most programs require you to choose a specialization such as experimental, clinical, de-velopmental, social, or biological psychology. This entails knowing your interests and aptitudes early, as your choice determines the programs to which you'll apply.

  For example, what are your favorite courses and why? What courses or learning experiences did you least en-joy? Do you have strong writing and research skills? Do you enjoy spending time in a laboratory? On what topics have you written papers? Talk to faculty members about the differences among the various specialties in a given field. Check out existing employment opportunities for the fields in which you are interested, including earnings, expected job prospects, the nature of the work, and work-ing conditions. A great resource for this information is the U.S. Department of Labor's Bureau of Labor Statistics website: www.bls.gov/ooh .

  This can also be a great time to use the career planning resources provided by your alma mater. At Bay Path University, our Career Development Office provides an online career assessment tool that allows you to map out potential career and educational options based on an assessment of your personality, skills, values, and leisure interests. Check with your college to find out whether it has a similar program.

- **Do you have what it takes to be successful in graduate school?**
  When I talk to students about how graduate school is different from their undergraduate experience, I hear many common themes, regardless of program or field of study; mostly, students tell me that graduate school is more intense and requires a higher level of academic commitment.

  In most graduate programs, students are expected to maintain at least a 3.0 grade point average. Some programs deny funding to students who fall below this GPA. Reading and writing skills are essential—you must be able to read and comprehend large volumes of information in a short period of time—as are critical thinking and analysis skills. Graduate school involves more independent learning, which means you must be sufficiently self-motivated and willing to advocate for yourself with your classmates and your professors. You also need to be good at multitasking, since you will be juggling many projects, papers, and assignments at the same time. Many students report back to me how overwhelmed they felt during their first semester in graduate school, and how little understanding they had about what they were getting into. Given this, it is a good idea to talk to students who are enrolled in the program you are considering. Ask them what they wish they had known prior to starting the program, and what they think is required to be successful in that particular program. Here are some tips from students I know who have been successful in graduate school:

  - **While you are still an undergraduate, do everything possible to strengthen your reading, writing, research, and critical thinking skills.** Most of what you learn in grad school will not come from classes, but from other activities, like doing research and attending conferences. You may work closely with a faculty member on his or her research. Graduate school is somewhat like an apprenticeship in which you learn how to think critically about the most important issues and problems in your field of study.

- **Approach your graduate school experience like a full-time job (even if you are attending part-time).** For students who breezed through their undergraduate experience with little effort, graduate school can be a shock. Your professors will expect you to take initiative for your learning and demonstrate commitment to your career. Create a support network that you can turn to when needed to sustain your motivation and commitment, especially during those challenging times that every graduate student eventually encounters.

- **More than anything, graduate school involves socialization into your chosen profession.** You gain the information and skills that you need to be a professional; however, this involves much more than course work and experiences. You will learn to think like professionals in your chosen field; you will learn the norms and values of your profession. Spend as much time as you can getting to know your instructors while you are still an undergraduate. This advice is not limited to aspiring teachers. Faculty members often are, or were, professionals in fields other than teaching. For example, a lawyer or corrections officer might teach a course on criminal justice, or a businessperson might teach a course on management. Your instructors might also be able to refer you to professionals in your chosen career. Ask them what it's like to work in their field. Not only will this help you know if it is the right field for you, but you will also have a head start on the socialization process.

- **Can you afford to go to graduate school?**
  One of the biggest concerns that students have involves finding the money to pay for graduate school. It can be expensive. The good news is that most students qualify for some form of financial aid. The first step is to contact the financial aid office at the graduate schools you are considering and find out what assistance is available. Common types of financial aid for graduate students include grants, scholarships, loans, and tuition reimbursements, which have been discussed in Chapter 9: "The Financial Aid Process."

  In addition, graduate and postgraduate students may be eligible for fellowships and assistantships.

  - **Fellowships**. Like scholarships, fellowships that are granted to graduate and postgraduate students do not need to be repaid. Both private organizations and the government offer fellowship programs in varying amounts. Fellowship funds can be used for research, tuition, and other school expenses, and may be granted based on merit or need. Fellowships will sometimes require that a recipient participate in an internship or conduct fieldwork or research on a particular topic.

  - **Assistantships**. Like the internships and work-study programs available to undergraduates, assistantships provide a stipend and/or tuition waivers for a student in exchange for work which the student performs, usually for the department in which she is studying. Assistantship programs vary from school to school; most often, students work as teaching assistants (TAs), who usually teach lower-level courses; or research assistants (RAs), who assist faculty with lab work, scholarly research, record keeping, data collection, presentations, report writing, and more; graduate assistants may also perform some administrative functions at their college or university. Assistantship funds may come from federal or state sources or faculty/institution grants.

Good Internet resources on graduate school funding can be found at:

- *www.studentaid.ed.gov/sites/default/files/graduate -professional-funding-info.pdf*

- *www.finaid.org/about*

Some students wonder if they should work while attending graduate school, an option that is more feasible in some graduate programs than others. There is no one answer to this question. Why? There are many ways to attend graduate school—and many graduate programs with differing cultures and rules. Take the graduate program that I attended. It was a part-time doctoral program, and students were expected to incorporate their real-life work experiences into their classroom discussions and learning. In other programs, working is frowned upon and sometimes forbidden.

In figuring out whether or not it makes sense for you to work while attending graduate school, consider the different enrollment options available:

- **Full-time graduate programs.** Students who attend full-time graduate programs are expected to treat their studies as a full-time job. Some programs actually forbid employment while you are enrolled.

- **Part-time graduate programs.** Part-time programs typically allow students to spread their course work over a longer period of time, thus enabling students to attend school and work at the same time. Keep in mind that even part-time graduate school enrollment requires a considerable academic commitment. I typically tell my graduate students to expect to work a minimum of two to three hours out of class for every hour in class. That means every three-hour class will require at least six to nine hours of preparation time.

- **Online graduate programs.** An increasingly popular option for graduate study is online learning. Online learning can be deceptive at first glance in that you do not usually have a set demand for class time. In fact, many students initially enroll in online programs assuming that such programs will be easier and require less of a commitment. Nothing could be further from the truth. Students who enroll in online graduate study have to be diligent about their use of time—perhaps more so than students in campus-based programs. Online students face similar reading, homework, and paper assignments as other students, but they also must set aside time to participate in class online, which may require that they read dozens or even hundreds of student posts as well as compose and post their own responses. Online learning offers great flexibility for those who want to combine graduate study with work; at the same time, it is not for everyone and typically requires an ever greater commitment of time and self-motivation than campus-based programs.

- **How do you get in?**
  Regardless of field of study or institution, most graduate school applications require the same basic elements:

  - **Transcripts.** Transcripts provide a record of your academic background, including your grades and the courses you have taken. Graduate school admissions officers will review your transcripts to get a sense of what kind of student you are. They will look not only at the grades earned, but also at the type of courses taken and their level of difficulty. You will need to contact the registrar's office at the school where you obtained your undergraduate degree to request that an official copy of your transcript be sent to each graduate program to which you are applying.

- **GRE or other standardized test scores.** Most graduate schools require standardized exams such as GREs (Graduate Record Examinations) for admissions. However, professional schools (e.g., law, medical, business) require different exams (LSAT [Law School Admission Test], MCAT [Medical College Admission Test], and GMAT [Graduate Management Admission Test], respectively). GREs and these other exams are standardized, meaning that they are constructed so that the results can be used for comparison purposes. The structure of the GRE is similar to the SAT and provides a sense about your potential for doing graduate-level work. Some graduate programs also require a GRE subject test, which assesses your knowledge in a particular discipline (e.g., biology). It is always a good idea to take practice tests ahead of time and to take GREs and other standardized tests as early as possible (typically, the spring or summer before you apply), as your results will determine to which programs you may apply. There are several good Internet resources for each of these exams, including practice tests, free test-prep software, and test strategies:

  - *For the GRE:*
    www.ets.org/gre/revised_general/prepare?WT.ac=rx46

  - *For the LSAT:*
    www.lsac.org/JD/LSAT/about-the-LSAT.asp

  - *For the MCAT:*
    www.aamc.org/students/applying/mcat/

  - *For the GMAT:*
    www.mba.com/the-gmat.aspx

- **Letters of Recommendation.** While your transcripts and test scores provide the graduate admissions committee with one perspective on your potential as a graduate student, your letters of recommendation will allow the committee to see you as a person and to understand the other components of your application. These letters are extremely important. Choosing the most appropriate individuals to write them is a critical first step. Consider asking professors who have had you as a student for at least two or more courses and who know you well enough to provide specific examples to substantiate their recommendations. (This is one reason that it is important to build good relationships with your professors during your undergraduate years and to seek out opportunities and experiences that will set you apart from other students.) For example, research experiences that you have had under the direct supervision of a faculty member who can attest to your potential for carrying out graduate-level work will be viewed favorably in the graduate admissions process. For applied fields such as education or social work, strong letters of recommendation from faculty who supervised your field experience can be especially helpful.

It is also important to provide your references with the information they need to write compelling letters on your behalf, including a copy of your transcript and other admissions application components, such as your personal essay. Keep in mind that they may be writing letters for several students at the same time. Make it easy for them to pull out the most significant things about your background.

If you have held jobs related to your field of study, you might wish to include letters from employers who can comment on your suitability for the field. You might also request a letter from an employer who can attest to your work ethic, motivation, and the quality of your work. It is generally not a good idea to include letters of recommendation from friends, spiritual leaders, or public officials.

- **Essay or personal statement.** Many graduate program applications require an essay or personal statement. This is your opportunity to stand out from other applicants to the program. Of course, you will want to introduce yourself and explain why you want to attend graduate school and why this particular program is a good match for you. It is always important to think about your words from the vantage point of the committee who will be reading your essay. What might they want to know about you to conclude that you are indeed a good fit for their program? This will depend in large part upon the type of program to which you are applying. Before you sit down to write, consider your personal qualities, skills, experiences, and accomplishments, and how they relate to the nature of the program to which you are applying. Be specific in describing your goals and what you have to offer to the program and to the profession that you are seeking to enter through graduate study. If the admissions essay asks you to write on a specific topic, be sure to fully address the topic. And have someone you trust proofread your essay and provide constructive feedback before you submit it. (See the "Resources" section at the end of this chapter for a list of books that provide advice on the application essay.)

One of the best online resources that I have come across on getting into graduate school is appropriately titled *Getting into Graduate School*. You can find it at: www .mastersdegreeonline.org/getting-into-grad-school

For many students, a bachelor's degree is a first step to either career advancement or a higher degree. Many professions today require a master's degree or even a doctorate. If you decide to continue with a graduate degree, you can refer back to this book for guidance through the next stage of your journey.

KEY POINTS TO REMEMBER:

- Use informational interviews to explore your career options after graduation.

- Many careers require a graduate degree; some also require work experience.

- Graduate-level studies tend to be more focused, intense, and demanding than undergraduate-level work.

- In addition to the types of financial aid previously discussed, graduate students may be eligible for fellowships and assistantships.

ACTION STEPS:

1. If you're considering a graduate degree, find someone who has achieved the degree you seek and talk to her about the challenges of graduate-level studies.

2. Refer to Chapter 7: "Finding the Right College" to compare schools with graduate and professional degree programs.

3. Talk to your faculty advisor about the costs and benefits of a graduate degree in your field.

JESSICA'S STORY

Fleeing an abusive situation, Jessica and her mother were homeless and forced to live in a green Oldsmobile while Jessica attended kindergarten. "I remember what the rain sounded like on the hood of the car at night," Jessica said. "I remember my mother crying when she thought I was asleep."

Her status took a toll on her studies and her self-esteem, and she dropped out of high school. Eventually, Jessica and her mother's financial situation improved, and together they obtained their GEDs. Her mother gave Jessica the impetus to continue her studies. "My mother enrolled at Bay Path in their One Day Program, and she advised [me to] check it out. . . I remember stepping onto campus that first time and walking into the beautiful buildings and feeling I wasn't . . . 'worthy enough.' But I pushed myself . . . I had to prove that I could do this. So I enrolled... [I]t was in the first couple classes there that I started to make connections with other women . . . Their stories were able to empower me and others, and I started to realize that all of us have . . . something in our backgrounds that can either prohibit us or push us forward."

Jessica was hesitant about sharing her own story until she decided to continue her studies in an MBA program. "I remember standing up in front of my peers and starting to read my story and crying and looking around the room and seeing everyone else in the room crying. . . They helped me understand that it was nothing to be ashamed of, and my story was powerful. And if I used that, I could go anywhere."

Jessica completed her MBA and went on to work at a local healthcare facility and then at a financial company as a "Continuous Improvement Consultant." She was recognized by a Western Massachusetts news magazine as one of the region's "Forty Under Forty" up-and-coming young businesspersons. She remains close to her alma mater, serving as an adjunct professor in the Business Department at Bay Path. She also serves on the boards of several local nonprofit organizations that deal with issues ranging from low-income housing to women's leadership. She now uses her journey up from poverty to inspire other women.

"I tell the story to my current students now and . . . I open up the door for others to share their stories . . . We support each other, and we help everyone understand. . . What is the piece that you feel is holding you back? . . . We confront it, and by confronting it you own it, and once you own it you can use it . . . to propel yourself forward. . . If it wasn't for education, for me walking on campus and enrolling in college, I never would have found the power that I had within myself. It was one of the most amazing things I've ever done. And through that, I've learned that my story is . . . everybody's story."

RESOURCES:

American Academy of Physician Assistants. (n.d.). *AAPA: American Academy of Physician Assistants*. Retrieved from www.aapa.org

American Bar Association. (2014). *ABA: American Bar Association*. Retrieved from www.americanbar.org/aba.html

American Occupational Therapy Association, Inc. (2014). *Considering an OT Career?* Retrieved from www.aota.org/Education-Careers/Considering-OT -Career.aspx

Asher, D. (2012). *Graduate Admissions Essays: Write Your Way into the Graduate School of Your Choice*. Berkeley, California: Ten Speed Press.

Association of American Medical Colleges. (2014). *Applicants*. Retrieved from www .aamc.org/students/applying

Association of American Medical Colleges. (2014). *Medical College Admission Test (MCAT)*. Retrieved from www.aamc.org/students/applying/mcat

Bodine, P. (2011). *Great Applications for Business School*. New York: McGraw-Hill.

Educational Testing Service. (2014). *Prepare for the GRE Revised General Test*. Retrieved from www.ets.org/gre/revised_general/prepare?WT.ac=rx46

Graduate Management Admission Council. (2014). *The GMAT Exam*. Retrieved from www.mba.com/us/the-gmat-exam

Kantrowitz, M. (2014). *FinAid! The Smart Student Guide to Financial Aid*. Retrieved from www.finaid.org

Lacey, L. (n.d.). *Survival Skills in Graduate School*. Retrieved from gradschool.nmsu .edu/workshops/survival.pdf

Law School Admission Council, Inc. (2014). *About the LSAT*. Retrieved from www.lsac.org/JD/LSAT/about-the-LSAT.asp

Masters Degree Online. (n.d.). *Getting into Grad School*. Retrieved from www.mastersdegreeonline.org/getting-into-grad-school

Princeton Review. (2012). *Medical School Essays that Made a Difference*. New York: Random House.

Reding, C. (2015). *Grad's Guide to Graduate Admissions Essays: More than 50 Real-Life Admissions Essays from Students Who Gained Admission to Harvard, Columbia, Stanford, Georgetown, and More*. Waco, Texas: Prufrock Press, Inc.

United States Department of Education. (2012, Fall). *Financial Aid for Graduate and Professional Degree Students*. Retrieved from studentaid.ed.gov/sites/default /files/graduate-professional-funding-info.pdf

United States Department of Labor. Bureau of Labor Statistics. (2014, January 8). *Occupational Outlook Handbook*. Retrieved from www.bls.gov/ooh

ON BEING A
WOMAN OF INFLUENCE

*W*hat is a woman of influence? She is someone who knows her skills, talents, heart, and mind, and uses that knowledge to improve her own life and the lives of others. A woman of influence does not necessarily need a college degree, but her options open considerably when she has one. In a June 2010 article in *Redbook*, Maddy Dychtwald, author of *Influence: How Women's Soaring Economic Power Will Transform Our World for the Better*, states that today women make up "51 percent of working professionals...represent more than half of all stock-market investors, and nearly a quarter of wives outearn their husbands."[1] The world has changed significantly in these last 40 years in other ways than just an increase in the number of women at colleges and in the workforce. Think of the power a woman holds today. Yes, don't be afraid to use the word "power." It is a good word if it's used to improve your own life and the lives of others.

Beyond achieving a college education, there are many other facets of our lives that we can improve. In turn, we can change the world of our families, the organizations in which we work, and the communities in which we live.

But how? Surely we must increase our own knowledge to be able to make a difference. A college degree will help broaden your knowledge in a variety of subjects, allow you to concentrate in an area that may lead to a job or enhanced personal satisfaction, and open doors of opportunity. But what else must you do to be a woman of influence in your career, family, and community? What else do you need to have as part of your personal portfolio?

How can you become a woman of influence on both the micro- and macro-level? In my opinion, several components of a woman's portfolio are integral to being a woman of influence. Could there be other components? Might you have some, but not all, to be a woman of influence? By all means. But if you have the key characteristics outlined in this chapter, you will be well on your way.

- **Communication Skills**

  If your college did not stress oral or written presentations, I strongly suggest that you figure out how to get this experience. One of the greatest fears is the fear of speaking in front of groups. With practice and coaching, this fear can be eliminated almost entirely. Toastmasters International is one organization that can help. Today, high-level positions in both career and volunteer capacities require excellent communication skills. Practice is key, and more practice ensures success.

  Whenever you have the opportunity in a class or in your job to speak publicly, take it, even though it may be frightening and painful. In the long run, it will help you become a woman of influence.

  On a personal note, it took me until I was almost 50 to feel comfortable speaking in public. I confess that I always had butterflies, or I forgot where I was going with a point I was trying to make, or I always had to read from notes. But after becoming president of Bay Path University, I was forced to communicate daily with my staff and faculty, the board of trustees, alumni, and community organizations. I was asked to be a speaker at local chambers of commerce and women's organizations. I needed to speak publicly almost daily. It was practice, practice, practice, and more practice that finally allowed me to relax.

Practice is also key to improving your written communication skills. As Suzanne Strempek Shea points out in Chapter 18: "Writing: Tips for Success," any professional-level position involves writing, from e-mail to letters to reports. Strong writing skills are critical to making your voice heard and understood.

Although you may hate to write those papers or speak in front of your classmates or your colleagues at work, take the opportunity. It will have incredible benefits in the end.

- **Leadership Skills**
  How can you become a leader or acquire leadership skills? These skills start with daily living. Are you managing your family's activities? Do you plan events or work with clients in achieving their goals? In a volunteer capacity, have you led a committee, a fundraiser, or an activity at your child's school? Have you had to manage the healthcare needs of an elderly relative and maneuver through red tape and bureaucracy? If so, you are leading. You do not have to be a CEO or department manager to lead. Leading is understanding what it takes to accomplish a goal and then achieving it with determination, delegation, and teamwork. We often misinterpret what leadership means when, in actuality, it is a part of our daily lives. The more we practice, the more we become better leaders and learn the joys and difficulties that come with leadership.

  Take the opportunities that are before you to hone your leadership skills. There are many seminars or workshops offered by women's organizations, or perhaps your own workplace, that provide ways to learn and improve leadership skills. Take advantage of every professional development opportunity to learn more. Volunteer at your workplace to run the holiday events or a fundraiser. You will quickly learn what leadership is all about. You might encounter some difficulty or challenge that will give you greater insight into what you need to do the next time to be successful or to avoid obstacles. Practicing and honing your leadership skills will help you become a woman of influence.

- **Financial Literacy**
  Another key factor to being a woman of influence is having the power of knowledge. While obtaining your education, you are accumulating a body of knowledge in a broad group of subjects as well as in a particular major or discipline. But there is a key piece of knowledge that many women do not take the time to consider: financial literacy. Financial literacy is an understanding of the basic concepts of finance, banking, investments, real estate, mortgages, loans, insurance, retirement funds, benefits, estate planning, and other financial vehicles or tools. For example, learning how to read the stock section of the local paper or *The Wall Street Journal* is a skill that few women have unless they are business majors or have had to learn in order to understand their own retirement plan or investment portfolio.

  Women are now an equal part of the workforce. Even if a woman is not the major breadwinner in the family, she needs to understand her own power as an investor. Why? Women may feel that their husbands or parents or lawyers will take care of their financial needs, and they (i.e., women) do not wish to be bothered by the somewhat tedious details. Often women who are married assume that their husbands are making smart choices and leave the financial oversight to them. In many households, the women control the spending for the household but have no idea if there is adequate insurance, or in what investment vehicles retirement or pension plans are invested. In some cases, husbands or other family members do not wish women to be involved and do not think it is necessary for them to be involved, so husbands or partners retain control over every aspect of the finances in a family. I have heard too many horror stories in which the husband has passed on and the woman has no financial support for herself or her family because there were no savings, no insurance, and no retirement fund. In some cases, there is no will, and an estate becomes tangled up in probate.

No matter what the circumstances, knowledge of financial affairs and how to manage on your own is key. The point is simply this: financial literacy and control over one's finances are essential to a productive and secure life now and in retirement.

I once heard Gloria Steinem share a story about a friend who had not worked and had depended on her husband's finances. The couple was supposedly wealthy. When Gloria remarked how lucky her friend was, the woman said, "I am one heartbeat away from welfare." She was not skilled in any field of work, except perhaps at a low-paying job. She had no idea what her worth was. If her husband were to die, she had no idea whether she would be on welfare or if she would be well-off. Because she had no idea, she always carried a level of stress.

Financial literacy is as critical to your overall education as your college degree is. While in college, take courses on financial planning. Attend a free seminar by a reputable financial firm (they sometimes offer these to solicit your business to buy insurance or stocks, but you have absolutely no obligation at the end of the seminar to purchase a product). College and university development offices offer assistance because they are looking for ways to encourage you to give back to your college at some point in your life (again, these seminars are usually free). There may be a women's organization that offers financial education as part of a professional development program.

Your employer may have a retirement plan for you. Be sure you know exactly what it entails. Make an appointment to have your human resources officer explain the details and the options for investments. Know the benefits of stocks versus cash versus annuities, and also know the risks. Take every opportunity to learn. As you learn the financial concepts and use them, they will become a part of your vocabulary.

If we, as women, improve our financial literacy, we will improve the lives of others. According to the *Redbook* article mentioned earlier, "[W]omen spend in different ways than men. The best research on this has been conducted in developing countries: A U[nited] N[ations] study found that 90 percent of women who earn income reinvest it in families and communities—by sending kids to school, or buying clean water and electricity for their communities—compared with only 30-70 percent of men."[2]

- **Community Activism or Involvement**

  Like financial literacy, community service is an opportunity and life skill that can bring great satisfaction. Many women serve on the boards of nonprofit organizations, or they volunteer their time for a cause while not taking a formal role in an organization. Volunteering can be as simple as a few hours a week or month. Not only will the organization benefit from your unselfish contribution, but you can reap many benefits. First, volunteering is good for the soul. Second, we often receive more than we give. Whether it is satisfaction that we are changing lives or improving the way an organization serves its clients, there is a side benefit that often occurs. We learn something: how to chair a committee or to speak in front of groups, how to organize a major fundraising event, or how to motivate others to assist in a needy cause. In so many ways, we can benefit from helping others and, in return, know that we have truly been women of influence, making a difference in others' lives.

- **Philanthropy**

  As we discussed above, community activism can lead to changes in our communities to benefit others. Once you have your degree, understand the importance of financial literacy as a life skill, and offer your time and talent to the many organizations that need volunteer help, you can also include your treasure, an element of philanthropy—namely, gifts of monetary value. At different stages in our lives, the ability to give money varies. Many believe that to be a philanthropist you must contribute thousands of dollars. I would like to dispel this notion. Organizations with worthy causes enthusiastically accept and appreciate gifts as small as five dollars. During your life, the organizations that receive your attention will change with your age, your stage in life, and your interests. The important point is that you see yourself as someone who can give, who has the passion to do so, and who can make a difference. As you complete your education and gain financial literacy, you can always find some way to give back.

As we approach our final act on this earth, we want to leave a legacy to our families and to charitable causes that will leave this earth a better place. In times like these, we will want to have the right advice from lawyers, accountants, and estate planners on how best to make those gifts of cash. In the end, there are many types of vehicles that can make our gifts work now or in the future; that can have great tax advantages, depending on your income level and tax bracket; that can provide for your family and a nonprofit organization at the same time. Many who have achieved a college education feel some obligation to return that privilege to others and establish scholarships in perpetuity (endowed scholarships) in their own name or in the name of their family.

In the end, we can all become women of influence if we accept the importance and the power of this concept. Why do I believe it is important? As women of influence, we can improve not only our own life, but we can improve the lives of our families, our workplaces, and our communities. My greatest hope is this: As women of influence, we can acquire more knowledge to add to our portfolio; we can gain satisfaction in knowing we are secure financially; we can seek new and better opportunities with our knowledge and our time; we can help organizations grow and thrive; and we can, perhaps, leave a legacy during and after our lifetime.

The point of this is to remember the journey—where you began, where you wish to be, and what you wish to do with your college degree. You can seek knowledge for knowledge's sake, and you can seek knowledge for the world's sake. The choice is yours.

KEY POINTS TO REMEMBER:

- Oral and written communication skills are essential to becoming a woman of influence.

- Pay attention to how you exercise leadership skills in your daily life, and work on honing those skills.

- Financial literacy is a critical skill that many women neglect.

- A woman of influence gives back to her community through community service and philanthropy.

ACTION STEPS:

1. Think of someone in your life whom you would define as a woman of influence. Interview her to find out how she achieved her position and what obstacles she overcame along the way.

2. Find biographical information on women you admire, past and present. Learn how they became women of influence, and think about what lessons you might learn from them.

3. Consider how you might take on leadership roles in your own life. Make a list of some actions that you might take in your personal or professional life to become a woman of influence.

4. Take some steps toward improving your financial literacy. Take a financial literacy seminar or read a book about personal finance, for example.

$\mathcal{G}$IA'S STORY

"Making the decision to return to college after so many years has given me the opportunity to believe in myself [and] build strong relationships with my classmates and professors," said Gia. "It has also allowed me to become grounded and fulfilled. My background consists of abuse, and in the beginning I was not able to speak about my experience because I was embarrassed. However . . . I am now able to speak and advocate for women who may be going through the same experience . . .

"I was able to maintain honors while balancing my personal life and professional life, and will graduate with a 3.85 GPA. This is a huge accomplishment, as I have faced many challenges in my personal life as well as my professional life. I did not have a stable family structure and was raised by parents that were consumed by drugs or alcohol. I did not graduate high school. As I grew up and became my own woman, I felt something was missing and needed to better myself. I began to work in an entry-level position in the legal field, but lacked the formal training to work at a higher level. . . As time passed, I obtained my GED and enrolled [in college]. . .

"I was afraid of the unknown; however, as I transitioned into college life . . . I became this disciplined individual, and my only goal was to be the best student that I could be, not exactly knowing what [being] the best student really entailed . . . [I formed] social networks and mutual bonds with my classmates. Many of these women called upon me for both personal and academic support and advice. Some of the women looked to me as their mentor . . . Helping my classmates and having them depend on me for guidance has been an empowering feeling. My mission in this life is to utilize the leadership skills that I have acquired . . . and become an advocate for the many women in our society who may want to embark on the same journey. Someone once told me that I was never going to amount to anything . . . all I can say to that person is 'Look at me NOW!'"

RESOURCES:

Dychtwald, M. (2010). *Influence: How Women's Soaring Economic Power Will Transform Our World for the Better.* New York: Hyperion/VOICE.

Toastmasters International. (2016). Retrieved from www.toastmasters.org

Women and Power—How to Get Some. (2010, June). *Redbook.* Retrieved from www.redbookmag.com/health-wellness/advice/women-and-power

NOTES:

1.   Women and Power—How to Get Some. (2010, June). *Redbook.* Retrieved from www.redbookmag.com/health-wellness/advice/women-and-power

2.   Ibid.

Afterword

The Journey's End and the Beginning of Another

Although this is the last official chapter of the book, it is truly the beginning of another journey. You have taken steps toward a college education. You may put this book down and not take the first step for a month, a year, or more. No matter when the time is right, the journey can begin, and the steps in this book can provide some clear paths for achieving your goal.

What is important is that you have this guide as part of your personal library. It may give you direction, but I also hope it gives you a sense of your potential as a woman with a college education. So many options will open. Perhaps it will take time, once you receive your degree, to obtain the job of your dreams. Perhaps you will not be able to use your education right away because of some life circumstance. In the end, the degree becomes like a badge of honor. It means you have undertaken a process of learning that has many milestones: beginning and completing one semester, one year, a degree, another degree. Your degree is a symbol to an employer that you are curious about life, that you have a passion for an area of interest and the desire to understand it and the world more deeply.

These chapters were written so that you would first understand what an educated woman is, why a college degree is important, and how you might become the CEO of your destiny, not only in obtaining a degree, but in how you look at your life and make your decisions.

These chapters also gave you an outline of the key college concepts and the departments that are there to help you on your journey. Remember: you are the consumer of a service, and colleges and universities are nonprofit institutions that serve the public good. They have an obligation to provide you with accurate and key information to assist you in obtaining a degree, even with all the twists and turns it may take to get there as an adult with many life obligations and responsibilities.

Finally, I hope this book gives you a sense that, beyond your education in a classroom setting, there are ways that you can use your education to become a woman of influence for your family, your workplace, and your community. The power of communication, leadership, and financial literacy skills will only enhance who you are as a woman and give you the confidence to step up and offer those skills to help others.

This book has an ending. But truly, your journey has only just begun.

"WE SHALL NOT CEASE FROM OUR EXPLORATION
AND THE END OF ALL OUR EXPLORING
WILL BE TO ARRIVE WHERE WE STARTED
AND KNOW THE PLACE FOR THE FIRST TIME."

—*T.S. Eliot, "Little Gidding"*

You will be changed forever when you have a college degree. You will start many journeys and explore much and yet be refreshed by the journey and know yourself again for the first time.

About the Author

A passionate advocate for women's education, Dr. Carol A. Leary is president of Bay Path University in Longmeadow, Massachusetts. Under her leadership, the University has established new baccalaureate programs, professional certificates and graduate degrees; introduced the innovative One Day A Week College for adult women; and launched The American Women's College Online, the first all-women, all-online baccalaureate program in the nation. In 2015, the University was recognized for the second year in a row as one of the fastest-growing private baccalaureate institutions nationwide, the only women's college on the list. Bay Path was also recognized in 2015 as #25 among the Top 100 Women-Led Businesses in Massachusetts by *The Boston Globe* and The Commonwealth Institute.

A hallmark of Dr. Leary's tenure as president was the launch, in 1996, of Bay Path's annual Women's Leadership Conference. Through the years, the Conference, with a yearly attendance of over 2,000 professional women and men, has featured such prominent speakers as Lady Margaret Thatcher, Dr. Maya Angelou, former U.S. Secretary of State Madeleine Albright, Barbara Walters, Queen Latifah, and Arianna Huffington, to name just a few.

Prior to joining Bay Path, Dr. Leary served as vice president for administration and assistant to the president of Simmons College in Boston. A Phi Beta Kappa graduate of Boston University, she earned her M.S. at SUNY, Albany, and her Ph.D. at American University in Washington, D.C. Dr. Leary and her husband, Noel Leary, reside in Longmeadow, Massachusetts, and Ogunquit, Maine. She is frequently called upon as an expert and commentator on women and higher education.

CPSIA information can be obtained at www.ICGtesting.com
Printed in the USA
BVOW08s0753160416

444306BV00001B/17/P